D0882845

A Buzzard Is My Best Friend

A Buzzard Is

MARGARET ANNE BARNES
My Best Friend

MERCER UNIVERSITY PRESS

2000

ISBN 0-86554-713-0
MUP/H532

Though the animals and events in this book are real, the names of people and places have been changed and characterizations are composites.

2000 Mercer University Press
6316 Peake Road
Macon, Georgia 31210-3960

Originally published by
MacMillan Publishing Company 1981

Dust jacket design by Jim Burt

∞The paper used in this publication meets the minimum requirements of American National Standard for Information Sciences—
Permanence of Paper for Printed Library Materials, ANSI Z39.48-
1984.

Barnes, Margaret Anne.
A buzzard is my best friend.
I. Title.
PS3552.A683B8   813'.54   81-8170
ISBN 0-86554-713-0

*For my sons, Steven and David, and my granddaughter Jennifer
with love and remembrance*

Contents

Preface

Years ago, my husband and I and our two little boys were living in the Virginia suburbs of Washington, DC. Life in the fast lane in the city and of the suburbs, filled with superficial things and meaningless tasks, became insufferable and we decided to go back to live on the land in search of the old values and old verities we had known growing up in the South.

When we moved to a splendid 112-acre farm in the Virginia hunt country, we thought we had followed the Yellow Brick Road to Oz. We expected it to be all Camelot and Currier and Ives. Instead it was Alice, not in Wonderland, but rather down the Rabbit Hole with 100 animals determined to break down the fence and run away. There was no help at all but the Buzzard, my early warning system, flying around in the sky, letting me know that trouble was on the way.

Before we moved to the farm, we expected to ride the horses in the morning, swim in the ponds in the afternoon, and sit on the veranda in the evening and count the fireflies. After we moved to the farm, we never ever saw the horses again. We were too busy...cutting...conditioning...raking and baling hay, because when spring came, the grass began to grow. The 112 acres turned into a sea of grass. It looked as though it stretched all the way across the continent on to Africa...and Asia and beyond...and every blade of it had to be cut, conditioned, raked, baled, and stored in the barn. It was time to make hay.

Until then, "making hay" had been nothing more than a cliché to me. This was no cliché. This was a nightmare. Coming from the suburbs, we didn't even know how to turn on the tractor. Before it was over, we had made 5,000 bales of hay...a million pounds!

We were still recovering from sunburn, bruises, and killing fatigue when the farmers began talking about a second cutting. I didn't even know what they were talking about. When they said we were going to have to cut hay again, I said "God and Jesus! What do you do if you don't want to cut hay again?"

The farmers thought complaining about plenty was pretty bad, but they said if we weren't going to make hay again, we'd better switch to the cattle business, and we'd better do it right away.

I had never seen a cow up close, only on a milk carton, but it didn't matter—anything was better than making another million pounds of hay.

Besides, all the farmers said there was nothing to grazing cattle: all I had to do was turn them out in the pasture and they did all the work.

Since I knew absolutely nothing about buying cattle, I had to find a cattle dealer. If you think gypsy horse traders and used car dealers are bad, you should have seen my cattle dealer. He was the greatest con-man I have ever seen, right out of P.T. Barnum, certain that a sucker is born every minute and he was *really* glad to see me.

I arranged for him to deliver fifty head of Black Angus cows and when they arrived, they were painfully thin. He said: "They got on their working clothes. You can't make no money buying pretty cows—you won't have nuthin' to improve." One cow was so crippled that she walked on three legs and dragged one. He said: "She won't be hard to catch." Another was blind in one eye. He said: "It's better if she only sees half of what's going on."

We turned the cows out in the pasture, which worked very well for a while. It was like having fifty mowing machines, and all I had to do was walk to the fence and say: "East fast, girls, eat fast."

But then I was obliged to buy a bull, a great big bull named Pericles who weighed 2,000 pounds. When he arrived, the cows were delighted, but so were the cows in the pasture across the road. They hung their heads over their fence and batted their big daisy eyes and mooed: "Yoo-Hoo," and the bull decided to go visiting and walked right through my 18-foot aluminum gate and turned it into a pretzel.

That's the way it was living on the land. We had expected to find the peace and quiet of the country, Camelot and Currier and Ives. In reality, it was the crisis center of the world, madness every hour, always on the cutting edge trying to find some sensible solution to some absurd situation.

We had a cow named Norma Nell who tried to jump the fence as she had seen the horses do. She only got half of herself over and ended up hanging across the fence like the Monday wash. Another cow stood in the pond until the mud turtle bit her tail off, and she didn't have anything left to swish flies with.

A goat named Dooma Lee ate the sleeves off all the shirts hanging on the clothes line. When Christmas came, we made the fatal mistake of taking her to church to be part of the live manger scene, and she ate Baby Jesus' bed.

They tell us to keep our eyes on the stars, but sometimes it is worthwhile looking down to see what is underfoot. When I did, there was Aesop in my own backyard. Living in close proximity to the animals, knowing their problems, seeing the perils they faced from the symbiotic balance and the forces of nature, I realized that their struggles and efforts were not unlike our own.

One winter afternoon when the ground was covered with snow and ponds were frozen over, I looked out my kitchen window and saw one of the ducks frozen fast in the middle of the pond. The ducks had a bad habit of lingering too long on the water. When the temperature dropped, ice froze around their legs and they were imprisoned on the surface of the pond. Then the foxes could simply walk across the ice and eat them.

The pond was not frozen to a sufficient depth for me to walk out on the ice and rescue the duck. The only thing I could do was keep watch through the window to make sure the fox didn't get him. The other ducks were nestled together on the pond bank chattering and worrying among themselves about their frozen-fast friend. Later, when I looked out the window again, I saw that they had all gone to join him on the ice. Watching, I thought...isn't that nice? At least he's not lonely out there.

But it was more than that. The ducks had the solution I did not have. By clustering around their frozen-fast friend, they generated enough body heat to melt the ice around their friend's imprisoned feet and by sundown that night, they had set him free. I marveled at their cooperation and compassion, and realized there was a lot the community of man could learn from the conduct of animals.

There were other animals and other stories, but most of all, there was the Buzzard. We finally learned what the other farmers already knew, to watch the sky. If the Buzzard was up there flying, there was either trouble in the pasture or trouble on the way. He was our early warning system, and the farmer's best friend.

The Buzzard and I became partners living on the land, and then one day, more than that. Out in the pasture one morning, I saw him trying to teach his young offspring to fly. When the baby buzzard faltered, the Buzzard swooped down and lifted his wing with his own until the baby buzzard regained his balance.

Watching, I realized that the Buzzard's efforts were no less than my own, which were somehow to give the young their wings and teach them the ways of the wind currents and the downdrafts and the exhilaration of soaring skyward.

After that day in the pasture, I knew we were all in this together, me and the Buzzard and the cows and the grass, and if we could somehow make it all mesh, we could make it all work. It was so easy to say, so hard to do. But the Buzzard was one of the strengths to be relied upon, because come crisis or chaos, he was the one constant I could depend on always to be there, doing his job as I was trying to do mine.

The memory of those times is treasured now. The children are grown, the cows are gone, the grass is someone else's problem to cut and bale. But the Buzzard remains like an icon in the sky, reminding me of a time and place where, early on, we learned some hard truths. We learned the extent of our own strength and we learned how to struggle with problems that seemed to have no solution. The harvest from living on the land: the old values and old verities…the only things that endure and do not depreciate.

To this day, I keep my electric fence tester hanging over my desk, and any time I think what I'm going through is tough, I am reminded of a time when it was worse, when a cow was hanging over the fence like the Monday wash, when there was a million pounds of hay to bale, and when Dooma Lee ate Baby Jesus' bed. And I always remember and shall never forget that the Buzzard really was My Best Friend.

Margaret Anne Barnes
July 2000

CHAPTER 1

Maggie Mae

I LOOKED AT THE BROWN AND WHITE HEREFORD COW crumpled by the fence. She was going to die if we couldn't get her out of the blazing July sun and into the shade. She weighed 750 pounds, and couldn't move. Her hindquarters were paralyzed.

Standing in the white board enclosure of the barnyard paddock, alone on a 112-acre Virginia farm except for my two young sons, I didn't know what to do. All I could think was, *Oh, God. How did I come to this?*

Only months ago, I was sitting at the bridge table with polished nails complaining about the deadening routine and plastic life in the suburbs, longing for life in the country. Now, I stood in the sweltering heat and limp humidity of a Virginia summer trying to fight desperation and overcome indecision.

Beside me, eight-year-old Billy-Wade turned his face up, his little

[1]

legs like pipe stems stuck in his boots, his dark hair a cap of damp curls, and his brown eyes as worried as those of the cow. "Mommie, what are we going to do?"

"We've got to get her in the shade," I said, repeating what the just-departed veterinarian had told me, "or Maggie Mae is going to die."

Studying the situation, ten-year-old Wayne propped his hands in the back pockets of his blue jeans, squinted his soft brown eyes against the blinding brilliance of the silver white noonday sun, and brushed aside a lock of blond hair stuck to his forehead by perspiration. He and his brother were competitors in everything, each one trying to be the first, the most, the best, but this was a competition he didn't want to win.

When we first moved to the farm, my husband, Larry, and I had bought each of them a Hereford heifer, so alike in size and markings that they seemed to be twins. Now Billy-Wade's cow, Maggie Mae, was about to die. Wayne's cow, Ida Belle, seeing what was happening, pushed up to the fence separating the pasture from the paddock and hung her head over, as saddened and concerned about the fate of her companion as Wayne was about his brother's cow.

"Do you really think Maggie Mae will die, Mommie?" Wayne asked, hoping for a better prognosis than what we had been given by the veterinarian.

We were first-season farmers, recently arrived from the suburbs where the death of something so small as a goldfish was cause for grief, and now we were in danger of losing Maggie Mae because of a difficult first birth.

"Bred too soon," the young vet had said when he first arrived. "The calf's too big and she's too small."

I worried when I looked at the vet. There was down on his cheek and not a line in his face. The young assistant with him was not a day older. Since my measure for experience was age, I despaired when I saw our crisis was to be handled by two young men who looked as though they had graduated from veterinary school the day before. I wished for grey-haired Dr. Caldwell, the seasoned vet who usually came, whose experienced eyes had seen a hundred things and whose capable hands had handled hundreds of emergencies. But he, they said, was still in surgery and had sent them to answer my emergency call.

Anything was better than nothing so I asked them, "Do you think you can save the calf?"

The first one, named Sidney, who seemed to be the spokesman of the two, gravely shook his skinny blond head and began meticulously laying out his instruments.

"We're going to be doing good if we can save the cow."

I knew it before he even said it, what we had helping us was the kindergarten crew.

He looked at the cow and lifted her eyelid. This convinced me that he was a novice. He wasn't even looking at the right end. "She's been in labor a long time," he said. "The calf's dead already." He looked at me with eyes that suggested negligence. "How come you didn't call sooner?"

"I didn't know . . . as soon as I saw what was happening. . . ."

We had found Maggie Mae in the deep shade of the trees at the edge of the back forty-acre pasture, her tail arched out, straining, one little hoof protruding. We had expected a joyous occasion, the very first baby calf from our very first herd of cows. In the fields all around us, the farmers' cows had dropped calves with what seemed to be no trouble at all. I had expected this too.

Thrilled by this coming event, I had called Ewell Early, our neighbor down the road, a farmer who supplemented his income by working for hire and who sometimes came to help us with chores we were still unaccustomed to. We had come to rely on Ewell for farming information, education, and advice. When I reported that one of our Herefords was about to become a mother, that I could already see one little hoof protruding, I expected congratulations. Instead . . .

"You got trouble," Ewell said, in a tone that sounded like doom. "I'll come up and take a look."

"What do you mean trouble?"

"You've got a breech birth."

Minutes later, he drove up in his ancient red pickup truck, the back fender flapping. Middle-aged, with streaks of grey in his light brown hair, his ruddy face was softened by bright blue eyes that had seen a lot in his forty years on the farm. Ewell was a man made lean by hard work, even though his best efforts never seemed sufficient to produce the income needed to maintain the farm and support his family. As taxes rose and farm prices dropped, he took on more and more work to supplement the falling farm income. Now, as he stepped out of his truck, his eyes looked tired from working all day in another man's field and late into the night in his own.

He let himself through the aluminum gate and into the paddock where we had penned Maggie Mae up. A look, a probe, a shake of his head, and he said, "You'd better call the vet. Maggie Mae is in trouble."

Dr. Caldwell answered the phone. When I told him the circumstances, he said, "All right 'am. Sounds like you need some help. I won't be able to come myself. I'm just on my way to surgery. Miz Montcliff's bitch got hit on the highway a little bit ago and I got to tend to her, but I'll send my two assistants out to your farm right away."

"Oh, Dr. Caldwell . . . ," I started to protest. I didn't want the two assistants. I wanted him.

Sensing my objection, he reassured me. "Now don't you worry. These two fellows know their business. I'm satisfied of that. They'll do you a good job."

Reluctantly, I managed to mumble, "If you say so. . . ."

"All right 'am. They'll be out t'erectly."

When they drove up, and got out of their car they were still consulting each other. They put on crisp white jackets, so new they had never been laundered. They carried brand-new black bags with gleaming gold initials, freshly done, and they still handled their instruments with awe and respect. I suspected that their textbooks, also, were still in the car for ready reference.

I watched Ewell Early watching them. Without his saying a word, I knew he thought what I thought: that this was a case that required experience, and they had none.

What would be required, the two vets said, was to remove the calf with a fetal extractor. A rope halter was slipped over Maggie

Mae's head and she was tied to the fence. They worked efficiently and well, and when Ewell was satisfied with what was being done, he nodded his head to indicate approval.

"Looks like Maggie Mae is in good hands," Ewell said. "I got to get on down the road. I promised Mr. Matthews I'd help him cut hay today." With a wave of his hand, he got back in his ancient red pickup truck and drove away. Wayne and Billy-Wade and I sat on the white board fence and watched the vets finish their work.

We had moved to the farm from the suburbs so that we could experience all of life and nature and growing things. This morning, we were getting a double dose. I worried that it was too heavy an experience for two little boys, but my husband, Larry, a daily commuter to the city, was not there to consult. As always seemed to happen, whenever a crisis arose he was forty miles away at work. Right or wrong, I had decided that if the boys were to learn about birth and death, and pain and joy, sheltering was not the answer. Besides, there was no way to shelter what was happening in the paddock this morning.

When the vets had finished, there was a puddle of placenta on the ground and Maggie Mae, overcome with her extraordinary efforts, had sunk beside the paddock fence, her hindquarters paralyzed.

We were stricken. "Is the paralysis permanent?"

They shook their heads. "Might go away in about two weeks."

"What must I do?" I asked the two young vets who were getting ready to depart.

"You've got to get her out of this sun and into the shade," the spokesman named Sidney said. "If you don't, she'll die."

My eye calculated the distance from the fence where Maggie Mae lay to the barn. It was a good forty feet.

"Could you help me get her into the barn?"

"No," they said, putting their equipment into their car, "we've got another emergency on down the road." Taking the dead calf with them, they drove away in a cloud of dust down the gravel driveway leaving the three of us and a crumpled cow in the hundred-degree heat of the paddock.

My first thought was to try to drag her the forty feet from the fence to the barn. Altogether, the three of us didn't come close to 300 pounds and Maggie Mae weighed 750, but I had read of instances where people under crisis conditions had lifted extraordinary weights like 2,000-pound automobiles. Surely, we could drag 750 pounds. We tried, with each of us taking a leg, but we couldn't budge her and I could see from Maggie Mae's agonized face that we were only adding to her misery.

If we couldn't bring her to the shade, then we'd have to somehow bring the shade to her. My first thought was the beach umbrella.

Wayne and Billy-Wade, smudged and sweating, were still trying to recuperate from their efforts to drag Maggie Mae.

"Go to the house and get the beach umbrella." I told them.

When they got back and we put it up, Maggie Mae was rolling her eyes. I couldn't tell whether she was about to faint or was utterly exasperated. In any case, the beach umbrella just wouldn't work. It wasn't big enough. On the beach it looked grand with its red, gold, and green stripes and its eight-inch fringe swaying in the sea breeze. In the paddock with Maggie Mae under it, it looked absurd. Besides, it didn't cover all of her. It left her legs and tail hanging out in the sun.

"You want me to go get your rain umbrella too?" Billy-Wade asked. It was already too insane seeing the cow sitting under a beach umbrella and I knew that adding my umbrella—no bigger than a parasol—wouldn't solve the problem. "No," I told him, "we've got to think of something else."

Billy-Wade's eyes lighted up with a suggestion. "Why don't we get the tent?"

Wayne shook his head. "That's not big enough either. That's just a Cub Scout tent."

A tent! That was a triumphant idea, but what we would have to do was build one. Wayne, anxious to fill a man's shoes, had already learned how to drive the tractor. I handed him the keys.

"Go get the tractor, and bring it into the paddock."

I sent Billy-Wade for the big piece of tarpaulin that we used to cover a wagonload of hay when a sudden summer rain appeared, and I went to the barn to find hay string for fasteners. By parking the tractor parallel to the fence and stretching the tarpaulin from the fence rail over the top of Maggie Mae to the tractor, we soon had the shade needed to save her, but her effort had been too great and our efforts had taken too long. Her big, broad, white face was depressed, her chin resting on the ground, her red brown hide trembling from weakness. Even to my inexperienced eye, it looked like sunstroke.

"Go get the water hose," I told them, scurrying them off. "We've got to cool her down."

The problem with this idea was that the spigot that filled the water trough in the paddock had no threads to hold the hose connection. This meant running the hose from the house, a distance of almost one hundred yards, and no hose we had was *that* long. It required piecing together all the hose we could find until we had a line that snaked its way from the house, across the grass, and into the paddock where Maggie Mae lay.

When we finally got it assembled, operating, and turned on Maggie Mae, the play of the cool water seemed to revive her. She raised her head and let the water run down her face, over her eyes and drip down her chin. Encouraged by this response, we got the electric fan and all the extension cord we owned and ran it out to the paddock. Soon, Maggie Mae was sitting in a cool breeze under her tent. We repeated the hosing down every fifteen minutes until alertness and life signs returned.

Billy-Wade, always willing to go the last mile, asked, "Do you think she'd like a glass of iced tea?"

Wayne scoffed at this absurdity. "Don't be dumb, Billy-Wade! Cows don't drink tea."

Billy-Wade jutted his chin out. "Cows don't sit under umbrellas either, and cows don't have electric fans, but *Maggie Mae* does."

"Come on, now," I told them, turning them in the direction of the next job. "We aren't finished yet."

There was still the placenta lying in a puddle in the paddock. We had to do something with that, and as they eyed it with distaste, I felt some explanation was necessary.

"You know, boys, that the mother cow carries her baby in her belly, and inside her belly the calf is in a protective bag called the placenta. Well that," I said, pointing to the puddle in the paddock, "is the placenta and what we've got to do is bury it, so go get the wheelbarrow and the shovels."

Burying the placenta was a lousy job. By now, the paddock was two-o'clock hot. The sky was white and drained of color. In the distance, forty-acres away, that would be our destination with the placenta, the heat lay in waves, distorting the stretch of green pasture bordered by trees and the foothills of the blue mountains beyond. The colors melted and mixed together like an impressionist painting, making the pasture look like a mirage.

Heat and the distance were not the only problems. The placenta, large as a laundry basket and the consistency of thick mucus, defied all our efforts to get it onto the shovel and into the wheelbarrow, each time rolling off the shovel and out on the ground again, gathering dirt and grime until it resembled a giant spitball. Finally, when it was corralled and rolled into the wheelbarrow, we bumped and bounced with it through the pasture to the area used for the disposal of refuse more than half a mile away. There, we dug a hole in the sun-dried soil and buried it.

Back in the paddock, Maggie Mae was much improved. With the fan blowing away the oppressive heat, we continued our water application with the hose at fifteen-minute intervals until the hot, gold brilliance of the day faded into red sunset streaks across the sky. Then, leaving Wayne and Billy-Wade to continue Maggie Mae's intensive care, I went back to the kitchen to prepare dinner, for Larry would soon be returning home from his day's work in the city. I was almost done when I heard the shriek from the paddock.

"Mommie! Come quick!"

I ran outside just as Maggie was making the last of a Herculean effort to push herself up from the ground on wobbling legs. Instead of sunstroke, she now had gooseflesh, having had six hours of shower baths, an uninterrupted stream of cool air from the fan, and constant care. She rose and stood unsteadily while we yelled encouragements, then staggered uncertainly toward the barn. We were all three so proud of Maggie Mae that we shouted with joy, and Wayne and

Billy-Wade began to scream, "Hurrah for Maggie Mae!"

Making her way toward the barn, Maggie Mae paused, looked back over her shoulder, and smiled. There was a look of triumph in her eyes and satisfaction clearly curled her lips. Also relief.

While Wayne and Billy-Wade fed her grain and hay in the barn, I ran back to call Dr. Caldwell.

"You won't believe what's happened!" I told him. "Maggie Mae is up and walking around."

The prognosis had been two weeks of paralysis, but Maggie Mae had made it in a single afternoon—likely, I thought, because she could not stand anymore such unaccustomed care. When I told Dr. Caldwell what we had done, he was full of accolades and congratulated us on the success of our treatment.

"Not very orthodox," he chuckled, "but what counts is that it worked. In forty years of practice, I never saw a cow sitting under a beach umbrella. That alone would have been worth a trip out to see. By the way . . . did she eat the placenta?"

In all my life, I had never heard of anything so horrible. *"Eat the placenta?"*

"Yes, she's supposed to, you know."

"Oh, God." I groaned.

There was concern in his voice. "What's the matter?"

"We buried it."

It was his turn to be shocked. *"Buried it?"*

"Yes," I admitted weakly. "Nobody told me . . . I didn't know."

"That's how the cow restores the nutrients taken from her by gestation and calf birth . . . *she eats the placenta.*"

When I thought how hard it was to get that lousy placenta in the wheelbarrow, how hard we worked in that blazing sun to dig a hole in that unrelenting soil, I was decimated with dismay. "What must I do?" I asked Dr. Caldwell. "Go dig it back up?"

His voice was as sharp as a rap on the knuckles. "For heaven's sake, no! Don't practice any more creative veterinary medicine today. I'll come by in the morning and give Maggie Mae a shot."

"What kind?"

"Fortified vitamins."

When Larry drove in from his day in the city, still crisp in his business suit, with his briefcase and umbrella, he scruffed the boys on the head, and asked, "What did you fellows do today . . . play?"

They rolled their eyes, flung out their arms, and fell writhing on the floor to indicate the absurdity of the suggestion that their day had been play.

Larry looked to me. "What happened?"

The longer we lived on the farm, the more difficult the daily accounting became. "Well, we have some good news and some bad news," I explained. "We saved the cow and we buried the vitamins."

He didn't even look surprised and he didn't even break stride as he walked to the sink and mixed himself a martini, because it was this way almost every day. This was the crisis center of the world. Every day, while he went off to work in the city, the boys and I were out on the cutting edge trying to survive as city transplants in the country. Knowing no more about farming and animal husbandry than we did, we were always winging it, trying to find some practical solution to some absurd situation.

In the beginning, moving from the suburbs to the country had seemed such a good idea, such a reasonable thing to do, but when we started out, there were only four of us, the family, and a dog named Suzie. Before it was over, the head count had risen to 104, and a buzzard was my best friend.

CHAPTER 2

The Suburban Strife

THEY LEANED ON THEIR PITCHFORKS and shook their heads as we drove past in our station wagon, moving from the suburbs to a farm in their valley. They and all their kin had lived there for more than a hundred years. They had seen city folks come and they had seen them go, and they could spot a loser when they saw one: a husband, a wife, and two small boys, eight and ten, taking over a 112-acre farm.

Standing in their field that ran for five miles along the road front, Clarence shook his big St. Bernard head and moved the straw he was chewing over to the corner of his mouth.

"They won't last the year," he predicted with a precision that was renowned for its accuracy.

Beside him, his brother, Claude, a wizened little man with skin like sun-dried fruit, not as tall and not much wider than his pitchfork, squinted his weak eyes and shook his head.

"Them's city folks. I say they won't last the winter."

The odds were awful. It was the first of February and spring was only eight weeks away, but at the time, we did not know about their awesome assessment of our abilities. We waved to them as we passed by leading the moving truck to our new driveway.

For us, it was the end of the rainbow, arrival at Oz, and Camelot all rolled into one. Life in the city's suburbs had been all orange juice and vitamins, Cub Scouts and Little League. Our expensive brick split-level was uniformly like our neighbors, well-tended, professionally landscaped, and without a blade of crabgrass.

Each morning with military precision, the husbands, carrying briefcases and umbrellas, drove off at exactly 7:30 A.M. to join Washington, D.C.'s going-to-work throng on the freeway into the nation's capital, inching along for an hour listening to weather and traffic conditions on the car radio. After eight hours of paperwork in the bureaucracy, they filled up the freeway again and reversed their struggle to inch their way home.

For their wives, like paper dolls all cut from the same pattern, it was kids, car pools, casseroles, and committees. Every day was just like the one that had gone before. The future was just like the past.

A generation before, the exodus had been from the rigid confines of the city to the freedom and open-air space of the suburbs. Now, suburban life had become as stifling as the city had been.

It was a deadly existence, processed, pasteurized, plastic. Something had to be done, before it was all over, before we died and all we would have ever done was rear children, kill crabgrass, and attend committee meetings.

We had already sat around and watched our dreams die. For years we had held on to the hope that one day we would move from the hated suburbs into the calm of the country. We would find a farm, and our two sons, Wayne and Billy-Wade, would have room to run and roam, explore and grow in nature's wildness. A ball could be thrown as far as the arm was able and there would be no irate neighbor holding them by the scruff of the neck, red-faced and shouting, "I was sitting in my living room reading the paper when this baseball came right through my picture window!"

For a long while we followed the newspaper's classified ads under "Farms for Sale." Every weekend, we packed a picnic basket, the boys, and little black Suzie, our miniature mongrel cocker, and headed for the country in search of this dream farm that would fulfill all our hopes and requirements.

Since we were financially dependent on Larry's salary as a minor official in the State Department, we could not move so far away that commuting to Washington was impossible. Since the boys' education was a primary consideration, and the youngest had already shown a marked preference for science, we couldn't jeopardize their progress by transferring them to a one-room schoolhouse with only the rudiments of reading, writing, and arithmetic. And, however serene the pastoral scene in Currier and Ives prints, the reality was that living on a farm would require more than a leaf rake, a lawn-mower, and a wheelbarrow to get the work done. It would require equipment and this was expensive . . . very expensive.

Some farms were too large and some were too small. Some farms were too far and some were too dear. It just seemed hopeless, and after a while, we quit looking under "Farms for Sale." We half-heartedly went about our suburban rounds and talked about "Some day. . . ." The possibility receded further and further, and finally we did not speak of it at all, for it reminded us of a failure to fulfill a dream that had died.

Then life took a 180-degree turn. Not all at once in one afternoon, but a little at a time. It began with a black velvet hunt cap worn by the golden-haired girl who lived next door. Her name was Lark and she looked like she had danced right out of the Sugar Plum Fairy. Although she was only eight, she had already won the heart of every little boy on the block. For the merest moment of her time, they offered her their life's treasures—marbles, catcher's mitt, candy, and cookies that they themselves longed to eat. If Lark would accept their offerings, the pleasure of pleasing her was far greater than the pleasure of having these things themselves, and whatever Lark did, they wanted to do too.

When Wayne and Billy-Wade learned that Lark had added riding lessons to her piano lessons, art lessons, and ballet lessons, and that the black velvet hunt cap that she wore was a requirement for riding, they came in from school and flung themselves groaning across the kitchen table. They were in pain. They were dying. What I was witnessing were the Death Throes.

"*Everybody,*" they wailed, "is going to take riding lessons. Everybody but us."

Wayne, with a larger grasp of language, added, "We're going to be the only disadvantaged kids in the neighborhood."

"Yeah," Billy-Wade pouted, "and everybody's going to hate us and not talk to us anymore."

For a time, Larry and I were able to withstand the onslaught of Lark and the riding lessons. After all, they had Little League, Cub Scouts, Junior Band, Boys' Club, swimming class, and Science Club. There was only one hour left on Saturday morning and they used this for looking at TV.

Then Nootie's mother gave way, and Nootie appeared one afternoon in a black velvet riding cap, riding boots, and a riding crop which he used to slap his boot tops as he strode about the street. When I saw Nootie's mother, Clara, she threw her hands up in abandon.

"We just couldn't stand it anymore. Nootie nagged Charlie so much that he got Charlie's golf game all off, and every time I played bridge, Nootie just stood there silently looking abused."

Nootie's new riding clothes were more than Wayne and Billy-Wade could bear. Nootie—called this because of the prodigious amount of Fig Newtons he consumed—was everything they longed to be. The biggest and oldest boy in the neighborhood, he was allowed things inaccessible to them. Over and over they chorused:

"Nootie is neat."

"Nootie is the living end."

If they died and went to heaven, they wanted to come back and be Nootie. Now, Nootie was going to take riding lessons and they couldn't. Unquestionably, they were being culturally deprived. A period of unassuageable grief set in every afternoon as they watched Lark and Nootie stride about in their black velvet hunt caps and riding boots.

Finally, we capitulated. Their only empty hour was at seven o'clock on Saturday morning. Secure in the belief that no one would teach a class at that unreal hour on Saturday, we told them, "If you can find a riding class at seven in the morning on Saturdays, you can take riding lessons, too."

Resourcefulness, when it was something they wanted, was their prime virtue. They found an old ex-cavalry sergeant who had ridden with General Patton who taught riding at the stables at seven o'clock in the morning. Because of his experience and expertise, his class was crowded with a waiting list to get in. Satisfied that they didn't have a chance, I drove them to the stables so that they could hear the refusal firsthand.

In the office we found the florid-faced stable manager sitting in a folding wooden chair behind a small cluttered desk with a large log book for signing out horses. "Can I help you?"

"I'm looking for Sergeant Massingale. I understand he teaches a class on Saturday. Can you tell me where I can find him?"

The stable manager hooked his thumb over his shoulder and from the corner a deep gruff voice said, "You found him. Right here." We turned and saw a broad-shouldered man of six foot three with his riding boot propped on the cold potbellied stove in the corner and wearing his cavalry hat pulled down to his brows.

"Sergeant Massingale?"

He took off his hat with a courteous sweep. "Yes, Ma'am?"

"My two sons would like to join your riding class."

I was just waiting for the blow to fall—his refusal—and then their despair, my concealed delight, and a trip to the ice-cream parlor to assuage their grief.

Sergeant Massingale bent his head down, studied the floor, and rubbed the back of his neck, figuring, I supposed, how to break it to them gently.

"I reckon we got room for two more."

I could only hope now that the hour of his class would conflict with something else they already had scheduled. "What time on Saturday?"

"We ride at seven o'clock in the morning. The kids have to be here at 6:30 to saddle up."

Wayne and Billy-Wade began some ecstatic jumping up and down to indicate their glee. "Are we going to get to sign up? You *promised!*"

There was no way out. "We'll be here."

"There's one thing," Sergeant Massingale said as we started to leave. "I don't take any latecomers and I don't put up with no foolishness from the kids and no meddling from the mothers."

How did he suppose I was going to meddle? I was ready to abandon the project already.

As if to soften his abruptness, he added in the gentlest tone his gruff voice could muster, "Them's my terms. Horses is serious business."

I nodded and thought on the way home that a good, tough, cavalry sergeant might be just what they needed to discourage them from this latest folly.

We got black velvet hunt caps. We got riding boots. We got riding crops. Lark smiled on them with approval. Their enthusiasm for life returned. There were smiles and laughter. But not for me.

The sun wasn't even up when we started out for the stables on Saturday morning. The sky was a murky grey and a morning chill hung on the air. A cross section of children from five to fifteen were milling about waiting for Sergeant Massingale to assign their mounts.

"I want Red Lady . . . I want Eloise . . . I want Diana. . . ."

"Keep still!" Sergeant Massingale commanded without taking his eyes off the job of adjusting a saddle blanket, tightening a girth, and shortening stirrup leathers for the younger riders. "You'll ride what you're told and I won't hear any complaining."

"But Sergeant Massingale," a little girl wheedled, "Red Lady is my favorite."

"That's why you're not going to ride her today. When you leave this class, I want you to be able to ride anything. Now get over there and mount up on Eloise."

"But Sergeant Massingale . . . ," and the blue eyes appealed for compassion.

Sergeant Massingale gave her one stony look. "One more word and I'll dismount you for the day."

Sergeant Massingale tipped his hat as Wayne and Billy-Wade and I arrived. "Mawn'in, Ma'am." Pointing to Billy-Wade, he said, "I'm gonna put that little fellow up on Sundance. He's easy and quiet. That other fellow," pointing to Wayne, "gets Diana."

Wayne was glassy-eyed with excitement. "Do I get to put the saddle on?"

"I'll show you how," Sergeant Massingale said with a slow smile, "but mind you don't get her girth too tight cause she'll faint."

"You mean *really* faint?"

"Dead away. Every time."

From behind a post, a brown-eyed, curly-haired boy of twelve popped his head. "You wanta see?" He directed his question to Wayne.

Sergeant Massingale stopped what he was doing, his face a declaration of intent. "You make that horse faint, Johnny, and I'll give you a hiding you won't ever forget."

"Yes, Sir," Johnny said, sliding back behind the post.

"That's one of my boys," Sergeant Massingale explained.

When the class was mounted and rode off down the hill to the riding ring, another problem arose. It concerned a large, sitting-size rock and what to do for the hour they were riding. Every vestige of accommodation had been removed from the office. There was only one folding wooden chair and the stable manager sat in that. It was senseless to drive the thirty minutes back home, turn right around, and go back again. There was only the riding ring at the foot of the hill and one large uncomfortable rock off to the side. The rest was scrawny pines growing out of eroded red clay. It was the rock that caused the trouble, and without realizing it at the time, life's circle changed again.

There was a polite jostling for position among the mothers to get the rock since it was the only place to sit down for an hour. After that, there was nothing left to do but hang on the fence like the Monday wash and watch the children ride round and round. Some mothers did, and as their children passed by they would call out corrections or encouragement. This got Sergeant Massingale agitated.

"Mrs. Tate!" he snapped, singling out the woman standing next to

me. "I made it perfectly clear that I would not put up with any meddling from the mothers. Now, if you want to teach this class, step forward and come take center ring."

Mrs. Tate sort of withered and died and slid down the post and as
I watched her, I wished for a better solution than the unseemly
scuffle for the rock and hanging like the wash on the fence. The
only other alternative was to rent a horse for an hour and sit in the
saddle.

At first it seemed insane, but it certainly beat the sun-baked bleach-
ers at the five-o'clock Little League game, and it was much more appealing than standing at poolside with a limp, wet towel, and not
nearly so nerve-wracking as the trumpet lesson and listening to "Mary
Had a Little Lamb." In fact, it got to be quite pleasant sitting there
in the saddle out under the open sky, and one day when Sergeant
Massingale said, "Why don't you come in the ring and ride with us?",
I did.

Looking back, I can see that life might have been simpler and remained relatively unchanged if I had just walked into the stable and
dumped the manager out of his chair and taken it for myself, or
shoved one of the other mothers off the rock down by the riding
ring. But I felt constrained not to do so and continued to sit in the
saddle instead. Along with Wayne and Billy-Wade, I began to like
the feel of the early morning air, creaking leather, and the strong
smell of horses. Saturday morning expanded to Sunday afternoon to
Wednesday after school and finally to every day in the week. We had
all come down with Horse Fever and nothing would do but that we
own our own horse.

"Horse!" Larry screamed. "What do you mean 'own your own
horse'?"

The boys and I had by this time become allies. We assured him
that none of us could live another hour without owning our own
horse.

"So go die somewhere—out of my sight—but don't tell me anymore about buying a horse."

For his birthday, the boys gave him a card with a horse on it, a
tie with a horse on it, and cuff links with horses on them. In his
craft class, Wayne made him an ashtray. Scrawled across the bottom

was the message: "I want a horse." But Larry was relentless. Just mentioning a horse put him in a fit reminiscent of St. Vitus's dance.

Then came Sergeant Massingale's cross-country ride, which was to begin with breakfast on the trail and lunch at a country store miles away. Wayne and Billy-Wade insisted that Larry ride along with us, and after many petitions, pleas, and persuasions, he grudgingly agreed. A short time later, *he* came down with Horse Fever, and we got a horse, a marvelous, red gold gelding with a flaxen tail and mane that we named Confederate Sabre. He was to be billeted at the stable and turned out to graze with the other horses in the pasture when he was not being ridden.

This joy lasted until spring came and Sabre decided to cut a little white filly named Poetry out of the herd as his own special companion. Poetry was the Marilyn Monroe of the horse world. Her silvery white mane was so long and beautiful, her eyes were so big and brown, that when she drew up her dainty foot like a chorus girl in ecstasy, Sabre would have fought an elephant for her favors. Another gelding named Sugar Foot had the same idea. A biting, kicking, stomping horse fight ensued which left both Sabre and Sugar Foot beat up and bleeding, and Sabre with the skin torn off his left ear and hanging like a tassel down the side of his head. It took the veterinarian and fifty-four stitches to put him back together again, and we decided that something simply had to be done. None of us could live through that trauma again.

With the horse fight, life took another turn. We began to think again about a farm and how much better it would be to have our very own paddock, our very own barn, and our very own field, so that we would never have to worry about a horse fight again. Looking for a farm on our own, we had not done too well. This time, we decided to call in a realtor. With professional help, we could surely find what we were looking for.

"We want a country place," we told Sure-Fire Realtors.

Their response was downright heartwarming. The agent was a Mrs. Gabriella and I could feel her smile over the phone.

"You just name it, honey," she said, "and I'll meet you anytime, anywhere, and take you to any place you want to see."

She was an energetic woman with a big pocketbook, bright eyes, and a quick smile. She said she adored our children, who were fighting in the backseat of her station wagon. She said she didn't mind at all taking along our dog, Suzie, who, with her head out the window, was trailing a thread of saliva down the side of her car. She also said that her family had no objections whatsoever to her leaving them on Sunday afternoon to help someone look for a country place.

Since the fee on country property and acreage was fifteen percent of the sale, her accommodation was understandable.

The country place she took us to was a twenty-five-room edifice that dwarfed Mount Vernon. The white-columned house stood on a sweep of manicured lawn overlooking a river. Included in the property were a farm manager's house, a thirty-stall horse barn, a cow barn, a hay barn, a grove of corn cribs, and an equipment shed that looked like an outlet for International Harvester.

Opposite the farm buildings stood a row of houses for the hired help, whose housing, utilities, hospitalization, dental, and medical care were provided by the owner.

"Now don't worry about the taxes," Mrs. Gabriella beamed cheerfully. "The oyster beds on the river front take care of that."

We didn't even ask the price, we didn't want to know. We just asked if we could look at something smaller that required fewer farm hands.

Mrs. Gabriella's eyes were a little less bright, her smile a little tighter, and she pointedly glanced in the backseat at the children fighting and Suzie's saliva trail.

"A farm, perhaps?" she asked, trying to maintain her Madison Avenue effort.

When we arrived, we found a lovely old house with a white picket fence and fruit trees in the front yard. The farmer and his wife, in their sixties, worked the 200-acre farm themselves. Their annual income from crops and cattle amounted to almost two thousand dollars, an effort that required of each of them an eighty-hour work week on the farm and in the fields.

"How," we asked the farmer's wife, "are you able to manage your housework with eighty hours in the field?"

Sitting in her shining, clean kitchen with sparkling windows and freshly starched curtains, she smiled brightly and said, "I have all my housework and canning done by five A.M."

To validate this statement, she opened up her pantry with 400 jars of canned, pickled, and preserved food, a sight to sink the heart of the most stalwart suburban housewife.

Rather quickly, we reminded the real estate agent that we could not go into farming as a full-time occupation; that after all, we were only looking for a place in the country.

"Place in the country!" She enunciated and accentuated every word. Her features sharpened, her eyes narrowed, her tone became abusive. "I *thought* you said 'country place.' "

"Well, country place . . . place in the country . . . what's the difference? It's just a matter of semantics."

"Scarcely." Her smile was completely gone, her eyes had lost their glitter. She kicked the dog and snarled at the children.

When we tried to explain that all we wanted was a place in the country with a house and some land to keep a horse, she said her only listing was 200 miles away on a mountaintop. She said she had heard of a little place down the road, but had no more time as it was her daughter's birthday and her family was waiting dinner. She left abruptly.

The "little place down the road" was a sharecropper's house surrounded by tangleweed sitting in the middle of a muddy field. Its windows had long since fallen out and when we opened the door, it came off in our hand and fell with a dusty thud. It was five miles off the main highway down a one-lane unpaved road that became impassable in winter.

We gave up in despair and drove back home to resign ourselves to the strife in the suburbs, an eternity of Little League, crabgrass, and horse fights forever. There was nothing else to do.

Then, just when it seemed that nothing would ever work out, an opportunity arose.

CHAPTER 3

Finding the Farm

THERE WERE SOME HOLDOUTS in our suburban neighborhood of brick ramblers and split-levels, landowners whose holdings had once been country but were now being encroached on by the city, who found themselves with skyrocketing taxes and surrounded by the suburbs. One such as this lived in our own neighborhood. Her name was Kate Cromwell and her big white two-story house still stood under an umbrella of red maples on the hill surrounded by fifty-two acres of land that had once been the family's farm.

She refused to sell even when land went to five thousand dollars an acre because she had begun married life there, raised five children, and spent forty years cultivating her flowers, rose bushes, rhododendrons and apple trees. Even though the fields lay fallow and the house was now too large for her needs, she still had no inclination to go off and leave it for someplace else. Instead, she called in her architect, Mr. Moffet.

"A two-story house is more than I want to keep up now," she told him. "I could do very nicely with just the downstairs, so what I want you to do is take off the top story."

Mr. Moffet was a resourceful and patient man, but not that patient.

"For God's sake, Kate," he protested, "let me build you something else. Just pick a spot . . . any spot . . . in your fifty-two acres and I'll put you up anything you want, but there's no way I can take off that top story without substantially weakening the structure."

She considered several areas—down by the stream, off near the woods—but could not, at last, go off and leave her forty years of flowers, shrubs, and trees, and stayed instead where she was, to tend them for she was happiest with a hoe in her hand, working her vegetable garden that later ended up in hundreds of jars on her pantry shelf; or in her big country kitchen, where there always drifted the aroma of freshly baked bread, cookies, and cake. These homemaker pursuits satisfied her and all those who were the recipients because she knew, and they could attest, that in the kitchen, Kate was without match.

In appearance, Kate, like most of the ladies of her generation, was no more flamboyant than a little brown wren. Her face was Ivory-soap clean, her steel grey hair was clipped short, and her grey eyes were steady and unblinking as a bird's, all of which gave no indication that here resided a great reservoir of courage, strength, and determination. Long before independence became popular or even acceptable in a woman, Kate Cromwell had a strong sense of self-worth and an independent frame of mind. She worked hard, did her share, and was more than fair, but fairness to Kate meant both sides, and that included hers.

During her children's growing up, their farm had been a working farm and her husband, Harshaw, who had a business in town, also kept a dairy herd. When the demands of raising five small children and milking cows became more than Kate could cope with, she told Harshaw, "You've got to find someone to help with the cows."

Harshaw promised he would, but never did, using his time instead to brag about his fine cattle to Casey Larue, his neighbor and cattle competitor, at the farm down the way.

"Harshaw," Kate warned once more, "I cannot manage the cows alone. You will *have* to get some help."

Again, Harshaw promised he would . . . again and again and again. One afternoon Harshaw came home from his place of business in town to find his barn completely empty. He raced to the house, burst in the kitchen, and demanded, "What happened to my cows?"

Kate never blinked once. "I sold them."

"Sold them! To whom?"

"Casey Larue."

"My neighbor! My competitor!"

Kate turned back to beating the cake batter. "He always said he wished he had them. I gave him the opportunity."

When Harshaw bought cows again, he put them out on a farm forty miles away. The barn that had housed the cows that Kate had sold still stood, empty now, all these many years.

Our need for such a barn increased as Sabre's fighting vendetta with Sugar Foot over the Marilyn Monroe mare continued unabated, with so much biting, kicking, and gnashing of teeth that the vet was on constant call to do the sewing, stitching, and repairing of all the resultant wounds. The situation become intolerable, and it occurred to me one afternoon as I drove past Kate Cromwell hoeing potatoes in her garden that she might allow us to rent her barn and ride in her fields. She propped the hoe handle under her chin and listened with unblinking eyes. "No cows," she said with a steely glint. After the history of the dairy herd, she was understandably reluctant, but we agreed to a trial basis and we had Sergeant Massingale haul Sabre over in his horse van. There, on the outskirts of the city, Sabre became our Suburban Horse.

What began as a trial basis developed into a relationship with Kate and finally into a lasting friendship. It began with a trade of housing for our horse in return for manure for her flowers and bushes, and then for the garden. After that, we helped Kate hoe the garden and she gave us jars of canned beans, corn, tomatoes, and eggplant in jewel colors of jade, gold, ruby, and amethyst. In the fall, we all sat on Kate's porch peeling tin washtubs full of red apples picked from her fruit trees, and when the moon was right and the frost had fallen, we made applebutter down by the barn in an enormous black iron pot over an open fire. This was an old handed-down skill that Kate supervised, for it required eight hours of stirring with an instrument resembling a sickle. In winter, after a snowy ride in the frozen fields we sat on the radiator in Kate's big country kitchen to warm ourselves while she restored us with freshly baked cookies and hot apple cider. She became our other-mother and added us to the five children she already had plus the ones that they had.

Then, unexpectedly, Harshaw died, and in settling his estate, some disposition had to be made of the farm he owned forty miles away. Kate already knew how we longed for a farm and how long we had looked for one.

"Why don't you move out to the farm?" she suggested. "It will probably take a year to settle the estate and this would give you a chance to decide if a farm is really what you want. It may not be, you know. It's a lot of hard work."

We had already had too many disappointments to be really thrilled about the prospects of another farm. We had seen it all, everything from Mount Vernon to Tobacco Road, and they were either too large or too small, too far or too dear, and our requirements for Larry's work, Wayne and Billy-Wade's school, and accessibility, we already knew were too numerous to ever find.

We left without much enthusiasm to go look at Harshaw's farm, for we felt that Kate was just humoring us. But she had generously offered to lease what she had available and the least we could do was drive out and take a look. We were in no way prepared for what we found.

During all the time we had known Kate, we hardly ever saw Harshaw except at family dinners when we were invited, and always he told stories about his mule down on the farm named Emma Jean, who was the bane of his existence.

"Emma Jean is the most cussed animal alive," Harshaw said. "When she gets it in her mind not to move, there's no way this side of hell to make her change it."

Holding up his finger and shaking it in remembered rage, he recalled, "Only once! And even then she ended up winning!"

Harshaw had a load of hay he wanted Emma Jean to pull out to the field, and after he had loaded the wagon and hitched Emma Jean up, she got it in her mind that she didn't want to move. Cussing, beating, and kicking Emma Jean did no good. Finally, in outdone rage and frustration, challenged beyond reason and refusal, he built a fire under Emma Jean.

"You know what she did?" Harshaw exploded. "She just moved forward enough to burn up the wagon!"

All we had ever heard were stories about Emma Jean. We had never seen his farm and didn't expect much what with a mule and a wagon of hay, but we took the freeway out of the city past dwindling suburbs to the small town of Victorsville and turned off on a narrow country road that wound through gently rolling hills and farmland with fenced pastures. In the distance were the foothills of the Blue Ridge, and overhead, the sky was country-wide and pale winter gold.

At the intersection, we followed the arrow to Forksville, a little hamlet whose corporate limits were two blocks long, divided in half by a railroad with a country store on one side and a one-room cinder-block post office on the other. The sign on the side of the road read: Population: twenty.

"Wow! Billy-Wade, did you see that?" Wayne exclaimed, hanging over the tailgate. "Twenty people! I've got more people than that in my classroom."

Up the hill and around the curve, the land fell in a flat plain that rippled out to hills on either side of the road. Stretched out before us was a quarter of a mile of white board fence. Behind it, a big, two-story white house with a barn stood on 112 acres of open land with a strip of woods bordered in the back by a wooded stream.

Larry leaned forward and peered through the windshield. "Are you sure this is the right place?"

"That's what it says on the mailbox."

It was just so splendid it was hard to believe. A winding drive past white gateposts and age-old cedars led up to the stately sixteen-room house with green shutters. Across the front downstairs was a bannistered porch; upstairs, a veranda. Recently renovated, the house was in mint condition with six bedrooms, four baths, and a huge country kitchen with a table for twelve that could be extended for twenty. There was beauty in every direction, out every window. There were two ponds back to back on one side; on the other, the back forty acres of pasture that sloped down to a woodline by a wide stream called Broad Run.

"Billy-Wade, look!" Wayne squealed. "Look what's outside!"

An outside spiral staircase led from the upstairs bedroom wing to the ground below beside the kitchen, and before Larry and I could get outside, they were both belly-sliding down the winding bannister rail.

"Stop that!" Larry snapped. "You'll break your neck." And they leaped lightly down and ran toward the barn.

Giddy with excitement, Billy-Wade grabbed Wayne's hand. "Let's go see what's inside the barn."

Behind the house in the three-story white barn we found four Dutch-door stalls, with stanchions and feeding racks, a grain room, and a loft so big that at capacity it held 5,000 bales of hay. Beside the earthen barn ramp in the back stood an equipment shed with every machine necessary to maintain the operation of the 112 acres. We knew we had followed the yellow brick road to Oz when we discovered a machine shop on the end of the barn stocked with every kind of tool necessary for making repairs.

We were breathless. "I can't believe it," I told Larry.

It was unreal. It was too good to be true. It was as if heaven had opened up and dropped all its treasures in one spot. But the fact was that Harshaw had been a hobby farmer all his life and it had been his pride to put all his leisure and considerable resources into making the farm as perfect as possible. The house, the barn, the fields, and the fences were flawless.

"Nothing can be this good," Larry said skeptically, overwhelmed as the rest of us were. "They probably don't have any schools out here."

To find out, we drove back to the little hamlet over the hill and a half-mile away, and drew up beside the country store, an oblong block made of concrete with a tin roof and a porch overhang that sheltered two antique glass-globe gas pumps. Inside, two farmers, with weathered faces and fleece-lined jackets, sat on nail kegs drawn up to a potbellied stove in the center of the store and held their work-worn hands up to the wood-burning warmth.

The proprietor, wearing a grey felt hat and a red wool muffler wrapped around his wrinkled neck, leaned up against a wall shelf stocked with snuff, chewing tobacco, sardines, and soda crackers.

"What can I do for you?" he asked, leaning over a counter worn smooth by fifty years of transactions.

His name was Matthew and the store, owned by his family, had served the surrounding countryside for more than half a century. He himself had clerked there for forty-six of those years.

"We're thinking of moving to the farm down the way," we told him.

"The old Hammond place?"

"No, the Cromwell farm . . . Harshaw Cromwell."

Matthew squinted his eyes and shook his head to correct our error. No matter how many times a farm changed hands, it was al-ways designated by its original owner. "That's the Hammond place. That fellow Harshaw bought it from Hammond." He shook his head again. "Too bad about him. He just had got that place all fixed up when he up and died." He paused and gave us a measuring look. "You say you're thinking about moving in?"

"Yes, and we wanted to know about the schools."

Matthew's eyes narrowed suspiciously as though the community's integrity had been called into question.

"You won't find none no better nowhere."

"Where are the schools?"

"Three miles down the track in Minniesville." He pointed in the direction that the railroad ran. "School bus'll pick'em up right at your gate. Miz Hardy drives the bus . . . fine Christian lady . . . don't put up with no foolishness . . . no sass either. You can figger when they ride with Miz Hardy, they gonna get to school safe and they gonna come home safe."

The two old farmers sitting on the nail kegs, listening and looking at the floor, snickered.

Matthew, with his arms folded over his chest, nodded in their direction. "Them's my brothers . . . Clarence and Claude."

They gave us the barest nod of recognition and went back to looking at the floor. Matthew, to explain their snickering, said, "Miz Hardy's a proper woman and ain't no boy hereabouts has growed so big he's willing to tangle with her . . . she's a strong woman . . . weighs right at 250 pounds . . . spent all her life working in the fields . . . would be yet 'cept high blood stopped her . . . drives the school bus now." His eyes mirrored approval. "Them big boys riding the bus know that Miz Hardy ain't gonna let none of them little kids be teased and took advantage of. If they're set on foolishness, it ain't gonna be on Miz Hardy's bus 'cause she'll lay 'em out cold, and don't nuthin' escape her notice." He directed his question to his two brothers by the fire. "Ain't that right?"

The two old farmers wagged their heads from side to side, as if a miracle they still couldn't believe had been spoken of.

"You done spoke the truth," the one named Claude said.

"And ain't she strong?" Matthew insisted, urging more testimonials.

"Onliest woman I know that can outwork a man in the fields," Clarence replied.

"Ain't nobody can hold a candle to her handling that bus neither," Claude added. "I seen her myself put them snow chains on the school bus without no help from nobody."

This raised another question. Snow in the suburbs was an agony and a misery, with stalled cars clogging the street, and the snow plow so busy clearing highways and freeways that it was sometimes three days before snow was removed from our suburban street.

"What happens when it snows?" we asked.

Matthew received the question with profound perplexity. It was as though we had asked him something as inane as "What happens when it rains?" He and his two brothers exchanged glances, trying to decide if this was some smart-aleck city question or if we were just so dumb we didn't know.

"Snow removal," we explained.

"You mean clearing the road?"

We nodded.

He leaned back against the snuff shelf and smiled. "That ain't no problem. The county contracts with the farmers and ever' one of them has a section of road to keep clear. Ain't no man's pride gonna let his neighbor get ahead of him."

The two sitting beside the fire nodded their heads in agreement. "Ain't it the truth," Claude said.

"Ain't no problem getting through down here," Matthew pronounced with finality and pride. "Now about them schools . . . why 'ont you ride over to Minniesville and see for yourself?"

Minniesville was three miles down the track and thirty years back in time. It, like the little hamlet of Forksville, had been virtually undisturbed by modern mores and the destruction of "progress," for it was a little rural village on a spur of road off the main highway beside a railroad loading dock where once the milk train had taken on its supplies. Now the pickup was corn, grain, soybeans, and other crops the farmers produced.

Here were all the necessities for country living: two churches, a school, a seed and feed store, a general store, a barbershop, and a bank, laid out on both sides of a tree-lined street so deserted that it was reminiscent of abandoned towns in the Old West. At two o'clock in the afternoon, the only occupant of the main street through town was a lone dog sniffing his way down the center line.

"Can you believe this?" I asked Larry.

"It wouldn't surprise me to see the Dalton gang ride into town and tie up at the hitching post."

At the sprawling brick schoolhouse, we met the schoolmaster, a recently arrived ex-marine colonel who, like ourselves, had brought his family back to the country in search of old values and a more meaningful way of life.

"Many of our teachers are the same," he told us. "They are experts in their fields and they, too, have come back to the land for the same reason." His smile was reassuring. "Our curriculum is good, our standards high, our teachers dedicated, and the school spirit and student enthusiasm are like something out of the long ago."

Realizing that he was beginning to sound like the Chamber of

Commerce, he brushed the top of his grey crew cut and grinned self-consciously. "It's really true," he told us. "If you move out here, you'll find that the community is a celebration. Everyone participates in everything—football, baseball, horse shows, cattle shows, and County Fairs. There are no sideline spectators. It's not permitted. If you're not in the game, you take up tickets, serve refreshments, or help count the cash box."

Besides the industry and activity at the school, we learned there were pancake suppers at the firehouse and ice-cream socials at the church. It was like turning back time and having a chance to start all over again. It got so good, it got scary. I kept thinking that either one or all of us were going to die or get killed and God had just decided to give us everything we had ever longed for before we were gone.

Before that happened, we decided to sign the year's lease for the farm, rent out our suburban house, pack up our belongings, and get ready to move to the country.

CHAPTER 4

The Christmas Pony

IT WAS JUST BEFORE CHRISTMAS when we made our epochal decision to move from our house in the suburbs to the farm in the country, and with that, life began its 180-degree turn. For the first time ever, we would be able to indulge ourselves in all the country pleasures we had always wanted. With 112 fenced acres of rich pasture land, a barn full of hay, two ponds stocked with bass, bluegill, and catfish, a fishing boat beached on the side, and woods and a wide stream at the end of the property, the possibilities of what we could do and have were endless.

From the outset, ten-year-old Wayne insisted that it would be a Black Christmas if he did not have his own horse. He envisioned a thoroughbred who effortlessly cleared five-foot fences and himself riding the Grand National. What we found was somewhat less than that. The cost of thoroughbreds who rode in the Grand National began in the hundreds of thousands. The one we found didn't look as though he would live another day. He was a dark bay named Brandy who had been raced on the track by a man who became so broke he didn't have the money to feed him any longer and turned him out in the woods to eat acorns.

We were led to him by a blacksmith at the stables who did horse trading on the side. The blacksmith, a tough, wizened little man who looked like he had been carved from a pine knot, was named Weasel and exhibited all the qualities and characteristics of the animal for whom he had been named.

"That horse is a steal," he told us, swiping his hand over his crafty, pointed face. "With care and good grain and hay, you won't even recognize him in a month."

It seemed unlikely, but the blacksmith insisted that Brandy's legs were good even though his hooves were not. His hooves were ragged and as fragile and brittle as old porcelain, but Weasel dismissed this as lack of care that could be cured with daily applications of burnt motor oil.

"Besides," Weasel said, seeing his sale slip away on the condition of a hoof, "where you gonna find a thoroughbred for three hundred dollars with a disposition that good? Most of 'em are so hot and high-strung, a boy like that"—he pointed at ten-year-old Wayne—"can't even sit on 'em, much less handle 'em. This here one," he said, patting Brandy on the neck, "is gentle as a cow."

It occurred to me that he was as "gentle as a cow" because he was so hungry, weak, and undernourished that he was utterly unable to move, and once restored to health would likely not be that way at all. But Wayne had already fallen in love with him. Having read the story of the abused plow horse named Snow Man, who under the right master, became a champion in open jumping, Wayne was already imagining triumphs of his own.

"This is a sho'nuff thoroughbred," Weasel said, holding Brandy's head up and admiring the sale he was trying to make, "and ever' one of them thoroughbreds that gets raced on the track has got a number tattooed inside the lower lip to prove it."

He pulled Brandy's lip down to show us, but the blue numbers

were so blurred we could no longer read them to check his registration. Weasel claimed he was twelve years old, which was a good, safe
number to choose since age after that can no longer be determined
by the teeth; but there were still vestiges of the fine bearing he had
once had, and Wayne was set on restoration, so we bought the three-
hundred-dollar thoroughbred and didn't wait to stuff him in the
Christmas stocking. Instead, we took him home and began immediate
intensive care.

This took care of Wayne's Christmas and what he wanted most to
take to the farm, but then there was eight-year-old Billy-Wade, who
would also need a mount to ride now that we were moving away
from the stables and the horses they had to ride.

Back in the fall, Billy-Wade had admired a little show pony named
Shenandoah who was owned by a blind hay man named Crookshank.
He was known as a sharp trader and he delivered hay to the stables
where we rode. Crookshank claimed he had been blinded by shrap-
nel in the Battle of the Bulge, but his glazed eyes looked more
drunk than damaged, and when I saw him back a truck loaded with
two and one-half tons of hay into the barn with only an inch to spare
on either side, I thought we would do well to watch Crookshank.

When we tried to buy his show pony from him, Crookshank said
there wasn't a way in the world he'd let that little mare go.

"Why she's so gentle," Crookshank said, "you could put a baby up
on her back. All you gotta do is point her at a fence, and she'll take
it clean ever' time."

He had had a special Steuben jumping saddle fitted just for Shenandoah, and his youngest daughter had already won a roomful of ribbons riding her on the show circuit.

"No, siree," Crookshank said, slapping himself on the chest in
testimonial, "there ain't a thing in this world would ever make me
give up that little hoss."

When we repeated this story to Sergeant Massingale, our riding
instructor at the stable who had known Crookshank for years, he spit
over his shoulder into the dirt and watched it turn into a wobbly little
dust bubble.

"Crookshank and everything he owns is for sale," he scoffed.

"Either the price ain't right or the time ain't come. Sooner or later, it's one or the other."

Before Christmas, hoping maybe one of these conditions had developed, we went to see Crookshank again, but he only repeated what he had said before: "No sirree, ain't a thing in this world would ever make me give up that little hoss."

We didn't want to buy a horse in haste, so we went ahead with our pre-farm plan to get Billy-Wade the ten-speed bicycle that we had put on layaway, and to buy him the pair of mallard ducks he wanted instead. The duck farm was some fifteen miles away and when we got there, the owner and his helper waded out into a pond full of quacking ducks to pick out the pair that Billy-Wade selected. There was a lot of quacking and squawking and flapping of wings, but we got them home and put them in the dog pen with a panful of water until such time as we could transfer them to the ponds at the farm.

The ducks were less than delighted with their new accommodations because the pan of water was only big enough for them to put one foot in the water and run around the outside rim with the other foot. Dissatisfied with the accommodations we had provided for them, they simply got up in the middle of the night and flew back home to their pond fifteen miles away.

When I told the man who had sold them to us that his ducks had returned, he sighed. "I'll have my helper catch another pair. Just come on out and pick them up."

In the pouring-down rain, we drove out to bring the ducks back home. When we arrived, the owner's assistant, as promised, had caught the ducks and they were ready. Having nothing handy to put them in, he had tied them up in a paper bag, and when he picked them up to hand them to us, the bottom fell out of the paper bag and the ducks flew away again.

Next, he searched out a burlap bag and waded out in the pond and the pouring-down rain again to get another pair of ducks. The ducks, by now conditioned to what was coming, all started screaming and flying away. The two who weren't so alert to the inevitable were the two he fell on and stuffed in the burlap bag. Back home again, we put the ducks in the dog pen and chicken wire over the top to prevent a repeat performance.

Inside, the phone was ringing. Crookshank was on the line saying that he had to sell his little show pony, named Shenandoah, right away.

"Why Mr. Crookshank! You said you would never ever—"

"That was before my oldest girl got married. Now I got trouble and I got to raise money in a hurry."

"What happened?"

There was pain in his voice. "Well, the weddin' was nice enough, but the groom got drunk on the punch and when he and some of his ushers came out to the house to pick up their suitcases they hit the hell out of the tree in the front yard, tore them and the car plumb up, and one of the women relatives at the house called the rescue squad."

He heaved a heavy sigh and continued. "That ambulance driver laid that si-reen wide open coming out and scared the horses so goddam bad that they jumped the fence. Then when he'd loaded up all them that was injured and started back to the hospital, he laid the si-reen open again and the horses ran right out in the road in front of the ambulance and tore it all to pieces. I got everybody suing me and I gotta come up with some lawyer money. That's how come I want to sell Shenandoah. You still wanta buy her?"

Without a moment's hesitation I said yes. Then I tried to figure how I'd get the toy store to take back the ten-speed bicycle so that Billy-Wade could have the pony for Christmas instead.

It wouldn't be possible to tell him the truth, for who would believe the madness about Crookshank and the horses and the drunk bridegroom? Instead, with a perfectly straight face, I went in to see the toy store manager and lied.

"My mother-in-law," I told him, "without consulting us once, has gone out and bought our child a ten-speed bicycle just like the one we have on layaway here. It would be absurd for him to have two, so do you think you could possibly take back. . . ."

It was close to Christmas and the toy store was crowded with last-minute shoppers ripping whatever was left off the shelves. A woman shopper who overheard my conversation with the manager in the middle of the store shouted, "I'll take it!" and that solved that problem.

Larry and I were delighted. Wayne's horse, out of necessity and need for immediate care, would not be a Christmas morning surprise, but Billy-Wade's would. With a great deal of persuasion and even more money, we persuaded the blacksmith to pick up the pony in his horse van on Christmas morning from Crookshank and deliver him to the foot of our driveway. There, the man in the neighborhood who played Santa Claus at the community house, dressed in boots and a fur-trimmed red Santa Claus suit, agreed to lead the pony, saddled in the fine Steuben saddle, right to the front door!

We couldn't get over how wonderful it was going to be.

"Imagine being eight years old and having Santa Claus bring your very own pony right to the door on Christmas morning," we marveled. "Why, if it had happened to us, we would have simply died on the doorstep!"

I began to worry about it. The shock of such a surprise might be too much for Billy-Wade. He might have a heart attack and die from pure delight. I decided I had better prepare him for it.

He was draped over the arm of a chair in the family room, with cartoons on the television and his tousled dark head buried in the latest comic book about Superman. I edged up and began gently. I didn't want to blow his little mind with so much joy.

"Billy-Wade, do you remember that little pony named Shenandoah that you liked so much last fall?"

Without looking up from the comic book, he bobbed his head up and down.

"Welllll," I said in an I'm-going-to-let-you-in-on-a-secret tone, "if you're *very* good and do all your chores and homework, Santa Claus just *may* see if he can bring you that pony."

I expected to see him have a seizure and faint. Instead, he looked up from the comic book he was so engrossed in and with no more emotion than refusing a second bowl of cereal said, "I don't want a pony. I want a cow."

"*A cow!*" I was so indignant after all that trouble, all that time, and all that money, I shouted, "Well, you can't have a cow!"

Crookshank and all the people who had been persuaded to

leave their own houses on Christmas morning had to be called up and told that the sale was off and the arrangements were canceled. By that time, all the bicycles had been bought from the toy stores and there was nothing left but broken dolls and busted-up train sets. I did find a little one-inch plastic cow, lost out of a toy farm set, and that's the cow Billy-Wade got on Christmas morning. When he fished it out of the toe of his Christmas stocking, he was shocked.

"I didn't want a play com," he complained. "I wanted a real cow."

"Well," we told him, "you put your order in too late. When we get to the farm we'll see about a real one."

In the meantime, the millennium had arrived. It was New Year's Day, and we began packing up household goods, horses, ducks, dog, and kids. A month later, we led the moving van from the house in the suburbs to the farm in the country. We were on our way to Oz, never realizing that the farmers leaning on their pitchforks in the fields were predicting our early departure. What they didn't know, and neither did we at that point, was that we were made of sterner stuff than that.

CHAPTER 5

Pavlov's Bell

WE WERE SURE WE HAD COME HOME to Camelot that first night on the farm. Through a silver winter frost on the kitchen windows, we watched the sunset blaze across blue hills and die behind the dark silhouette of winter green trees in a red and blue glory that turned the ponds pink. We saw the evening star break through and shine in solitary splendor in a velvet blue sky. In the back pastures, we saw the moon rise and gild the fence posts and frost the grass gold, and we sank into a deep winter sleep lulled by soft country silence.

We were awakened out of this slumber by a knock at the door. I reached for the light switch, squinted against the glare, and looked at the clock on the bedside table. Five A.M. Larry groaned and covered his head with the covers. The knock was insistent.

Pulling on my blue flannel robe, I struggled across the living room to the back door and switched on the porch light. Standing in the white glare on the back steps was a very small woman bundled up in a very large overcoat, wearing boots, with a knitted orange scarf wrapped around her head looking very like a winter bird on a pair of toothpick legs. I couldn't remember what a grinch looked like, but I thought this must surely be one because she had a pointed beak of a nose, yellow eyes, a mouth that seemed to disappear into a straight line, and no chin at all. She was holding a jar of jelly.

When I opened the door, she stepped forward and chirped, "Good morning. I'm Henrietta Early."

If this was some kind of joke, I saw no humor in it. *Henrietta Early?* Nobody could be named Henrietta Early. It was just too absurd.

"I'm your neighbor at the next farm down and I brought you some jelly for breakfast."

She plopped the jar in my hand and pressed forward. I looked down at the still-warm jelly and the dark outside and tried to think of something appropriate to say for a present delivered at this hour. I couldn't.

"That's very nice of you. Won't you come in?"

I fully expected her to refuse and tell me she would come back at some later time, but she didn't. She stepped right through the door and went straight for the kitchen and began looking around. Her eye took in and cataloged everything.

"I saw you moved in yesterday." She stuck her head around the corner to look in the living room at the packing boxes stacked clear to the ceiling where the movers had left them. She turned back to me clearly appalled. "You haven't finished unpacking yet?"

I did not like being on the defensive at this hour of the morning with a perfect stranger, but I found myself shrugging and saying, "The movers didn't leave until after seven last night."

She gave a knowing nod, rejecting this as no excuse, and went back to the kitchen.

"Anybody sick?" Henrietta asked, hoping to find the secret of such a hopeless household.

"Why, no. Why do you ask?"

Henrietta looked at the green kitchen clock on the wall, now at five minutes past five. "Well!" she said, as though I were unable to recognize the obvious, "when I saw your kitchen light wasn't even on and you hadn't gotten up yet, I thought somebody must surely be sick."

Henrietta unwound the knitted orange scarf from around her head and smoothed down her thin brown hair. She had pale yellow eyes and pale yellow skin with a network of veins that should have been blue, but were pale green instead. Her eyes glittered as she stepped over to the kitchen counter and flicked away an imaginary spot.

"You know," she smiled, "out here in the country, you have to get up and get ahead of the sun if you're going to get your work done."

The comparison was invidious and almost immediately, I realized I was not going to find it very easy to like Henrietta, but it was five o'clock in the morning and no reliable time to make judgments. The only time I had ever been up at that hour of the morning was after dancing all night at a New Year's Eve party.

Having made her point was not enough for Henrietta. She walked about the kitchen with quick, short steps and found another imaginary spot to brush off the kitchen table, smiling indulgently as she did so.

"I've already put up thirty-five pints of preserves this morning. . . ." She paused and added, "after I finished my housework."

I found myself singularly uninterested in this piece of information, but forced to rally with a response. "Really? What do you find to preserve at this time of year?"

"Strawberries from the freezer . . . the ones I grew in the garden last spring. Back then, I was putting up a hundred pints a day. These are just the ones I had left over."

She was bragging and I knew it, but at this hour of the morning, I just had no tolerance for it. I was not about to be drawn into a contest on who could get up the earliest and put up the most preserves and get the most housework done. If this was Henrietta's idea of throwing down the gauntlet, she could just pick it back up and take it home.

She took the cup of coffee that I offered her, but before drinking it, she turned the saucer over, examined the markings underneath, took her napkin and polished the spoon, then drank the coffee all in one gulp.

"Well," she said, standing up and wrapping the orange knitted scarf around her head again, "I've got to be going. You're already far enough behind in your work this morning. I'll get along now so that you can get on with it."

I tried to force some sincerity into my voice. "Thank you for coming by. I do appreciate the preserves."

Henrietta gave me the kind of sympathetic smile reserved for failures. "Just remember . . . to succeed out here in the country, you have to get up and get ahead of the sun."

Her eyes glittered triumphantly and I saw that they had no more depth or warmth than a pair of glass beads. With a cold winter bird's quick short steps, Henrietta was out the door and gone. As I looked after her, I decided my first reaction was right. I didn't care what time it was or how unreliable judgment at this hour might be, I was not going to like Henrietta.

When I went down to the country store that morning to buy milk, Matthew was leaning against the snuff shelf muffled in his red scarf against the cold. His mouth was hidden, but I could see from his eyes that he was smiling.

"I see Henrietta's done got the drop on you already."

Matthew had his arms crossed over his chest rubbing his shoulders to keep warm and was rocking back and forth on his heels to increase his circulation. The potbellied stove in the middle of the store was radiating so small a circle of heat that none of it reached the counter where Matthew was standing behind the cash register.

"What do you mean?"

"I mean she's done called on you already."

I was surprised. "How did you know?"

Matthew pulled the scarf down with his finger so that he could talk. "First off, I was helping Clarence and Claude feed the stock this morning when I seen her turn into your driveway. Second, I know Henrietta. Anytime there's a new neighbor, she always stakes out territory right away. She don't let no woman get up and get ahead of her, and from where she lives down there on that rise, she can see 'most every kitchen window in the valley, and she sees to it don't nobody beat her gettin' up and gettin' started."

"Well, it was five o'clock in the morning, for Heaven's sake!"

"That don't matter none," Matthew grinned. "If you had of got up at four o'clock, Henrietta woulda been there at three-thirty. She likes to live up to her name and takes it serious."

"Is she *really* named Henrietta EARLY? That seems so unlikely."

"Might be unlikely, but it shore suits."

"I find it hard to believe."

"Well, it's the God's truth. Old Jubal Early, the Confederate general in the Civil War, was some sort of relative of theirs . . . leastwise, Henrietta claims it was so."

Matthew paused to catch his breath and change gears. "Now Ewell, her husband, ain't like that atall. He's as nice a fellow as you'll find. Don't make much money 'cause he ain't got the heart for tradin' . . . honest as the day is long . . . full measure for everything . . . and he ain't about to change."

"What's wrong with that?" I asked.

"Keeps him in a whole lot of trouble with Henrietta 'cause she don't understand nothing 'cept dollars and cents, and a lot of times you'll hear her lay the sharp side of her tongue on the raw side of his back for not tradin' hard."

"That's too bad."

Matthew shrugged. "Henrietta's just thata way."

Out in the country, they had a way of accommodating everybody's faults and eccentricities. With failings of their own, they didn't hold hard on someone else's, and Matthew no more faulted Henrietta for her meanness of spirit than he would have faulted her for having been born with a clubfoot. To him, "Henrietta was just thata way."

"Ewell," Matthew said, drawing his conclusions to a close, "is a good neighbor. Willing to work and willing to help."

I found that what Matthew said was true. Ewell Early drove up later in the day in his ragged red pickup truck and offered whatever assistance we might need in getting settled. Over a cup of coffee in the kitchen, I learned that he had grown up on the land and that during the Depression, he and his family had lost their "home place" with a bank foreclosure but had been hired back as tenants to work the land that had once been theirs. The pain and humiliation of this was still in his eyes. He passed his hand over his mouth to wipe away the hurt, tried for a smile, and said, "Now, Henrietta and I, and our three boys, live with her father at the next farm down. If you need any help, just give us a call."

I decided to forget about Henrietta, but Ewell, I could see, would be a good and reliable friend. We waved good-bye and I got back to the business of beginning to live on the land.

We soon learned the cadence of the country: Larry, leaving before light on dark winter mornings to drive into work in the city; Wayne and Billy-Wade, catching the yellow school bus at the gate by the foot of the driveway to go over the hill to the schoolhouse in Minniesville three miles away; and I, running the farm until they all returned.

In the afternoons at four o'clock when the boys were back from school, we rode the horses over fences and fields, manicured and clipped in the fall and held fast in their winter beauty by winter's cold frost. We gave ourselves over to unmitigated indulgence and sampled every simple country pleasure we had so long anticipated.

Wrapped in our cocoon of cold and snow, we spent long winter evenings by a blazing log fire with little black Suzie curled up on the hearth beside us. Mongrel that she was, Suzie was a delicate little dog with ruffles and curls down her shining black coat, and a white lacy jabot at her throat. Despite this, she ran like a fox hound beside us on our rides through the woods, coming home exhausted and stretching her tired little body as close to the hearth as she could get, her chin resting on her black fluff feet, the curls on her ears tangled and tumbling down on the rug.

Outside on the pond, the ducks quacked and flapped their wings in undiminished glee. They not only had a pond to swim in again, they had a pond all to themselves . . . not one . . . but two, back to back . . . and if they chose, a his and hers pond. They were very possessive of their new acquisition and if another animal or someone unknown to them approached their ponds, they began to scream and yell and carry on and give voice to their objections. At first, we thought there might be danger, and every time we heard a riot down at the pond, we went running out to see if they were all right. Finally, we overlooked their outbursts of outrage and watched through the kitchen window as they cut wakes across the pond's surface and threw epithets at anyone who tried to intrude or interfere.

The horses figured they had died and gone to heaven and now dwelt in the Elysian fields, for they had a hundred acres of pasture behind the barn, all their own—enough grass for a herd of horses, and every blade belonged to them. By now, Brandy's sleek thoroughbred lines had returned and he had rounded out and become the color of fine cognac held up to sunlight. Sabre, satisfied and satiated, became so content that neither he nor Brandy wanted to come to the barn to be fed until the last light left the pasture in a purple haze. In the afternoons when we wanted to ride, we had to go to the pasture and hunt them down.

Right away, this became a problem. Calling them did no good. They were too busy enjoying themselves to be bothered. When they heard the call, they looked up from a hilltop away and went right back to grazing with no thought whatever of responding. When Sabre saw us coming through the pasture with halters and lead shanks, knowing it was time to work instead of play, he frolicked off to the next hill to graze and gaze at the sky and do nothing at all but what pleased him. Seeing this, Brandy followed, and what should have been a wonderful afternoon of riding turned into an angry afternoon of playing chase all over the hills.

It would have been a pity to take away their freedom of a hundred acres and lock them up in the paddock just so they would be available to ride, for we loved watching them run free in the gold of the afternoon across the pasture. Besides, one of their jobs, which was also their joy, was to keep the grass in the pasture clipped, and this couldn't be done shut up in the paddock. It was clearly a problem.

In all our previous experiences, problems had been solved by practical application. This would have to be, too. The solution we sought was how to make the horses *want* to come to the barn when called—want to so much that their desire would overcome their reluctance to work and leave play.

Seeking a solution, I remembered Pavlov's dog and his principle of conditioned response. In the laboratory, Pavlov rang a bell each time he fed a laboratory dog to produce anticipation and, thereby, salivation. It seemed to me that his principle of conditioned response would work well on the horses too.

There was a fine cast-iron bell on the farm that had been used in an earlier age by previous owners to call hands in from the field. This would serve well as our bell. By temporarily penning the horses up in the paddock, and ringing the bell every time they were given grain, the association of being fed grain with the ringing of the bell should produce the anticipation and thereby the conditioned response we desired: running in from the fields so that we didn't have to spend the afternoon chasing them down to ride.

I was rather sure of the results because Sabre, our red gold gelding with the flaxen tail and mane, had one absolute failing: he would do anything to get grain, and when he did, it was so exquisitely delicious to him that he literally couldn't stand it. At the grain box in his stall, he always drew one foreleg up to his barrel chest and stood trembling on the other three as he ate the delicious morsels of corn, oats, and sorghum. All things considered—like loyalty, obedience, reliability—his stomach came first.

All I had to do was train him and Brandy on Pavlov's principle and Sabre would be a pushover. He would immediately run in from the pasture to get grain.

Since the horses were bigger, stronger, and faster, it was necessary to work on weaknesses. Brandy had his, too. Now that he had found a buddy in Sabre, Brandy had a hang-up about being left alone. After all those years by himself in the woods eating acorns, he didn't want to be left alone again. Wherever Sabre went, he dogged along behind. Even out in the pasture with all the grass in the world to choose from, he ate at the same spot that Sabre did. Once in a while, he would stray a short distance away, but never so far that he couldn't keep Sabre in sight.

Even out riding, if one got separated from the other, they had a system of calling to each other: a loud whinny that meant, "Here's me. Where's you?" The response was immediate: another loud whinny giving location.

Sabre learned easily, but he wasn't as shrewd as Brandy. We figured if we pulled Pavlov off on him, Brandy would follow him back to the barn. For two days, we went out to the paddock every hour, rang the bell, and gave each of them a handful of grain. Sabre thought this was super. We didn't even have to close the gate to keep them locked up. They just hung around the paddock fence and waited for the next bell to ring.

The third day, we turned them back out in the field. By then, Sabre had lost all his enthusiasm for anything but bell ringing. He hung around the paddock fence for hours waiting for the bell and the grain. When it didn't happen with the regularity of the previous days, he began to pout, sticking his lips out like big pie plates and sulking around the fence until finally, he stalked out to the pasture and began to graze.

At four o'clock, when we went out to ride, we rang the bell. It was like thunder out of the west. Sabre ran so hard back to the barn that his feet were working some six inches off the ground. Seeing this, Brandy started off right behind him, then, with his long, easy thoroughbred strides, beat Sabre to the barn. A handful of grain, a pat, and we hitched them to the hitching post, groomed, saddled, and rode them with no more trouble.

The idyll we had all imagined was coming true. Every afternoon when the school bus came over the hill and deposited Wayne and Billy-Wade at the front gate, there was a snack waiting at the kitchen table, and then at four o'clock, it was Boots and Saddles.

We had found a little bay pony named Winchester at the sales barn in Minniesville for Billy-Wade to ride. In color and conformation, he looked like a miniature of Brandy, whom he adored and tried to emulate in every way, making his little legs fly to keep up with Brandy's long-legged stride. Sabre didn't much care for Winchester and considered him a little upstart, and whenever the opportunity arose, Sabre took his nose and belted Winchester in the belly. Winchester soon learned to stand on the off side of Brandy, who afforded him protection from Sabre's contemptible temper.

Under saddle, they forgot their differences and we rode through the winter woods down by Broad Run and watched the icy water swirl over ancient rocks. Where the water ran smooth, we saw the bare trees bending over the mirror of the stream admiring their reflections in the water. We galloped over the smooth winter grass of the pasture and jumped fences while squirrels in nearby treetops watched and complained to each other about this intrusion on their quiet.

Little black Suzie ran right alongside, her fluff feet racing to keep up, her curly black ears flying, her pink tongue hanging out the side of her mouth. When fatigue had just about overcome her, we picked her up and carried her across the saddle as we relaxed, dropped the reins, and rode the buckle back to the barn. On the way, we stopped at the persimmon tree, heavy with fruit, and stood in our stirrup irons to reach the topmost icy orange balls, sweetened by frost.

As we rode up and over the hill, the barn was silhouetted black against the red setting sun that had turned the ponds pink and it was time for evening chores. While I cooked supper, the boys fed and watered the horses, then Billy-Wade had the additional duty of taking corn down to the pond to feed his ducks.

We were gathered at the kitchen table one night, waiting for his return from the pond, while Wayne described Brandy's latest jump across the fence to his daddy. The kitchen door burst open and Billy-Wade rushed in. His face distorted with shock and pain, tears running down his cheeks.

"Somebody ate them!" he cried.

"Ate what?"

"The ducks!"

The foxes had come during the night and feasted on Billy-Wade's two ducks, leaving only feathers and bones on the bank of the pond. It was our first experience on the farm with death and we were all profoundly shocked and saddened.

In the suburbs, pets were precious. They lasted for years and became family members just as Suzie had. In the country, back to nature, things were different. There was the symbiotic balance. Everything fed on something else. Life was cheap, full of challenges and predators. Before we moved to the country, on our summertime rides from the suburbs, the farm animals standing in the pasture and the ducks swimming on farm ponds always looked so secure and peaceful. Until now, we never realized how vulnerable they were and what perils they faced from the forces of nature. This was just the first of many lessons we were to learn about nature and mortality and the short span that every living thing has. We saw animals born and we saw them die and we saw them replaced by others who themselves gave way to those who succeeded them. It was nature's way of replenishing the species. Each one had his brief moment. Some of them languished it away, and others seized center stage and made the most of it.

For the moment, Billy-Wade couldn't understand this. All he could understand was that the ducks he had loved and cared for were gone, eaten by the foxes, with only bits and bones left on the bank of the pond, and all he could do was cry.

Word of what happened to Billy-Wade's ducks traveled fast through our country community and the next afternoon, Ewell Early and Henrietta drove up in his ragged red pickup truck. Ewell stepped out and tipped his hat. "I hear you had a problem down on your pond."

When I told him what the foxes had done to Billy-Wade's ducks, he shook his head sadly. "Happens all the time. The ducks stay out in the water till it freezes around their legs. Then the fox walks right out there on the ice and eats them."

Clinging to my side, Billy-Wade's big brown eyes filled up with tears.

"No use in doing that, sonny," Henrietta snipped, her yellow glass eyes hardened by all she had seen. "Animals come and animals go and you can't waste time getting all soppy and sentimental."

A sob caught in Billy-Wade's throat and Ewell opened his mouth to say something to Henrietta, then closed it again and turned to the back of his pickup truck, taking out two big-breasted Muscovy ducks. He bent down and handed them to Billy-Wade.

Billy-Wade wiped his eyes on the sleeve of his white sweatshirt, reached up and smiled. "Thank you," he managed to say.

Ewell gave his shoulder an understanding pat. "You're welcome."

The warmth of the exchange was too much for Henrietta. She

quirked the corner of her straight-line mouth and turned back to the truck. "Can't waste time on sentiment, I always say. 'Course, Ewell don't listen to what I say, that's why. . . ."

Ewell took her gently by the arm and put her in the truck. "Come on, Henrietta, we gotta go home."

The two Muscovies, black and white with little red beads around their beaks, were content on our pond and utterly devoted to each other, and because they were, we named them Othello and Desdemona.

As word went around our little community that the foxes had eaten the only two ducks that Billy-Wade had, other farmers shared their bounty with us. Carlyle Hayes, a big, robust dairyman from over in Minniesville, brought us two of the white Peking ducks from his pond, and an old man named Joe Frost drove over in his wood-slated cattle truck with a black duck of undetermined breed.

Joe looked like a poor man's Jimmy Durante, with a nose so long and that hung down so far that it almost pulled his eyes shut. He was a poor, emaciated, ragged little man, barely five feet tall, thin as a fence rail, wearing a worn jacket with tattered sleeves. I hesitated taking the duck because it seemed likely that this was one of his few remaining possessions. He insisted and I accepted.

"This here is a powerful duck," he said, handing me the black duck he had tenderly cradled in his arms. "You'll need a good name for him."

"How 'bout Black Power?"

His old eyes crinkled into folds and his nose hung down like a drain spout. "I think that sounds plumb fittin'."

Down at the country store that afternoon, Matthew's brothers, Claude and Clarence, having finished with their work, were sitting on nail kegs pulled close to the potbellied stove, their dog, a black and white Border Collie named Frances, lying at their feet. When I walked in, they looked up, gave me a barely discernible nod, and looked back at the floor. Frances did too. I was still "the new girl" in the neighborhood and they hadn't yet decided if it was fit to pass the time of day with me. They were already satisfied that the rigors of the country were going to send me screaming back to the city sooner or later, and it was hardly worth getting to know somebody who was going to be so soon gone.

Although Matthew was the oldest of the three brothers, Clarence was by far the biggest, a big ox of a man with a day's stubble of beard, and triangular white sideburns that hung in pendants below his ears. Born on the farm, he grew up and grew old on the land he farmed and there was nothing he didn't know about crops, cows, and how to make them grow. He and his brothers lived in the house next door to the store with the equipment shed behind that and the red barn behind that. For nearly sixty years, he had farmed the same land, season after season, as his father before him had done, and his father before that. When it came to doing what he did, he was an *authority* and he didn't like anyone disputing his word or thinking they could easily do what for sixty years he had done.

Matthew had always been sick and weakly from a blood condition and had never spent a day in his life out in the field. It therefore fell to Clarence to be in charge and to Claude to do what he was told. It was also Claude's lot to agree with whatever Clarence said. Claude's general endorsement on everything was: "Ain't it the truth!" This seemed to satisfy Clarence and when Clarence spoke ex cathedra, as he did on everything, he could always be assured of an affirmative response from Claude in the Amen Corner.

To further distinguish his position as leader of the clan, Clarence wore a black and white striped engineer's cap, indoors and outdoors. This was an authority symbol and out in the country it stood for something. It meant you knew what you were doing, and if you didn't, it made you look like you did. Claude wore a knitted wool ski cap that made his little onion-size head and his sun-wrinkled brown face seem smaller yet.

Another indulgence that Clarence had was wearing white athletic socks under his brogans with the red cuffs turned down over the top. Everybody else wore black so that the dirt wouldn't show, but Clarence liked red, so much so that he bought a red tractor, painted the barn red, and chewed Red Dog Chewing Tobacco. This flair for red gave him the reputation of being something of a rake, and he cherished that and jealously guarded his position and prerogatives, wrapping himself in an exclusivity that precluded the necessity for passing pleasantries with just anybody who came in the store.

After a perfunctory nod at me when I came in the door, Clarence and Claude were satisfied to sit, bent over their nail kegs, their arms crossed and resting on their knees, listening but not looking. Their dog, Frances, did too.

With Matthew, it was different. He was a storekeeper, and in his own rural way, he understood about public relations, and business, and people, and knew he couldn't act like Clarence and Claude if he expected to keep his customers. *They* were farmers and they could sit there like two fenceposts if they wanted to, but he couldn't. He smiled and asked after his customers' health, and how things were going down on their farms.

This affability and the flow of people in and out all day had made Matthew's store the meeting place of the community and the public forum for the countryside. This was where all the news was gathered, discussed, considered, and passed on in judgment. Matthew presided over it all standing behind the big brass cash register and leaning up against the snuff shelf. The cash register didn't work anymore, but it looked impressive and official, and Matthew kept it there in its place on the counter where it had been since the store opened in the early 1900's. He now used a King Edward cigar box to keep his cash and meticulously wrote down each sale with the tax on a Blue Horse note pad. After I paid for the loaf of bread I came to buy, Matthew took the yellow Micado pencil from behind his ear, licked the point, and wrote out a receipt for the sale. He had his receipt pads specially printed in Richmond, announcing across the top: *MATTHEW MADDOX, Dealer in General Merchandise, Shoes, Dry Goods, Seeds and Feeds.*

Since his customers bought in cash and on credit, the reverse side of the receipt carried this legend:

> *TO OUR CUSTOMERS:*
> *You need your money*
> *And I need mine,*
> *If we both get ours*
> *It will sure be fine.*

But if you get yours
And hold mine too,
What in the world
Am I going to do?
Think it over.

Every sale, no matter how small, was made a matter of record, laboriously noted on the Blue Horse pad and written out on a receipt that was given to the customer. When our business with the bread was finished, Matthew crossed his arms over his chest and leaned back against the snuff shelf. "I heard you had trouble down on your pond," he said, tilting his head back and looking at me through smudged, steel-rimmed glasses.

I told him what had happened to Billy-Wade's ducks and how warm and wonderful the neighbors had been, and how this poor old man named Joe Frost had come in a broken-down cattle truck and brought us this one black duck. "I hated to take it," I told Matthew, "because from the looks of him, I expect it's all he had."

Clarence and Claude, silent until now, broke out laughing and rolled around on their nail kegs and almost fell on the floor in a fit. I looked to Matthew to find out what this meant.

Matthew grinned and threw his head back so that when the light hit his glasses, his eyes looked like two silver dollars. "Don't waste no time worrying about Joe. He's probably the richest man in the county. Owns ten miles of land along both sides of the highway and more cattle than he can count."

"But he *looks* like . . ."

Matthew shook his head. "He goes around looking thata way so nobody'll think he's got nuthin'! Since he's little, and old besides, he ain't able to fight for what he's got, so he figgers if folks thinks he ain't got nuthin', they won't try to take nuthin' off of him."

Matthew smiled and tried to make it sound polite since Clarence and Claude were still rolling around in uncontrolled laughter. "So don't you worry about Joe being pore. He's a country fox . . . a rich one."

The notion of "pore Joe" and my misplaced sympathies struck near hysteria in Clarence and Claude. They hooted and hollered and laughed all the harder. Frances, seeing her masters struck with such joy, got up and wagged her tail. Clarence grabbed his sides so his belly wouldn't shake so hard, and Claude's wizened little face disappeared in laugh wrinkles. "Don't that beat all!" Clarence yelped, enormously enjoying the foolishness of my misjudgment of Joe. "Joe . . . pore!"

"That's enough!" The command came like the crack out of a rifle.

While we were talking, I had heard the store door open behind me, and when I turned around a massive woman in a red and black lumber jacket, pegged black trousers, and a two-inch leather watchband stood in the doorway. Her brown hair at some point in time had been treated to a cheap permanent wave, and now fringed her red knitted cap with a border of brown fuzz. Her face had never known makeup and was as solemn and granite-hard as the statue of Constantine.

Matthew looked up and smiled. "Hey, Maude, this here is our new neighbor down the way." Turning back to me, he explained: "This here is Maude Hardy. She drives the school bus."

Maude took no notice of what Matthew was saying. She had her eyes riveted on Clarence and Claude still rolling around the floor saying, "Joe . . . pore!"

"How was she to know?" Maude demanded.

The two of them laughed all the harder.

Maude took one step forward. "Get up and get out of here."

Clarence stopped laughing for a moment and shook his big St. Bernard head. "But, Maude. This here is *our* store."

Claude endorsed the objection and babbled, "Ain't it the truth!"

In one swift movement, Maude reached down and grabbed Claude up off the nail keg by his overall strap, holding him up to eye level dangling above the floor. "I said . . . git!"

She dropped him back on the floor like a cat held by the nape of his neck and moved over to deal with Clarence, but Clarence just curled his hulk up inside his overcoat and turned away toward the door. Frances, sensing this indignity, tucked her tail and went along with them.

As they skulked out the door, Maude Hardy said, "Shame on the both of you . . . treatin' a newcomer that way."

Matthew, enormously enjoying the action in the arena, grinned when they were gone and said to me, "Didn't I tell you, first time I seen you, that Maude Hardy don't put up with no foolishness?"

She held out her hand and shook mine with a wrenching squeeze. "Welcome to our community." There was warmth in the welcome and friendship in her eyes.

"Thank you," I replied.

She jerked her head toward the door where Clarence and Claude had made their exit. "Them boys get to carrying on every once in a while and have to get put in their place, 'else they'll get out of hand."

Matthew, fearing he might be next, hurried to pass over it with a strained smile. "Now, Maude, you know they didn't mean it hard."

Maude fastened a steady look on his face. "I ain't having nobody make light of ladies . . . or anybody else for that matter." Then, turning to me, she addressed herself to the current topic of the community. "I hear you had trouble down on your pond."

The personality of the pond changed completely with the arrival of the new ducks. Having been residents of farm ponds, they were accustomed to visitors who stopped to rest and replenish themselves on their spring flights north after a winter in the southern sun. Whenever our ducks saw an interesting flight overhead, they quacked and squaked and flapped their wings and told the flight leader, "Come on down. Stay with us. We have plenty of room."

Their hospitality was legion. At times it looked as though the United Nations had arrived, because there was something of everything on the pond . . . Canadian wild geese, wild swans, and once even some egrets that we had only seen before in Florida, feeding beside cattle in the pasture and standing on their backs to pick lice from their hides.

We especially wished that the wild swans would stay, but the time came and they raised their magnificent wings in mighty grace and disappeared into the blue sky from whence they'd come.

Billy-Wade, meantime, had decided to employ Pavlov's principle to the ducks. Instead of having to walk to the pond each night with a bucket of grain to feed them, he wanted them outside the kitchen door waiting after he had finished his ride. Ringing the bell obviously was not going to work with the ducks. So he had to think of another sound association. Standing on the bank of the pond and employing an imitation quack didn't work. The ducks only looked askance and whispered to themselves, "Who does that dummy think he's trying to fool?"

One night, by chance, he was humming his then-current favorite song, "Bridge Over the River Kwai." This struck some responsive chord in the ducks. They all swam to the pond bank and followed Billy-Wade and the grain bucket up the hill to the kitchen door, marching straight as an arrow, one behind the other, in time to Billy-Wade's rendition of "Bridge Over the River Kwai." . . . Da-dum . . . da-da-da-dum-dum-dum . . . da-dum . . . da-da-da-dum-dum-dum. . . .

One morning we woke to bitter cold. The temperature had fallen to five below and the snow that had fallen two days before had turned to glacial ice, freezing everything . . . water pipes, water trough, and ponds. The wind-chill factor was fifty below, and Wayne and Billy-Wade, cherry-cheeked and wrapped like two little round mummies in sweaters, coats, scarves, and caps, waited for the school bus beside the protective branches of the giant cedar at the foot of the driveway.

Delayed not more than a minute by the crippling cold, Maude Hardy arrived driving the school bus and whisked them over the hill to the schoolhouse. Busy with burst pipes, I did not look outside again until I saw the yellow school bus drive up in the driveway.

Wearing her red and black lumber jacket, a red ski cap over her scraggles of brown hair, and a pair of thin leather ballet slippers on her feet, Maude Hardy stood on the running board of her bus.

"Won't you come in?" I asked.

"Can't. I haven't got on my boots. My feet are killing me today." She smiled good-naturedly. "They never have been big enough to support the rest of me."

I noticed for the first time how very small and delicate her hands and feet were and I searched for an appropriate response, but Maude had gone on to other business.

"I thought I'd better tell you, in case you haven't noticed, one of your ducks is frozen fast in the pond. I saw it as I drove past your place this morning."

I just wanted to cuss. I had trouble enough already without a frozen-fast duck. "I guess I'll have to go out there with an ax and chop him loose."

Thunder was in Maude's face. "Don't you dare do such a thing!" she commanded like a sergeant correcting a recruit. "That's how people drown in farm ponds. You get out there on that ice, and the next thing, we'll be looking for you. Just keep an eye on him out the window and make sure the foxes don't get him before the ice melts and he can work himself loose."

Without another word, she got back under the steering wheel of the school bus and took off like a big yellow zeppelin down the driveway.

With everything else to be done, the water pipes burst, and the house in chaos, now I had to babysit a duck. There was nothing else to do but pull on fleece-lined boots, fleece-lined jacket, and everything else I could find to keep warm and walk down through the frozen pasture. It was Black Power, frozen fast to a mother-of-pearl pond.

"Quaaaaaaaack."

When he saw me, he made so sad an appeal for help that I wanted to go out on the pond and get him anyway, but the pond, completely iced over, was not sufficiently frozen to support my weight. There was no way in the world to free him other than going out and chopping a hole in the ice, and with Maude Hardy's warning still ringing in my ears, I decided against taking the risk.

The other ducks, nestled into the bank out of the icy wind, chattered and worried among themselves about what had happened to Black Power, but there was nothing to do except what Maude had suggested.

Later that day, as I kept watch out the kitchen window, I noticed that the other ducks had walked across the ice and joined Black Power in the middle of the pond, clustering around him to keep him company. I thought, How nice. At least he's not lonely.

But it was more than that. The ducks had the solution I did not have. By clustering around their fast-frozen friend, they generated enough body heat to melt the ice around Black Power's imprisoned legs. Before sundown, they had their friend free, and at nightfall, they were all lined up outside ready to receive their grain.

I marveled at their community cooperation. It was the best I had ever seen, and when Wayne and Billy-Wade got home from school, I told them what the ducks had done.

"I think that's neat," Wayne grinned.

I so approved of what the ducks had done, I thought it worthy of a pronouncement. "There's a lot the community of man might learn from the conduct of animals," I told them.

"You mean do as good as the ducks?" Billy-Wade asked.

"Right."

When feeding time came, I told Billy-Wade, "Give the ducks a double portion of grain tonight."

"Are they getting a reward?" he asked.

"Yes, for cooperation and compassion."

That night, Maude Hardy called on the phone. "I see your duck got loose."

"Yes, and I want to thank you. That was especially nice of you to be watching the fields and let me know."

"Nothing special about it," Maude said. "All us farmers watch the others' fields and call in when we see something. You'll be expected to do that, too."

The idea we had had, on first moving to the farm, of being out in God's wilderness forty miles from nowhere with no one knowing what was happening, was largely a myth. Actually, everyone was looking as they drove up and down the road and as they worked in the fields. To know what was going on afforded the nucleus for the day's conversation, but it also afforded protection. Out in the country with so much to look after, there were other eyes helping guard what was your own, and at the first sign of trouble, they called to alert or warn you of what you might not have seen.

Raw recruit that I was, I began to train my eye to scan the horizon until I could spot the barest movement of a brown thrush in a brown field. By then, the worst of winter was over.

We had survived, at least, thus far, and for this we were held in a new regard by Clarence and Claude and the other farmers in the fields around us. Instead of shaking their heads as we drove by, they began, tacitly, to nod their heads in greeting. Nothing really enthusiastic, or even cordial, just recognition that we were still part of the community, that we had lasted longer than they thought we would.

The real test was yet to come. They knew it, but we didn't. We were still enjoying the long quiet of winter hibernation, but our plans were already made.

In the spring, we would fish for bass in the pond and plant a garden . . . corn, beans, peas, tomatoes, okra, cabbage, cucumbers, squash, watermelons, and pumpkins. There was almost nothing in the seed catalog that we weren't going to try. Summer would be early morning rides, dips in the pond, sitting on the upstairs veranda sipping tall glasses of tea and lemonade. Besides all this, we were going to make hay for the horses' winter feed. This, we thought, would be jolly good sport, a reenactment of Currier and Ives.

Our only contact with hay had been what we bought for the horses at the feed store already baled, but on our Sunday rides in the country we had seen from the car farmers in the fields making hay. It looked like marvelous fun, riding through the fields on a wagon stacked high with hay. We'd do it, too.

All of the equipment necessary for making hay was stored in the now almost empty barn. One day in summer, when the notion struck us, we would get it all out and make hay, but that was a season away. For the moment, we stretched in front of the fire and contemplated all the summer pleasures.

Then one morning in early spring, there was a knock on the door.

CHAPTER 6

Is This Oz?

A STRANGER STOOD ON MY PORCH, a man I had never seen before. As I peered through the windowpane onto the porch outside, I saw that he was wearing a narrow-brimmed grey hat with a small red feather tucked in the band, a wool plaid shirt, baggy pants, and dusty shoes. He appeared to be in his mid-sixties and reminded me of childhood memories of my grandfather.

When I opened the door, he swept off his hat with a courteous flourish, showing a wisp of grey hair on top of his head. Behind his glasses, his brown eyes were warm and friendly.

"Is Mr. Cromwell home?"

The question came as a surprise. Mr. Cromwell, Kate's husband, Harshaw, who had owned the farm we leased, had been dead for several months.

The man was looking at me expectantly, waiting for a reply.

"Why no," I said slowly. "Mr. Cromwell is dead."

"Dead!" He blinked his eyes and stepped back as though he had received a physical blow.

"Yes. More than four months ago."

He passed his hand over his mouth to wipe away the shock. "Nobody told me," he said, in a voice so full of sorrow that I apologized for being the one to break the news. He looked suddenly very old and so pale I thought he might faint.

"Won't you come in and have some tea?"

He hesitated, and held on to the door frame.

"Please do," I insisted. "I was just going to have a cup myself."

"Why, thank you, I will."

He followed me into the kitchen and sat down at the table as though this was his accustomed place.

"I hope you'll forgive me for breaking in like this," he said, massaging his forehead with his hand. "This was just so unexpected. Why the last time I saw Harshaw . . . that is, Mr. Cromwell . . . he was fit as a fiddle, and to find. . . ." His voice trailed off.

I poured the tea and he told me that he and Harshaw had been friends since boyhood. When Harshaw bought the farm, he had sold him all his farm equipment, and came back from time to time to service it.

"This," he explained, "is why I haven't seen Harshaw for a while and didn't know what happened. I travel from one area to another all over the countryside and haven't been back here for a while."

He told me his name was Jim Finley and he was interested to know about us and how we had come to live at the farm. When I told him, he said, "You've done farming before?"

"Not at all," I replied. "As a matter of fact, I don't even know how to turn on the tractor."

Mr. Finley rattled his teacup setting it down.

"And you with a hundred and twelve acres to take care of!" he exclaimed, worry settling on his brow. "We'd better go do something about that right now. Have you got a pair of boots?"

I nodded.

"Get them and let's go to the barn."

We walked to the back ramp of the barn where the tractors would pull the hay wagons inside for unloading. Mr. Finley pushed open the double sliding doors.

At that moment, my education in farming began. In his grandfatherly fashion, speaking slowly, as though he were instructing a small child, he explained all the equipment and its uses.

I learned about eight-foot cutter bars, bushhogs, hydraulic lifts, hay conditioners, and manure spreaders. There were two tractors in the barn, a big blue Ford and an old grey Jubilee.

"This," Mr. Finley said, patting the hood of the big blue tractor, "is the workhorse. You'll want it for all your heavy work like bushhogging, pulling the manure spreader, and baling hay."

"What's a bushhog?"

"That's the big mower you'll use to clip your fields, but we'll get to that in a minute. First I want to tell you about this old fellow." He rested his hand on the steering wheel of the old grey Jubilee parked alongside the blue tractor, as though he was going to introduce me to an old and trusted friend. "This one's your helper. It can pull wagons and carts and you can use it for conditioning and raking hay, but I'll warn you right now, don't put too much strain on it. It's like an old man with a bad heart, it's got to be cared for and coddled."

In order to cut hay, I learned, the first step was attaching the eight-foot cutter bar with rows of red shears like lobster claws to the blue tractor. This would fell the grass in great clean sweeps. When this was done, the next step was to use the conditioner, an attachment with two cleated metal cylinders that picked up the cut hay and rolled it through the cylinders, crimping the cut grass and mashing out the moisture. This would be followed by the rake, an attachment with rotating prongs that picked the grass up and piled it in neat windrows for the baler. This marvelous piece of machinery cut the hay, packed it into bales, tied it with twine, and dropped it in the fields to be stacked on the wagon and taken to the barn. Inside, a conveyor the size and height of a fireman's ladder would pull the bales of hay to the top of the barn to be stacked.

Listening to Mr. Finley, it all sounded deceptively easy; in fact, downright simple. I was sure we would have no trouble making hay. In one afternoon, I had learned all I needed to know about farming. All we had to do was play Farmer in the Dell.

Winds and rain washed winter away and the grass, yellowed by snow and freezing cold, now began to show fresh flecks of green as spring thrust through the ground. The clipped carpet of grass began to inch up the horses' hooves, and as the days grew warmer, it was knee-high, then hip-high, and winter's smooth pasture became a green sea of grass, rolling and billowing like ocean waves forming far out at sea under a summer sun. Farmers in fields all around us had begun their work. It was time to make hay.

Knowing this, Mr. Finley came to call again. Driving up in his battered maroon Chevrolet, he waved and got out smiling. Over coffee in the kitchen, he said, "Since you're new at this, I thought I might come out to see how your grass is doing. You know, there are three things that are important: when to cut, when to rake, and when to bale."

Seeing that I had no idea what he meant, he went on. "You've got to cut before the grass tassels or your food value is gone, then you've got to wait till it's cured by the sun or you'll foul your rake, and if you bale it when it's green, you'll burn your barn down."

This no longer sounded like Currier and Ives. It all began to sound horrible and I had nightmare visions of the barn in flames because of our lack of experience and our utter ignorance on what to do and when to make all these vital decisions. The first pangs of panic appeared.

"How am I going to *know* all these things?"

"Come on," Mr. Finley smiled, "I'll show you."

I followed him out to the field to where the sun was warming the waves of waist-high grass.

"You see," he said, pulling a long stem of grass out of the ground. The grass seeds are still intact. When they drop, you'll see a fuzz in place of the pod, and you'll know it's tasseled. You want to cut before that happens, and it looks to me like you ought to start now."

The idea of making hay no longer seemed so simple. The rolling hills of grass seemed to stretch all the way to land's end, clear across the ocean, and on to England and Africa. I realized for the very first time that every last blade of this great expanse I was looking at would have to be cut, conditioned, raked, baled, and brought to the barn. It might take the rest of my life, and even then I might not finish. I was overcome with despair, but Mr. Finley was saying, "Get me the tractor key and I'll cut some down for you this afternoon, then tomorrow I'll show you what I mean about being cured."

I stood at the gate to the fields and watched him go over the hill on the tractor, the grass falling in smooth rows before the advancing cutter bars, the land honeysuckle-sweet with the scent of freshly mown hay. Rabbits and ground-nesting birds who had chosen the tall grass to raise their young now scampered away from the clatter of the cutting blades, running wild-eyed through the field to safer, more secure ground.

"That's something you've got to watch for," Mr. Finley said, as he came past the gate on his second round. "Make sure nothing gets in front of that cutter bar. All farm equipment is dangerous, but that cutter bar will tear anything to pieces before you know it. Just make sure your boys stay out of the field when you've got a mowing operation going. Every season somebody gets careless and every season somebody gets hurt."

Gloom blotted out the brightness of the day. I began to wonder, *Is this Oz?* To despair was added danger lurking over every hill. Seeing my concern, Mr. Finley leaned over the steering wheel of the tractor and pushed his hat back on his head. He smiled, and his brown eyes behind his glasses were warm with confidence. "Don't worry, just be aware of what you're dealing with. I been farming better'n fifty years and nothing serious ever happened."

I wasn't persuaded, but I did appreciate his efforts at reassurance even though I knew I would never again think of making hay as a jolly jaunt through the fields. Now I had something to worry about.

Mr. Finley put the tractor in gear and the clattering of the cutting blades began again. "While I'm here, I'll get some of this down for you."

The fields were fenced so that there were forty acres on one side of the farm, sixty acres on the other, and ten acres fronting on the road where the two ponds were located.

Mr. Finley had begun in the forty-acre field and all afternoon he went round and round on the tractor until the whole forty acres was cut. The farmers in the field across from ours were shaking their heads again. I didn't know what this meant until I went down to the country store that evening to buy baling twine. Clarence and Claude were sitting on the nail kegs in dusty overalls chewing tobacco beside the fireless potbellied stove that warmed them in winter.

"You got a powerful lot of hay down today," Claude observed when I came in.

I was pleased that so much of the work had been done, but Clarence was shaking his head gloomily. "If a rain comes up with all that hay down, you'll lose it all."

Claude nodded his positive approval of what Clarence had to say "Yeah, ain't nuthin' worse'n ruint hay."

The list was getting longer; now I had to worry about the weather. Until we moved to the country, I had never bothered with a forecast. There was just summer and fall, winter and spring . . . time for swimsuits or sweaters, sleds or Easter bonnets. The once important evening news was ignored. The only thing that mattered now was what the weatherman had to say.

Claude and Clarence dismissed this too. "Them fellows with all their fancy instruments don't know what they're talking about. What you gotta do is watch the sky. That's the onliest way you can know what's gonna happen."

Claude and Clarence were part of the brotherhood of farmers who had lived on the land all their lives and who had experience I was not privy to. Looking at the sky, I could only tell the obvious, like sun, rain, and snow when it was falling. Claude and Clarence could tell when rain was coming and accurately predict its arrival to the moment of the first raindrop. I decided that I would just have to rely on God in his great mercy taking pity on me trying to get that hay out of the field and into the barn because I had no way of knowing what the others already knew.

The next day Mr. Finley came back to condition the hay and after that to see if the sun had cured the hay. The test for curing was the requirement that the hay should rattle. We walked all over the field picking up lengths of long cut grass, listening for the dry rattle of dried-out hay. Satisfied that this condition had been met, Mr. Finley hooked up the rake to the stabilizer bar on the tractor. This required expertly backing the tractor until the hook-up connections, circles the circumference of a penny, matched and the lynch pin could be dropped into the hole.

From the gate I watched again as he made his rounds in the fields, the giant round prongs of the rake throwing the hay together into knee-high rows that ran up and over the hills in a perfect line.

"That's what you call windrows," Mr. Finley said on his first round past the gate. "What you want to do is make them straight as an arrow so that when you get in the field with the baler you don't have to zigzag all over creation. Makes a farmer look like a fool to do that. You watch Claude and Clarence across the way. They can drop a bale on a dime . . . every time."

The sun was down when Mr. Finley finished and a faint lavender streaked the melon-colored sky. Dropping the tractor keys in my hand he looked at the sky and said, "Looks like we're in luck. The weather ought to hold. Get some help to pick up the hay and I'll be back this weekend to help you and Larry bale."

That afternoon I went down to the country store to ask Matthew where to look for help in the hayfield. Matthew was behind the counter leaned up against the snuff shelf and Clarence and Claude were in their usual places on the nail kegs having an R.C. and a chocolate moon pie. Clarence was looking out the door at whatever was passing by and Claude was looking at the golden-haired girl on the Coca-Cola calendar.

Of the three bachelor brothers, Clarence was the only one who had entered the matrimonial circle. He had been married once for six days, but when he found out what his wife was going to make him do about leaving his muddy brogans outside the kitchen door, hanging up his overalls, and being on time for dinner instead of sitting around the country store, Clarence decided that he liked living with his two bachelor brothers better and would just visit her on Sunday.

Matthew's blood condition made him too frail for the rigors of marriage, and Claude, after he saw what happened to Clarence, decided he would not subject himself to such a misadventure. Instead, he contented himself with looking at the golden-haired girl on the Coca-Cola calendar. After a long time of looking, he'd break away and grin, "She's still up there swinging, ain't she?"

This, along with an R.C. and a moon pie, was the only indulgence Claude ever allowed himself, which wasn't much. The R.C., or Royal Crown Cola, came in a huge green bottle and was what Claude and the other country men called "a belly-wash," and was the most preferred drink since it gave the most for the money. The chocolate moon pie, two saucer-size graham cookies with marshmallow creme squashed in the middle, was covered with chocolate so cheap that it stuck like adhesive to the mouth, teeth, and gums, a condition made worse by a cold R.C. This suited Claude for refreshment, and sitting on the nail keg in the country store was his recreation. The rest of the time was working. If this was a narrow world, it apparently never seemed so to Claude, for he never complained, and he enjoyed, undiminished, the three things he did have.

"I've got to have some help in my hayfield," I told Matthew when I got inside the store. "Can you tell me where to find it?"

Before Matthew had a chance to answer my question, Clarence responded for him. "There ain't none. This time of year with hay season in full swing, it's all took up."

Claude smacked off another piece of moon pie. "Ain't it the truth! Things done got so bad, John Enos down the way had to hire a dairyman that won't go on daylight saving time. Dairyman said he ain't about to fool with the time God gave him. He says it gets him confused and gets the cows confused, too."

Clarence took a long swig of his R.C. and wiped his mouth on the back of his hand. "It ain't the dairyman that's confused, it's poor old John Enos. I seen him yesterday wearing two watches. One of 'em has got his time, the other one's got the dairyman's time."

Matthew frowned. "How come he can't tell it's just an hour later than what the dairyman says?"

"All that figurin' on what time it is has done got him addled. All the rest of the dairymen are gettin' up at four o'clock to milk the cows, but that new dairyman John Enos has got, that won't go on daylight, is gettin' him up at three o'clock. Gettin' up at three o'clock is enough to get anybody addled."

I didn't care about John Enos and his dairyman that wouldn't go on daylight, all I was interested in was getting help in the hayfield.

"I wouldn't care if they were on Tokyo time," I told them. "I've just got to have some help."

"It's all been spoke for," Clarence said, closing the book on the discussion.

I looked at Matthew who was wearing his summer hat, a racy little number, the kind men used to wear on the golf course forty years ago. Even though it was warm now, he was still rubbing his arms and rocking back and forth on his heels to keep his circulation up.

"You might try the Turners down the way. They got a big family and a bunch of boys. They ain't none of 'em very big, but you might hire enough of 'em to get the job done."

"Making hay's a man's job," Claude, who was not even as big as I, snorted smugly. "They won't do nothing 'cept drink Co' Colas and mess around in the hayfield."

Matthew shook his head. "Them's good boys. You can give 'em a try."

I left the country store in black despair. I could just see myself with an army of Lilliputians and a whole continent of hay to bale. I wished I had never thought farming was a good idea. I wished I had never seen a horse or a saddle or a pair of riding boots. I wished I was back sitting in air-conditioned comfort holding a deck of cards. That lasted for only a moment. I didn't really wish that. I only wished I didn't have to make hay.

I drove down the road to the Turner's house, a big, rambling old white frame house sitting on a grassless knoll rubbed bare by the play of so many children. Out back were five very long strands of clothesline strung from tree to tree, all filled with freshly washed clothes drying in the sun. Mrs. Turner was sitting in a screeching porch swing hung from the ceiling by rusted chains. She had a lap full of peas and a pan that she had almost filled up and even as she looked up to greet me, her plump, almost childlike hands flew down the pods of peas like perpetual motion. She was as round as a pumpkin, pushing at the seams of her flowered, flour-sack dress; and she had a jack-o-lantern smile. Her eyes were warm and full of welcome and her two front teeth were missing.

"Howdy," he grinned. "Come on in. 'Scuse me, if I don't get up."

The porch was full of children, a baby crawling on the floor, a toddler playing with a ball, three young boys hanging on the porch rail, and two girls who came to the screen door when I drove up. I told Mrs. Turner who I was and where I lived. It was always necessary in the country to establish credentials and domain.

"I seen you driving by and I figgered you was the new neighbor down the way."

"Matthew down at the country store told me I might be able to hire some of your boys to help me in the hayfield," I told her. "I've got a whole field of hay down and nobody to help."

A light frown creased her smooth face and she shook her head. "All the big boys has been done took for haying in other fields. The only ones left are Timmy, Tommy and Tad."

Matthew had told me that she had a penchant for naming all her children with names starting with a "T" . . . all thirteen of them.

Her husband was named Thaddeus, she was named Thelma, and there were Tillie, Tessie, Tammy, Tony, Trixie, Trudy, Toddy, Terry, Teddy, and Townsend. Her husband worked for the county on road maintenance shoveling gravel into the cement mixer, and to supplement his small salary, they grew a huge garden to help feed the children. They had little else but love and this was all they needed. I could see it in the shine in the children's faces and feel it in warm swirls when I walked up on the porch.

"Tommy, Timmy and Tad can help you," she said, lifting her hand from shelling the peas and pointing to the three little boys hanging on the porch rail. They were eight, nine, and ten. My heart sank. They weren't any bigger than Wayne and Billy-Wade. They probably didn't weigh as much as the bale they would have to lift. I had opened my mouth to decline the offer when the one named Tommy spoke up.

"We might look little, but we can lift a lot," he grinned, with bright eyes that promised what he said he could do.

"Yeah," Timmy and Tad chimed in. "We work good. Mama taught us how."

Mrs. Turner accepted her accolade with a nod of her head and another jack-o-lantern smile. "They're good boys," she said. "They'll do you a good job."

I wasn't happy with the prospect, but it was the only prospect I had, so I made arrangements to come pick them up the next day, and drove back home lamenting the army of Lilliputians that would have to do what was unquestionably "a man's job," as Claude had said.

I was still lamenting about it when Larry came home from work.

"Why don't we call some of our friends in the suburbs? They are so anxious to come out to the farm and play Farmer in the Dell, let them come out and make hay."

That was a triumphant idea. I would call Clara and Charlie and Lark's parents, and two teenage girls in the neighborhood that I had taught how to ride. Pat and Jeanette were big and strong, loved horses and hay and the whole outdoors. When I called them, they said they'd love to come make hay. Lark's parents, Karen and Ted, said they would come too, and Charlie thought it the finest suggestion he had heard in a long time.

"Working in the sun and drinking in the shade," Charlie guffawed. "That's what I like. We'll be there."

Working in the sun and drinking in the shade didn't sound like too good an idea to me, but I wasn't going to quibble with willing help; I'd just hide the liquor until the work got done.

This idea didn't work too well, because Charlie brought his own gallon jug of Bloody Marys with him and he had been drinking all along the way as they drove out in a caravan. They arrived looking like they were going aboard for a yachting party. Clara and Karen wore white silk slacks and halter T-tops.

"So," they explained, "we can get a suntan while we make hay."

I looked at their bare shoulders and their perfumed skin. "It will be more like sunburn. Didn't you bring any clothes for making hay?"

They looked down their white silk slacks to fragile strap sandals with polished red toenails peeking out, not understanding what I meant. "Clothes for making hay?" This was an outfit they had never heard of.

"You know . . . jeans and long-sleeved shirts and sturdy shoes?"

They shook their freshly coiffeured heads. "Oh, no. We wouldn't wear anything tacky like that."

Passing along my recently learned information, I told them, "Without any protection on your arms, you'll get all scratched by the hay . . . after all . . . we're only going to the field."

"Well!" they sniffed, as though I had already gone to seed, but they certainly would not. "We wouldn't even go to the field looking like that."

Right then I scratched Karen and Clara off the duty roster; they weren't going to be any help at all. Charlie and Ted weren't much better. Charlie had on his red Hawaiian shirt which matched his red, Bloody Mary face. This shirt, brought back from Honolulu, was what Charlie wore for special occasions. Ted was wearing his Gucci loafers.

I looked at Heaven and could see no end to this madness. "Really, Ted! How can you make hay in Gucci loafers?"

Ted smiled. "This is my old pair."

As this caravan arrived and got out in their city clothes, Claude and Clarence, properly attired in long-sleeved work shirts, overalls, brogans, and straw hats to shade off the sun, didn't even try to be discreet. They got off their tractors in the field across from ours, walked to their fence, and hung there gazing over to our field in frank amazement. They couldn't *believe* what was going to go to the field with me.

Pat and Jeanette had already arrived, suitably fitted out in jeans and tennis shoes, and right away went to the barn and began currying and kissing the horses. Pat was big and strong and wore her straight brown hair in a Cromwell cut. Jeanette was big and fat and wore her glistening blonde hair in ringlets with a little blue satin baby bow set slap in the middle of her mass of curls.

Pat did the currying and Jeanette did the kissing. Pretty soon, Brandy's bay coat was shining like the morning star and Sabre's white blaze was covered with lipstick. They were a good deal more interested in riding the horses than riding the hay wagon, but we finally got them disengaged from the currying and the kissing and began to herd everybody up to go to the hayfield.

Wayne and Billy-Wade were sitting on the steps with their lips poked out because Nootie and Lark hadn't come out with their parents. The fact that Nootie was off at camp and Lark was visiting her grandparents didn't matter. What mattered was that they weren't there to join them in what, until now, had been thought of as a great adventure.

The three little Turner boys, Timmy, Tommy, and Tad, did what they could to dissuade them of their ill humor. They had been outside waiting to begin work since sunup. When they knocked on the door, announcing their arrival, I told them, "I was going to drive down and get you."

Spit-polish clean with their hair slicked back, they grinned. "Mama said it wasn't no use in that, for us to go ahead and walk. It wasn't but five miles."

In the midst of all this, Mr. Finley, who was going to drive the blue tractor and do the baling, arrived. When he took a look at what I had assembled as a hay crew, he removed his hat, rubbed his handkerchief across his balding head, and said, "Well, well. What have we got here?"

I explained that these were our friends from the city who had come out to help in the hayfield. To his everlasting credit, he had the composure and restraint not to burst out laughing. Instead, he scratched his head and said, "Well. Let's see how we can work this thing out."

The operation, Mr. Finley explained, would require dividing the hay crew into two crews. We would use two wagons, two tractors, and the baler. Mr. Finley, driving the big blue tractor pulling the baler with a wagon hooked on behind, would take one crew to the field. When this wagon was loaded with baled hay, Larry, driving the old grey Jubilee tractor, would bring his hay crew to the field, unhook, swap wagons, and drive the wagon loaded with hay back into the barn to be unloaded and stacked. Mr. Finley always made everything sound so easy and simple and effortless. This was going to be simple. I couldn't think why I had been so concerned.

Looking over the assorted group of young, old, and indifferent, Mr. Finley said, "I'll take the five boys on the wagon with me. Larry, you take the rest on the pickup wagon with you."

Now that the time had come to really make hay, Wayne and Billy-Wade had brightened considerably and they jumped on Mr. Finley's wagon with the three Turner boys determined to compete to see who could get the most work done. The enthusiasm on our wagon was measurably less. The sun was coming up hot overhead and Karen and Clara began having little beads of perspiration around their carefully coiffeured hairlines. Charlie wanted to go back for one more slug out of his Bloody Mary jug, and Jeanette wanted to go back and keep on kissing the horses. When we finally got them all aboard, with Karen and Clara daintily decorating the hay wagon, Larry, enormously enjoying his job as driver, jerked the tractor into gear and we were off.

"Wait!" Karen cried. "I've got to go back and get my sunglasses."

She walked mincingly back through the hayfield in her white silk slacks and strap sandals and decided to cross the barbwire fence instead of going through the gate. The next thing was a scream.

"Oh, God! Oh, Ted! Come quick! I've slashed my finger on this rusty barbwire!"

We all rushed over to see what had happened to Karen's finger. Mr. Finley, seeing all the commotion from the field, turned back, too. Karen's finger didn't have so much as a pinpoint of blood on it, but she continued to wail, "Oh, Ted! Do something quick! Get me to a hospital. Get me a tetanus shot before I get lockjaw . . . hurry!"

Mr. Finley came over to take a look and all the others crowded around. "Now, young lady," he said, with calm and reassurance, "that's not too bad. You don't need a tetanus shot unless you have a puncture."

"Puncture!" Karen screamed. "Oh, God, Ted, do something!"

Ted was now supporting her fast-failing ability to stand and trying to lead her back to the car as she leaned on him heavily for support, holding her wounded finger like a broken dove.

"There, now, Sugar," he said comfortingly, "you just bear up until I can get you to a doctor."

Witnessing the scene, nine-year-old Tommy Turner said, "Don't need nuthin' but kerosene. Mama always puts kerosene on everything . . . cuts, burns, scratches and scrapes. Mama says kerosene'll cure anything."

Only suggesting an amputation would have seemed worse to Karen. She gave one last horrified gasp and got in the car and they were gone.

The rest of us got on our hay wagons and went back to the field, loading and stacking hay, bringing it back to the barn. The only pleasant part was riding the wagon back to the barn from the fields. Loaded seven bales high all around, we rocked along on top resting and recovering until we got back to the barn.

There, everybody had to get off and help push the wagon up the steep earthen ramp through the double doors into the barn. As Mr. Finley had pointed out earlier, the old grey Jubilee tractor was like an old man with a bad heart. It just couldn't stand the stress of pulling that much strain alone, so we all got out and helped, heaving as hard as we could while the old grey Jubilee coughed and sputtered and almost died on us every time we went up the ramp.

Inside, we unloaded the hay onto the conveyor and stacked it again in the corner, taking care to pattern it in the prescribed manner: one bale butted against the other like a checkerboard, so that when it reached the roof of the three-story barn it wouldn't tumble down like jello.

When this operation was complete, the hay wagon had to be un-coupled from the old grey Jubilee tractor and hand-rolled back down the earthen ramp because the grade was too steep and the Jubilee too light to back it down without the tractor's front wheels bicycling. To hand-roll it, Larry took the tractor tongue and guided the wagon and the rest of us hung on pulling our weight against it so that the wagon wouldn't fly down the hill and run into the pond. This meant everyone literally had to pull his own weight.

We had just finished stacking the second load of hay and were rolling the wagon down the ramp when Charlie's strength completely gave way and he turned loose his side of the wagon. With that, the wagon's momentum snatched it out of our hands and even as we ran after it, it ran down the hill and sank in the pond. We got there just as the bubbles closed over it.

Charlie, embarrassed by the unmanly thing he had done, decided to have an attack of something to mitigate his situation. He dropped to his knees, clutched his shirt pocket, and held his breath until his already red face turned redder. The only thing really wrong with Charlie was that he was so terribly out of shape and had done too much drinking in the shade before he began working in the sun.

"Oh, Charlie!" Clara cried, dropping down beside him. "Is it your heart?"

Charlie then decided to give it a little theater, squinted his eyes shut and said, "I can't tell."

"Let's take him back to the house," I suggested, "where it's cooler."

Clara shook her head. "I think I'd better take him home." And they were gone.

Our original crew of eight was now down to four and we had to go get the wagon out of the pond. Larry tried wading in and pulling the wagon tongue but the wheels were held fast in the soft, sucking mud of the pond bottom. He went back to the barn, got the old grey Jubilee, backed it into the water, hooked up the wagon, and tried pulling it out. All this did was to cause the front wheels to bicycle, and the more he pulled, the more it looked as though the wagon would pull the tractor over backwards. We had to go to the field and get Mr. Finley to come with the blue tractor to pull the Jubilee pulling the wagon. When we got it out of the pond it was a godawful mess of mud, but we took it to the field anyway and began work again.

Morale on our pickup wagon wasn't doing too well. There were just me and Larry, Pat and Jeanette left. On Mr. Finley's wagon, the morale was doing fine. He laughed and teased and joked with the boys, and they were filling up hay wagons faster than we could unload them. As the day wore on, Pat set her jaw with grim determination and Jeanette's rosebud mouth began to pucker in a pout. I could tell Jeanette wasn't going to last too much longer. She was hot, tired, and miserable just like everybody else.

Inside the barn, the heat was insufferable, and I began to wonder why the Weather Bureau that could so accurately estimate the wind-chill factor in winter couldn't estimate the sun-scorch factor in summer. I had put casseroles in ovens that weren't as hot as that barn in the afternoon.

Everyone was coming unglued, so we stopped for a cold lemonade break poured from a gallon thermos into paper cups. When I handed Jeanette her cup, I saw two traces of tears run down her dusty cheeks.

"Why, Jeanette! What's the matter?"

"I'm hot," she wept, "and I'm tired and my arms are all scratched from hay and I want to go home."

Pat, quiet and grimly determined to get the job done, snapped, "Well you can't. I'm driving and I'm going to stay until the job is done."

With this, Jeanette jumped up and ran back to the house wailing all the way, "I want to go home."

Watching her go, Pat curled her lip in disgust. "She dissolves all her problems with tears."

We went back to the field and worked on and on until the sun slid down behind the hills and we had 517 bales of hay stacked in the barn. Mr. Finley, as cheerful as he had been when the day began, parked the blue tractor and said, "I'll be back tomorrow to bale some more."

The very thought of making more hay again tomorrow made me want to kill myself. I just couldn't stand it, but for the moment I knew I simply had to hold on to the ragged edge of composure. I thanked him and when the boys, full of pride and enthusiasm over the work they had done, dashed up and wanted to take a cool dip in the pond, I said yes. With shouts of glee, they ran down the hill, throwing their clothes off as they went.

Larry and Pat and I dragged ourselves back to the house, and when we got to the kitchen, Larry, with his day's work done, took off his hat, laid it on the table and said, "What's for supper?"

That seemed the most unreasonable question I had ever been asked. After all day in the field, I was tired beyond my strength and pushed past my endurance. "Supper!" I screamed. "What do you mean . . . supper!"

Larry looked at me in utter astonishment. "I mean what are we going to have for dinner tonight?"

All I could think of was this cartoon I had seen a long time ago of a husband returning home from work and reading a note on the dining room table. It said: *"Gone berserk. Your dinner is on the ceiling."*

I thought if I had to cook dinner after that devastating day in the field, it would be served on the ceiling.

"Don't you know," I said indignantly, "that you can't take the cook to the field?"

The words hung in the air, and like so many things said during crisis conditions, were never forgotten. In fact, the phrase became part of the family vernacular, and ever after that, if anyone was asked to do more than he possibly could, the response was always, "You don't take the cook to the field."

Somehow, we managed to survive that first weekend of making hay, and when it was over, we sank into exhausted heaps at the kitchen table, plastered with perspiration and hayseed, sunburned, scratched, and sore, too tired to eat. Our conclusion was that friends don't make good farmers and what we would have to do was find more help. I didn't know where I was going to find it, but I was ready to take up piracy, white slaving, or body snatching, whatever it took to get the job done.

Mr. Finley had been more than generous with his time, but he had his own fields to cut, and we could not expect him to continue to help us. Now that we had been taught what to do, it was up to us to get it done.

Because of Larry's job in the city, he, of necessity, could only help after work and on the weekends. This left us with a problem and at cross-purposes.

"You've got to wait for the weather," Claude and Clarence and every farmer we knew said. There were no creative shortcuts in making hay. You waited for the sun and then it was just long, unrelenting labor until the job was done. If conditions weren't right on the weekend, all we could do was wait for conditions to improve. Often, by then, the weekend was gone.

Larry had made it unquestionably clear that his job at the State Department was primary and the farming, secondary, but one Tuesday, when the weather was right and twenty-five acres of hay lay flat in the field ready to be baled, I called him at his office in Washington and asked:

"Do you think your boss will let you off this afternoon?"

You would have thought I had asked him to cut off his left ear lobe.

"LET ME OFF!" he yelled, so loud that the telephone lines trembled all the way from Washington down to the farm.

"I have all this hay down," I tried to explain, "and the weatherman says that a storm. . . ."

"Have you *any* idea what's happening in Rhodesia?"

I didn't give a hell about what was happening in Rhodesia, all I knew was that I had twenty-five acres of hay that had to be gotten up off the ground before the rain came and ruined it.

So, I took to standing down on the road at the foot of the driveway and watching the pickup trucks go by, looking for likely prospects to pick off for the hayfield, but this didn't work too well, because by the time I had sighted one, he was over the hill and gone. I decided then to take up my station in the country store. This was the center of the ebb and flow of the community. If I sat down there long enough, I would surely find someone to help in the hayfield.

Claude and Clarence were none too happy when I pulled up a nail keg and joined them in the middle of the store beside the cold potbellied stove. It was as if I had intruded uninvited into the men's locker room. They sat there tense and all drawn up and rubbing their chins, but Matthew was affable, and introduced me to everyone who came in the store.

"This is our new neighbor down the way," Matthew explained. "She's looking for help in the hayfield."

The answer was always the same: "Ain't none. It's all took up."

I went home in grim despair. When the phone rang, I decided not to even answer it, I was too busy having a decline, but it kept on ringing and ringing. When I got up to answer it, it was Larry calling from the city.

"I've got you some help for the hayfield."

I had had it with people from the city. *"No more friends."*

"You'll be pleased with this one."

I didn't even answer. I didn't want to hear it.

"Remember Colonel Swagnagle?"

Remember him? My memory was branded.

Colonel Swagnagle was the most overbearing, overwhelming, overpowering man I had ever known. He fancied himself another General George Patton, and patterned himself on that model. He was a thirty-year career man and was fond of saying, "You know, George and I were classmates at the Point." His heart had always been in the horse cavalry and when this was replaced by tanks, he would have preferred being a tank commander, but unfortunately went into ordnance instead, where he repaired tanks instead of riding in them. He had been Larry's commanding officer when Larry was in the army.

"Well," Larry was saying, "Colonel Swagnagle is in Washington for a convention. We ran into each other today, and over lunch I told him about the farm and the hay."

I hated to hear what was going to come next.

"And," Larry said triumphantly, "Colonel Swagnagle is going to come out and help you in the hayfield. He says there's not a piece of equipment in the world that he can't make run."

I would have preferred having Hitler.

"Tell him we've already got somebody. Tell him we've moved. Tell him anything. . . ."

"I can't. He's already made arrangements and is coming home with me tonight."

I could only make a suffering sound.

There was surprise in Larry's voice. "I thought you'd be glad."

Glad? I wanted to run away from home. All I could do was besiege Heaven: *Deliver me from General Patton in the hayfield.*

CHAPTER 7

General Patton in the Hayfield

I LOOKED AT THE CLOCK on the kitchen wall and hated every minute it ticked off because within the hour, Larry would arrive with Colonel Swagnagle. I dragged myself disgruntled around the house, putting fresh sheets on the bed in the guest room and trying to figure out what I was going to use for a spittoon, because Colonel Swagnagle chewed tobacco—not just out in the field with the men, but in the parlor with the ladies, too.

He never apologized for this indecent habit, but bragged about it instead: "When you've been out on the front like I have, you know you can't sit there smoking cigarettes on the battle line, it'll give your position away . . . that's when you learn how to chew tobacco."

Well, World War II was over, and Colonel Swagnagle had long since retired from the army, but it never occurred to him that now he was dwelling in drawing rooms instead of war zones and that he might give up or at least refrain from this squalid habit in mixed company. But Colonel Swagnagle remained ever the same. Everything was done as it had been done during the war. Peace, progress, and garrison duty had done nothing to change him.

Mrs. Swagnagle had endured his excesses and eccentricities for better than twenty-five years, but the repressed anger and anxiety induced by so many outrages had been too much for her heart and she had, in recent years, gone on to God's Greater Reward.

I first knew Mrs. Swagnagle when Larry went in the army for his two-year obligatory tour of duty and was assigned to Colonel Swagnagle's battalion. Mrs. Swagnagle was a little bitty bird of a woman, silent and solemn as a little grey wren sitting in the rain. She kept her own counsel, and never said a word when Colonel Swagnagle was around.

Out of his presence, she talked all the time. It was the only opportunity she had. But when she talked, it was almost inaudible and utterly incomprehensible. She spoke in a whisper out of the side of her mouth, her bird-bright eyes darting back and forth as though Colonel Swagnagle might catch her talking and kill her.

This wasn't too bad on casual meetings at the commissary or the P.X., but Colonel Swagnagle requested that all the officers in his command be in attendance at his table at the Officers' Club each weekend for the Saturday Night Dance. When Colonel Swagnagle "requested" something, that meant he ordered it done. If he "ordered" something, he sent the firing squad to enforce it.

Every Saturday night, Colonel Swagnagle held court at his table on the balcony overlooking the dance floor below and directly opposite the bandstand downstairs in front of the fireplace. From this commanding view, Colonel Swagnagle could see *everything* and count how many officers other commanders had at their table.

Upstairs at his table, we could hear *nothing*. The sound of the music richocheted off the wall behind us, making conversation impossible. This didn't deter Mrs. Swagnagle for a moment. While Colonel Swagnagle took all his officers to the bar to prop his foot and regale them with war stories, the wives all sat at the table and tried to look charmed to be sitting on the balcony listening to that thunderous music.

My instructions from Larry were: "Be nice to Mrs. Swagnagle. He can make life miserable for me."

When the last of the men had left to go prop on the bar, Mrs. Swagnagle slipped into the chair beside me and began to talk. I had no idea what she was saying and there was no way to judge whether it was good, bad, or horrible because I could never get a fix on the expression in her eyes, as she continued darting them back and forth watching for Colonel Swagnagle's return. When this happened, she always lapsed into a deep and respectful silence and only listened to what *he* had to say.

It was desperately frustrating not knowing what I was being told, only knowing that it was important because Mrs. Swagnagle had said it, and that she must in no case be offended in the slightest measure. I sat there wishing to God I had taken lipreading instead of literature in school and not knowing what to do.

I finally settled on sitting there looking vacantly pleasant while she chirped away. This seemed to satisfy her and things went along all right for a while. Then, her darting stopped and her eyes came to rest on me and I realized she expected a reply to what she had just said.

I tried to look pleasantly confused. "I beg your pardon. What was it you said?"

Mrs. Swagnagle began again, chirped on for a while, and when she stopped, I was obliged to say "I beg your pardon" again. The third time it happened, I could see she was getting annoyed, and I knew for Larry's sake I mustn't let that happen, so I decided to change tactics and say, "Oh, that's fine. I know you're glad." This seemed to please her. It worked so well, I continued to say this at every pause until finally she said something else inaudible and incomprehensible and I said, "Oh, that's fine. I know you're glad."

Her eyes fell on me and flared with indignation. I was obliged to say, "I beg your pardon. What did you say?"

In the clearest voice I ever heard her use, she replied, "I *said* my mother-in-law has epileptic fits and we are afraid to leave the children with her."

That ended it with me and Mrs. Swagnagle and very nearly ended it for Larry. He wasn't court-martialed, but Colonel Swagnagle made it so miserable, it was almost as bad.

Apparently, by now Colonel Swagnagle had forgiven him all that was past, for he had volunteered to come and help in the hayfield. I just couldn't believe it. It was just too unreal. I kept hoping that Larry's phone call was nothing more than a nightmare and that I would soon wake up, but as I watched the clock hands work their way around the dial, I knew it wasn't a nightmare. Not the kind you wake up from. Only an hour ago, coming home from the country store, I had thought things were already so bad that they couldn't possibly get worse. Now I knew they could get incredibly worse.

When Larry drove up and they got out, I saw that Colonel Swagnagle had changed little since last I saw him. In the army, they had called him "Old Ironass," and this had gotten broader, his bristle-stiff hair whiter, and his rough-skinned face redder. He was wearing his highly polished brown riding boots, his riding breeches, his campaign hat, and was carrying his ebony crop under his arm. Larry was carrying his luggage.

"Well, Little Lady," he boomed at me, "I've come to rescue a damsel in distress."

I wanted to say something obscene and then kill Larry, but I forced a smile instead. "You really shouldn't have put yourself to so much trouble."

"No trouble at all," he boomed in a voice that filled up the world. "We'll have these fields cleared off in no time." Colonel Swagnagle was retired now, and for lack of another challenge had decided to take on our hayfield.

Wayne and Billy-Wade, hearing what must have sounded like the voice of the Lord thundering in the kitchen, left their television program and ran downstairs to see who had arrived. One look at Colonel Swagnagle and they were struck completely dumb. He was well over six feet tall, 250 pounds of hulking flesh, with a big red bulbous nose and a florid face from having drunk up most of the liquor in the world. His eyes were a blurred blue, the whites having long ago turned a dull red plaid, but they were still piercing and powerful.

Wayne and Billy-Wade were so overcome that they couldn't think what to do, so they eased their hands up in a timid salute.

"Well, well," Colonel Swagnagle boomed. "What's your name?"

He looked down at Billy-Wade with that demanding, intimidating look, and poor Billy-Wade, standing there in his untied tennis shoes, was so overcome he either could no longer remember his name, or did not want to disclose it, so he said, "Wayne."

Swinging around to Wayne, Colonel Swagnagle said, "And what's your name?"

Wayne was helpless under that unrelenting look, so he said, "My name is Wayne, too."

Colonel Swagnagle seemed genuinely disturbed, and swung around to Larry. "That's a damn fool thing to do, Larry. How come you to name both those boys the same thing?"

Larry looked embarrassed and tried to manage a weak smile. "I didn't really," Larry tried to explain. "This one," laying his hands on Billy-Wade's thin shoulders, "is really named Billy-Wade."

Colonel Swagnagle frowned and focused all the intensity of his look down on Billy-Wade. "Don't you know you're supposed to tell the truth, boy?"

Poor Billy-Wade was melting like a little candle under the heat of Colonel Swagnagle's gaze. Confused and uncertain what to do, he blinked his eyes, bobbed his head, and looked down at the floor. Colonel Swagnagle took this for disorientation and turned on Larry.

"That's your fault, Larry. Trouble with that boy is he's addled . . . giving him two names like that . . . he doesn't even know who he is. What made you do such a damn fool thing?"

Larry stiffened and tried to explain. "Well, he's named for both his grandfathers, and neither one would hear of his being called by the other's name, so we call him Billy-Wade."

Colonel Swagnagle's face was a study of disapproval. He pierced Larry's chest with his pointed finger. "*That's* what you get, listening to what old men have to say."

The situation was going to hell in a hurry, and I could see from Larry's frozen expression that something was going to have to be done right away, so I turned to him and suggested, "Why don't you take Colonel Swagnagle to the barn to see the horses?"

"Good idea!" Colonel Swagnagle boomed. "I'd like a little ride before supper."

Wayne and Billy-Wade faded into the wallpaper and slithered back upstairs. Larry and Colonel Swagnagle went out to the paddock, and I started figuring how I could end this awful situation. It just wasn't going to work. Colonel Swagnagle had already pulverized the children and put them in such a state of shock they didn't even know who they were, and I could see that he was going to depend on deference to age and rank and press my manners to the wall. Before I was driven to do something irreparable, I meant to get rid of Colonel Swagnagle.

It seemed to me that the easiest and most humane way was to ruin his digestion. If I could send him back to the city with nothing more than a bad case of heartburn, I felt we would come out of this with the least possible damage to everyone concerned. When we had known him in the army before, he had been very picky about what he ate, insisting on very lightly seasoned food and no pepper at all. It seemed to me the best place to begin was with the meat sauce for the roast. I went to the spice shelf and got the Tabasco, the chili powder, and the red peppers and poured them all in the meat sauce.

Then I went upstairs and told the children, "Don't touch the meat sauce at dinner tonight."

"What's wrong with it?" Billy-Wade wanted to know.

"I made it for Colonel Swagnagle."

"I hope you put grasshoppers in it," Wayne said, still smarting from his encounter with Colonel Swagnagle.

"Yeah!" Billy-Wade agreed. "Snails, too."

"Now, boys," I said, hoping God would forgive me for hypocrisy, "it's not nice to talk about company that way."

With the children put on the alert about the meat sauce, I went to the paddock to join Larry and Colonel Swagnagle. Before I even reached the fence, I could see that the horses had already had it with Colonel Swagnagle. Sabre was standing there rolling his eyes around as though the fool of the world had arrived. Brandy wore the pained look he had when he wasn't going to put up with much more.

He was much more worldly than Sabre. Sabre liked to flash his temper and show how annoyed he was. Brandy didn't indulge in such demonstrations. He had a tolerance level beyond which he would not be pushed. He was, after all, a thoroughbred, and once past his thoroughbred threshold . . . watch out. There was no accounting for what he might do.

We had had a visitor once before that Brandy had not taken a liking to. He was out riding Brandy in the field when Brandy decided he had passed his tolerance level. Without a moment's notice, Brandy dropped into racetrack strides and raced up and over the hills, under the trees, and across the fields at breakneck speed. It was the first time in my life I had heard a grown man scream. If Brandy was contemplating such a coup with Colonel Swagnagle, I didn't think it was going to work. He could run like a Race for the Roses from here to East Istanbul and he'd never get Colonel Swagnagle to scream.

But Brandy had assessed the situation much better than I. When Colonel Swagnagle stepped up in the stirrup iron and threw his full weight in the saddle, Brandy's hindquarters simply sank down like a cat sitting on its haunches and Colonel Swagnagle, not at all expecting this, slid rather indecorously off onto the ground.

His face flushed, he glared at Larry and demanded, "What in the hell kind of horse is this?"

Larry hurried over to help him up off the ground and tried to dust him off and smooth over the situation by saying, "He's a thoroughbred off the track and accustomed to carrying light weights."

Colonel Swagnagle turned a sour look on Brandy and said, "That's the goddamdest horse I *ever* saw."

Brandy just stood there looking arrogant and indignant and Sabre had turned his head away so that Colonel Swagnagle could not see his utter enjoyment at what had happened. The situation was getting out of hand again and before it deteriorated any further, I thought it best to get Colonel Swagnagle out of there and back in the house.

"Dinner's ready," I said, interrupting Colonel Swagnagle's determined attempt to get back on Brandy and show him who was boss. "Come on in."

Unsaddled, the horses ran out to the pasture as fast as they could and hid in the woods. Inside, we sat down at the table for dinner. I thought about the meat sauce I had prepared for Colonel Swagnagle and, for a fleeting moment, I wavered with an attack of conscience and guilt. But when I saw Wayne and Billy-Wade, not knowing what to expect from Colonel Swagnagle next, sitting at the table afraid to swallow, I knew I could not indulge in those Christian virtues. Colonel Swagnagle was a disaster, and if he was left alone to continue, the whole place would be in shambles. We were up against survival. This was the moral equivalent of war.

I passed Colonel Swagnagle the roast and then the meat sauce. It seemed to appeal to him and he poured it all over everything. Wayne and Billy-Wade knew there was something wrong about the meat sauce, but they didn't know what. Larry knew nothing. They watched out of the corner of lowered eyes as Colonel Swagnagle cut off a huge hunk of roast covered with meat sauce and wolfed it down. I held my breath waiting for the end to come.

Colonel Swagnagle smacked his lips. His face turned redder. He smashed his fist down on the table. "Goddam!" he boomed. "What have you got in this meat sauce?"

I was so upset I was on the point of confession. Larry was frowning and glaring at me with a look that said now I had *really* made his life more miserable.

"Er . . . ah . . . ," I began, grasping for an excuse or explanation, like maybe the spice shelf fell off in the pan while I was cooking, but Colonel Swagnagle was roaring again.

"Damn stuff tastes like it's made out of gunpowder."

Larry was glaring at me again, hostile this time. He was not only cross, he was positively put out with me for not having done better for company, but Colonel Swagnagle was wolfing down another forkful, smacking his lips, and letting his taste buds judge the contents.

"Damn good stuff. I'd say the only thing it needs is a little more Tabasco."

I was stunned. I had never expected him to say that. I thought, the army was wrong. They should have never named him "Old

Ironass," they should have named him "Old Irongut." I had put enough flaming hot seasoning in that sauce to melt a gun barrel.

Relieved by Colonel Swagnagle's reaction, Larry was smiling again. "Get Colonel Swagnagle some more Tabasco," he told me.

"I'm afraid I used it all."

"Mustn't go too light on the seasoning," Colonel Swagnagle advised me as he wolfed down more and more of the meat sauce.

"I didn't know you liked hot seasoning so much."

"Never did till me and my wife had a tour in Mexico. After that I never could get enough."

Billy-Wade, having heard the reference to the sauce tasting like gunpowder, and watching the relish with which Colonel Swagnagle was eating it, simply could not resist sticking his finger in the sauce and taking a quick lick. As soon as it touched his tongue, he screamed, clapped both hands over his mouth, fell off his chair onto the floor, and writhed.

Colonel Swagnagle looked down at Billy-Wade and then back to Larry. "Larry, you ought to do something about that boy before it's too late to change him."

I rushed Billy-Wade into the bathroom, washed out his mouth, and salved his tongue with ice, butter, and unguentine. He stood there with his tongue hanging out like a gargoyle and visibly swelling.

"I *told* you not to touch that meat sauce," I scolded.

"You didn't tell me you made it out of gunpowder."

"I *didn't* make it out of gunpowder."

"Colonel Swagnagle said. . . ."

"Forget Colonel Swagnagle. You just do what I tell you to do."

He remembered his tongue again and began to cry. "I want a Band-Aid."

"You can't put a Band-Aid on your tongue."

His eyes filled up with tears and ran down his cheeks. He looked so pitiful and I felt so bad that he had been the casualty that I decided to humor him.

"All right, but it's not going to stay on."

I put one Band-aid on top of his tongue and another underneath to hold it on and we went back to the table with his bandaged tongue hanging out.

Colonel Swagnagle took one look at him and boomed, "What in the name of God has that boy got on his tongue?"

"Band-Aids."

Colonel Swagnagle took his napkin, wiped his mouth, folded it, and put it beside his plate. Then he addressed himself to Larry. "My boy, I think we need to have a little talk after dinner tonight. I don't think you realize it, but everybody here seems to be ready for a Section Eight."

When dinner was over, Wayne came to me and asked, "What does he mean, Section Eight?"

"He thinks we are all ready for the Funny Farm."

"What do you mean Funny Farm?" Billy-Wade wanted to know.

Wayne answered for me. "He thinks we're all crazy."

I *was* crazy to think I could run Colonel Swagnagle away with a bottle of Tabasco. It didn't ruin his digestion at all. It just gave him vigor and zest and that night he slept like a lion in his own lair, but we didn't sleep at all. It's just possible that none of our neighbors slept either, because Colonel Swagnagle's snore roared through the house, rattling the windows and the tin roof of the barn. The animals all stood around outside bleary-eyed and out of their minds with fatigue, unable to rest.

It was just before dawn when I finally drifted off, but this didn't last more than a minute. Colonel Swagnagle, rested and refreshed, was stomping through the house booming, "What time is reveille?"

I turned my head on my pillow and looked at Larry. "Larry, I'm leaving you."

Larry, utterly fatigued by a sleepless night, tried to grapple with the thought. "What for?"

"For bringing Colonel Swagnagle out here."

"You said you needed help."

"I don't need *anything* that bad."

Larry plumped his pillow up and rolled over into it utterly exhausted. "Oh, he'll settle down."

But Colonel Swagnagle was not about to settle down. He was outside our bedroom door pacing up and down the living room rug. "What kind of outfit are you running here? Letting the troops stay in bed 'til the sun comes up? Time to rise and shine."

I just lay there and wished I knew some really terrible cuss words. The ones I knew weren't nearly bad enough to fit the occasion.

"Rise and shine," Colonel Swagnagle roared again. "The sun's almost up."

Hearing all this static about the sun, it occurred to me that what I should do was unleash Henrietta Early on Colonel Swagnagle. All her talk about "getting ahead of the sun" was just the right sport for Colonel Swagnagle. They could have a public competition and see who could outdo the other one getting up the earliest. Making book on that, I'd put the odds at even. Getting up the earliest was the characteristic that Henrietta had cut out as her own and she wouldn't let even Colonel Swagnagle beat her on that. On second thought, I knew I wouldn't be able to stand Colonel Swagnagle and Henrietta too, so I let that idea rest.

It was the sun that caused the next crisis. Not the getting-up sun. The working sun.

I wearily dragged myself to the kitchen and began to cook. Being from the Deep South, my solution to settling nerves, a weak stomach, or insomnia was a bowl of hot grits in the morning. Being an army man, and a Yankee besides, Colonel Swagnagle was accustomed to having fried potatoes, ham, eggs, hot bread, fruit, cereal, milk, coffee, and pie for breakfast. To me, Thanksgiving dinner wasn't nearly that much trouble to cook, but I decided to forgo the grits and try to comply with what he had been accustomed to. As I did this, he walked out to the pasture to survey the work that had to be done. He stood on the crest of the hill in the grey dawn light in his riding boots and breeches, his leather gloves buckled across his wrists, his hands propped on his hips in the pose made classic by General Patton. Once more, he was master of all he saw, and he looked like Caesar surveying all of Gaul.

"We'll get started as soon as breakfast is done," he announced when he came back in.

This was impossible. Every farmer knew that you had to wait for the sun to burn off the morning fog and dew. This dampness, which had settled on the cut hay during the night, made the hay limp and moist and would foul the rake and jam the baler. The hay had to be dry enough to rattle. It had to be cured. This meant ten or eleven o'clock in the morning, not just after dawn.

"We have to wait for the sun," I told Colonel Swagnagle.

"If we had waited for the sun in World War Two," Colonel Swagnagle snapped, "we would have never gotten on the beaches in Normandy."

"I know that, but this is a hayfield."

Colonel Swagnagle looked at me and smiled as though I didn't have good sense. "Don't you worry about a thing, Little Lady, the job will get done. I'll see to that."

Nothing strikes more dread and certified terror in my heart than the phrase "Don't worry about a thing." I long ago learned never to take anyone's word for that. This is precisely the time to start worrying. Worrying hard. Historically, this is the time when everything starts going to pieces.

"Well, you see, Colonel Swagnagle," I tried to insist gently, "the first thing we have to do is rake the cut hay into windrows. If you start while the hay is still wet, it will foul the rake and you won't get any farther than the barn."

Colonel Swagnagle was sure he knew everything and certainly didn't need some woman to tell him what to do. He received my bit of information rather badly. He put on his bold commander's look that meant he wasn't going to brook my disputes and told me again, "Don't worry about a thing."

I decided to hell with it, it was his funeral, and he went out the door to the barn to begin his siege of the hayfield.

CHAPTER 8

Hell on Wheels

FROM THE KITCHEN WINDOW, I watched Colonel Swagnagle's military march to the barn, his chest thrown back, his eyes riveted on his objective, his strides matching the cadence of a drumroll. To me, it was as ill advised as a march through a minefield, but he was and always had been "old Hell on Wheels." It was damn the dawn, out of the trenches, and over the wire. After the beaches of Normandy and crossing the Rhine, unquestionably, a hayfield was nothing for Colonel Swagnagle.

His first task was to hook the rake up to the old grey Jubilee tractor, and this was his first problem. The old grey Jubilee didn't like early morning starts and snuffed and snorted and died on him about forty-five times before, through sheer force of will, he got it started. Then it died again. The cussing coming from the barn was so bad, I kept Wayne and Billy-Wade inside the house so that they couldn't hear it.

I didn't know what to do, whether to go to the barn and see about Colonel Swagnagle or stay inside the house and hide. I knew that would never do, so I pulled on a pair of Keds, walked through the dew-wet grass that was ankle deep, around the barn and up the ramp where Colonel Swagnagle had thrown open the barn doors and was standing over the grey Jubilee. A shaft of early morning sunlight beamed through the opened doors and spotlighted him standing there, his white, bristle-short hair quite literally standing on end, his face in flames, his highly polished brown riding boots layered with dust, and a greasy smudge on his expensive riding breeches. I could see that he was not only enraged but deeply offended by this tractor that wouldn't work. He always stuck to the notion that there wasn't a piece of machinery in existence that he couldn't make run. The truth was that Colonel Swagnagle had never run or repaired a piece of machinery during his whole thirty years in Army Ordnance. He had just bulldogged others and made them do it. He was trying to bulldog the old grey Jubilee now, but the old grey Jubilee couldn't be bulldogged. It had to be treated gently, encouraged, and cared for, as Mr. Finley said.

I didn't dare suggest this to Colonel Swagnagle, for he was in a black rage. He was not accustomed to anything or anyone not doing what he wanted *instantly*. As far as he was concerned, this was insubordination, and in Colonel Swagnagle's outfit, this was a capital offense. I was not sure but what he might not decide to strike me dead from pure provocation on his part and temerity on mine for having the unmitigated gall to speak to him when he was in such a state as this.

"Colonel Swagnagle," I began tentatively.

He didn't even listen. He turned on me with unspeakable fury. "There's something you ought to know, Little Lady, in case you never knew or have since forgot. You can only go as far as the horse you're riding. I learned a long time ago in the horse cavalry that you have to shoot the stragglers. For the sake of efficiency on this farm," he was shaking his fist at the old grey Jubilee, "I'd shoot that one."

The most absurd picture popped into my head. I could just imagine Colonel Swagnagle taking out his .45 and shooting the poor old grey Jubilee and it slumping to the barn floor in one last fatal sigh. I knew then I had to get out of there and get a hold of myself. This was making me crazy. I had begun hallucinating.

I hated to suggest it but I did think it ought to be said one more time. "All the farmers say you have to wait for the sun. Maybe then. . . ."

I could see that Colonel Swagnagle wanted to say something a whole lot worse, but he restrained himself and shouted, "horse . . . feathers! We've got a whole field of hay to rake, bale, and put in the barn. We can't wait for the sun or anything else. We've got to get started . . . now!"

I thought, *So let it be written, so let it be done.* I had said everything that was safe to say. He was like a force of nature, nothing could stop him. If he wanted to go out there in the field and tangle with the elements, then, let him have at it.

"I'll have the pickup crew and be ready to bale when you are," I told him and left him to his own reward.

The hay that Mr. Finley had cut earlier was lying in great sheaths all over the ground, covering hill after hill in the pasture. The task that confronted Colonel Swagnagle was raking this into windrows with the rake's giant rotating prongs throwing the hay together into a row to be baled. Under optimum conditions during the right time of day with a hot sun coming down, it was just a matter of sitting on the tractor, keeping it straight, and guiding it over the sheaths of hay.

I didn't even have to look out the window to know what was going on in the pasture, but when I did, it was just as I expected. Colonel Swagnagle had gotten no farther than the corner of the barn. The damp, sticky hay was not only matted and twisted, it was plaited around the prongs of the rake. Colonel Swagnagle, with his pocketknife, was very tediously and laboriously cutting the tangled hay loose, his face angry and red and very near stroke-stage.

The best I could do was go to the country store and get some cold soft drinks to cool him down when he got through. When I got there, Claude and Clarence, in their straw hats and overalls, their morning chores done, were hanging around waiting for the sun to get hot enough to bale.

Their division of labor was always a puzzle to me. Clarence was a big bear of a man with huge ham-size hands capable of lifting large weights like one end of a tractor. Claude was a bantam by comparison, so skinny and small he hardly looked strong enough to board a hay wagon let alone load it, but that's what he did. Clarence had the prestige position of sitting on the tractor and doing the baling. Claude stood on the wagon and did the loading—which may have accounted for his having dwindled away to practically nothing.

Always at the country store, it was Clarence who made the pronouncements, Claude who made the endorsements, and Matthew who did the mediating when mediation became necessary. Out in the field, Clarence also made the decisions on when to begin baling and when to quit, and Claude unquestionably followed his judgment. Whatever Clarence did, "Claude did too." He was Clarence's shadow, not a long shadow like the afternoon sun, but a small shadow, like the overhead sun.

This morning, Clarence was waiting, not resting, and therefore not sitting in his usual place on the nail keg. Instead, he was standing by the door, leaned up against the penny-candy case, ready to go the moment the sun was right. Claude, in a similar attitude, was lounging up against the glass display case that held ladies' combs, cosmetics, and other unguents on the opposite side of the door.

The moment I walked in the store, Clarence turned to me.

"What's wrong with that feller out in yore field?" he wanted to know. "Don't he know better than to try to rake dew-wet hay? How come you ain't told him about waiting for the sun?"

The barrage of questions was almost like an accusation, as though I had not done my part to protect the community and keep it clean.

"I told him."

Clarence drew his bushy brows together in a studied frown. "How come he don't listen?"

"It's against his nature."

His frown turned into a scowl and his voice was full of scorn.

"Must be one of them know-it-all city folks that thinks they can do any man's job."

Claude, lounging up against the glass display case on the other side of the store, unrolled the toothpick he held between his teeth to the side of his mouth and turned his wizened little face up to me.

"Sho looks like it . . . all fancied up in them riding breeches and boots. You wait'll he's been out in that sun for a while . . . he ain't gonna last long."

Promise me that, I wanted to say, but I thought the better of talking about company and went to the back of the store where Matthew kept his rusting old ice chest in the corner beside stacks of baling twine and boxes of store-stiff blue denim overalls. Matthew swept the floor and the sidewalk first thing every morning, but he never dusted anything. He couldn't see it. The merchandise lay under layers of dust in the dark in the back of the store. The only light in the rectagonal building came from the two windows on either side of the front door and one fifteen-watt bulb hanging from a drop cord from the ceiling. This was hardly better than a small candle.

"Can you find what you want?" Matthew asked.

"I'm looking for grape, orange, and strawberry soda, but it's hard to see."

Now that summer had come and Matthew had removed all his layers of winter clothing, he wore a short-sleeved shirt that exposed his frail, white arms. Self-conscious about them, he kept them tucked across his chest so as little as possible of them could be seen, and unwound them only to aid a customer or make a transaction. Untangling them now, Matthew leaned under the counter and pawed around. "I'll bring the flashlight."

Matthew was very frugal. He figured it was better to keep a flashlight to search out a purchase that a customer wanted to make than to burn up a lot of money using electric lights. He rummaged around the ice chest until he found what I was looking for and took it back to the counter for me.

"Are you going to drink them here or are they to go?"

"I'm taking them to the field."

Matthew reached under the counter again and this time took out a sheaf of newspapers cut in half and a huge ball of thin laundry string and began wrapping the bottles up one by one. I thought this was likely another economy and I told him, "You don't have to go to all that trouble if you don't have any bags."

"Won't be worth drinkin' if they get hot," Matthew said, continuing to wrap the bottles up. "I always do this for my customers, soon as the hot weather sets in."

I gathered up my bundles of soft drinks and as I got to the door, Clarence couldn't resist one more comment. He leaned back against the candy case and crossed his arms across his bib-overall front. "Is that feller gonna try to bale that green hay?"

I didn't want to take any responsibility for what Colonel Swagnagle was doing. "He said he was."

Clarence shook his big, St. Bernard head in silent amazement, as though he had just heard the wonder of the world. "That's a sorrowful sight. I ain't never seen the likes of what's happening in yore hayfield."

"Ain't it the truth!" Claude added. "Makes me just want to come watch."

They didn't mean it badly, but I took it badly because it translated into the fact that we had become the sideshow of the community, and it didn't get better, it got worse. A farmer measured his pride by how straight his windrows were. It was done with slide-rule precision the same as planting crops. The aesthetic effect was important because everything out in the country was under constant scrutiny and the work was out there for all the world to see. Straight windrows were equally important from a practical viewpoint because the baler had to follow the windrows and the pickup wagon had to follow that. All it took was driving the tractor in a straight line, and with application, anyone could do that.

By nightfall, Colonel Swagnagle, having finally untangled the rake, had all the hay in windrows, or rather what were supposed to be windrows. There were all these dizzy lines of hay that zigzagged up and over and around the hills. Instead of driving the tractor straight down the field, he kept looking back and cussing. Every time he did, the tractor zigged off course, then he would have to zag back. I had seen what was happening, but I wasn't about to do anything to stop it. I couldn't have if I had wanted to. Once Colonel Swagnagle made up his mind, God himself couldn't stop him. I thought if we could just somehow get through this awful experience, I didn't care if he raked the hay in circles.

When it came time to bale, it was almost as bad. Since it was midweek and Larry was at work, there was only me, Wayne and Billy-Wade, and the three little Turner boys to act as hay crew. Colonel Swagnagle, ready to take command of the situation, strode out in boots, breeches, and campaign hat. He took one look at the boys and said, "Well, I see the children are here, where are the troops?"

"We *are* the troops, Colonel Swagnagle."

I saw the muscles in his cheeks harden. *"That?"* He flung his hand at the five little boys and they dwindled into dwarfs at his utter disdain. "That's all we have for troops?"

I tried to keep my voice even. "All we could muster."

He blew his breath out in unspeakable exasperation. "All right," he snapped at the boys, "hop to it."

Wayne and Billy-Wade and the three Turner boys jumped on the hay wagon hooked up behind the baler and got as far away from Colonel Swagnagle as they could without falling off the back of the wagon, and we headed for the field. The problems began with the first bale of hay. The tension on the string that fed through the baler and bound the hay always had to be adjusted. It was as routine as adjusting the string on a guitar, and as necessary. I had tried to recommend this to Colonel Swagnagle earlier. He dismissed it out of hand as female meddling, and when we picked up the first bale, the hay poured out the sides and back on the ground. The same thing happened with the second and the third bale. This was an exercise in futility.

"Colonel Swagnagle," I yelled, over the clacking and chopping of the baler.

"What now?" He looked back and saw Tommy Turner standing there with the just-baled hay spilled out both sides and nothing but the hay strings in his hands. "You can't send a boy to do a man's job," he said with black annoyance.

"It's not that. It's the tension on the hay string."

He made a very elaborate display of getting off the tractor, lifting the lid of the baler, and winding the tension as tight as he could get it.

We began again. Now the string was so tight we couldn't get our hands under it to lift it onto the wagon. We tried working in pairs, lifting the hay like footlockers with one of us on each end. It was insane and inefficient and we weren't going to last a half hour doing this.

"Colonel Swagnagle, . . ."

He slammed on the brakes and threw the three Turner boys off the wagon. The blue tractor almost stood on end and the red baler jackknifed behind that. He jumped off the tractor and stormed back to where we were on the wagon, hands on his hips, striking his General Patton pose, execution in his eyes.

"What in the hell is it now?"

I hated to tell him. I could see that he would like to have us all drawn and quartered and maybe drowned after that. "The tension is too tight," I told him. "We can't get our hands under the hay string."

All the attributes of the old field commander rose in his stance. His voice had the cold cutting edge of command. "I don't want to hear that word another time today. 'Can't' doesn't get a damn thing done. All you've got to do—" He reached down to snatch the bale off the ground, but he couldn't get a hold of the string either. Stung by this, he wrapped both arms around the bale and threw it up on the wagon. "—is pick it up." He turned away and went back to the baler and adjusted the tension again.

Baling hay with Mr. Finley, we had learned that a well made bale of hay should be sweet, sun-dried, and firmly packed, with the hay strings on each end tightened to just enough slack to pick it up and stack it. What was coming out of the baler now was green, damp, and so loosely baled that it looked like lumps of Monday wash tied up in bed sheets.

It was no longer safe to speak to Colonel Swagnagle about this again. He was hell-bent on getting the baling done no matter how it was done. All five faces turned to me.

"What are we going to do?" Wayne asked.

I would like to have said, "Guillotine Colonel Swagnagle," but I knew not to put such notions in their heads, for I could already see that if things continued the way they were going, I might have a mutiny in the hayfield. Browbeating only lasts so long, even for little boys, and after that, it's Watch Out time.

"Stack it as best we can," I answered, "and take it to the barn anyway."

Timmy, the oldest of the Turner boys, stood his ground and shook his head. "Ain't gonna work. That hay he raked ain't cured. You stack green hay in the barn and it'll burn it down."

"How do you know?" Wayne asked.

"I seen it happen."

The words on green hay were familiar. Mr. Finley had said the same thing, the gases that formed from stacking green hay would cause spontaneous combustion. I was wondering if I could take the whole load down to the county landfill and have it buried, but Tommy was running his hand inside the bales testing for dampness.

"It ain't so bad that salt won't help," Tommy said.

"*Salt!*"

"It'll draw the moisture."

That night I went down to the country store and told Matthew I wanted twenty-four boxes of salt.

He pushed his hat back on his head and blinked his eyes. "Lord a'mussy. What you gonna do, pickle the world?"

"No. I'm going to salt my hay."

I expected him to look profoundly shocked, but he didn't. He acted as though it was the most natural thing in the world and said, "You don't want boxes of salt, you want bags of salt."

With that, he loaded up my station wagon with twenty-pound bags of salt and we went home and salted all the hay in the barn, so that it wouldn't burn down during the night.

The next day we went back to the field again. By this time, I was no longer speaking to Larry. The last thing I told him was, "If you don't get rid of Colonel Swagnagle, I won't be responsible for what happens."

Larry, who had spent the day in peace and serenity in the city, tried to make light of it and chuckled and said, "Oh, he means well."

"Means well hell!"

"He's just trying to be helpful."

"I'd rather have help from Attila the Hun."

"Now, now."

It was the patronizing and placating that did it.

With a cheery wave, he was off to the city and as we went back to the field with Colonel Swagnagle, I decided I would never speak to him again.

For us, the day began as the day before had begun . . . locked in mortal combat. The boys were getting grey-faced from discipline and restraint. As we followed the weaving windrows dizzily up and down the hills, Billy-Wade, overcome at last, began to cry.

"I want to go home."

Wayne, past enduring anything more, turned his frustration on Billy-Wade. "You *are* home, dummy."

"I want to go home back in the house," he wailed.

"Me, too," Tad, the youngest of the Turner boys, added.

"Now, boys," I told them, we've got to stay until we. . . ."

Suddenly, there was a crash and a crunch. The left front side of the hay wagon fell down and all the hay slid off on the ground. The constant weaving back and forth following the winding windrows had been too much for the wagon's axle. It had broken off. We all held our breath as Colonel Swagnagle got off the tractor to inspect this latest disaster. He was a man straining for control. I expected hell to fall on all our heads and the fields around us.

Colonel Swagnagle took off his campaign hat and bent down to take a look. In that moment of leaning down, there was something about the way the sunlight hit his bristle-white hair, the aging slack in his jaw, and for the barest moment, a fleeting sadness and defeat that flicked in his eyes. With all the aggravation to the contrary, I suddenly felt very sad about Colonel Swagnagle. He was an old warrior who had likely known defeats before but had been younger and stronger and more able to mask them and recover from them.

Here was a man who had kept whole brigades rolling during World War II, who had pushed troops across the Rhine, and whose iron discipline and single-mindedness of purpose had kept his men going and contributed measurably to the victory in Europe. The very qualities that had served so well in war, now had no place in peace, and I suddenly realized that Colonel Swagnagle was a man who had lived beyond the world's need for him. His way of seeking a solution, solving a problem, and bringing it to a resolution was a hold-out in yesterday's armament. He had operated on the principle of war that if he was tough enough on his troops, they would be too busy hating him to be afraid of the enemy, and it gave him strength and a sense of pride to think he was tough enough to endure this dissent. But now the flags were gone, the purpose was gone, his valuable asset, so necessary in peril and in time of war, was now a liability no longer needed in peace.

There were no longer troops, but five sullen children and one unmanageable woman. The solutions for the battlefield were not the solutions for the hayfield, but for Colonel Swagnagle there was no way to change. It was all mixed up with how he viewed himself and how he viewed others viewing him. The bluster and bravado had been there too long and Colonel Swagnagle was locked in his own armament. He could no more change the way he was than he could have changed a war wound or an amputation. He was a casualty of his own career.

With battlefield tactics, Colonel Swagnagle had tried to overcome the elements of nature, and the farmers had long ago learned that you couldn't do that; you had to work *with* the elements of sun, rain, and humidity. Colonel Swagnagle had tried to overcome all of nature and it had defeated him. He knew it and I knew it and we both knew there was no need for acknowledgment because it was the kind of silent defeat that rankles inside and whose memory never goes away.

The problem now was how to salvage an old man's pride and get him out of the hayfield as quickly and painlessly as possible and back on the golf course at the Officers' Club where he could remember with old cronies the glories of the past. But when Colonel Swagnagle looked up from where he stooped beside the broken axle on the wagon, I could see that long ingrained habit was going to make him see it through, that he was going to keep on until the job was done, even if it killed him, and there was no need for that.

Before he could say anything, I told him, "That's all right, Colonel Swagnagle. The boys and I will go get the old grey Jubilee tractor and the other wagon and follow you."

The boys were none too pleased. They were ready to quit, and, if pressed, mutiny. I got them back to the barn and we sat down for a conference on the tumbling-down hay.

"Look, boys," I told them, "Colonel Swagnagle is an old man, and somebody who has been our friend for a long time. It would hurt his feelings and end our friendship if we were to quit on him now, and hay isn't worth that."

The five of them sat there in assorted attitudes of silence and resistance, their mouths clamped into a tight straight line, their eyes making the refusal their lips did not. Finally, Timmy, the oldest of the Turner boys, said, "I don't see no use in doin' something that's gonna have to be done again. Ever' one of them bales is made too loose, and before first and last, it's gonna come tumbling down right here in the middle of the barn. He won't listen to nobody tell him how to do it right."

"I know, Timmy, but it's not a matter of who's right and who's wrong about how the hay is made. It's a matter of what's important . . . the hay or an old man's feelings and pride."

He still couldn't quite accept this until Tommy came to my rescue. "She's saying the same thing Mama always tells us when Grandma comes to visit and does everything the old-fashioned way. Mama just lets her go ahead and then goes behind her and does it again."

"I don't see no use in doin' things twice," Timmy complained. "Mama says we gotta respect old folks and their way of doin' things . . . even if it ain't the best way."

"Your mama's right," I told them, "and that's exactly what we're going to do. As soon as the hay is finished and Colonel Swagnagle is gone, we'll just back the baler up in the barn and rebale the whole lot."

Wayne slapped himself on the forehead with the palm of his hand. "All 750 bales?"

"All 750 bales."

That's exactly what we did. We somehow managed to endure until the last bale was put in the barn, and when Colonel Swagnagle asked, "What about the other sixty-acre field?" I told him, "That's going to be winter pasture for the horses." He didn't question that and I didn't explain because I knew he didn't want to cut it and I didn't want him to, but it left us with a good parting place.

"That's just as well," Colonel Swagnagle said, gathering up his luggage to leave and looking relieved. "I've got to get back to the golf course and practice. There's a tournament for retirees next week.

We shook hands. "I wish you luck," I said, and he was gone back from whence he came. His pride had been salvaged and nothing but nerves had been damaged. When he was gone, we backed the baler in the barn, rebaled all the hay, and stacked it tight to last the winter.

I was proud of the boys, and in the end, they were proud of themselves, for they finally reached an understanding of what had happened and why we did what we had done. As troops, they might not have looked like much, but they had conducted themselves like real soldiers.

As for me, I was never going to be persuaded ever again to let friends help in the hayfield. On this, Larry agreed, and when it came time to cut the sixty-acre field, we would hire somebody with experience to do the cutting and baling, somebody who knew what he was doing. For this, I turned to our neighbor, Ewell Early, who helped others and was willing to help us by working for hire. It was a condition that hurt him since all the other farmers but tenants were able to make it on farming alone, but he hid his feelings as best he could under enforced cheerfulness and hard work.

Ewell Early had three sons who had grown up in the hayfield and who helped him, the oldest, a boy of sixteen, called Goochie. The two younger boys, Hank and Frank, were hardworking and reliable, but Goochie liked to hot rod. When his father wasn't looking, he flew across the fields on the tractor like Mario Andretti on the racetrack. He had broken bones, equipment, and his father's patience, but nothing really irreparable had happened until he came to work in our fields.

CHAPTER 9

A Portrait of Courage

BALING HAY WAS BAD ENOUGH, but it was the cutting of the waist-high grass with the eight-foot cutter bar that was the most dangerous. Early on, when Mr. Finley was cutting the forty-acre field, he had warned us about this. Now that it was time to cut the sixty-acre field, we took every precaution.

For the mowing operation, the cutter bar with fifteen red, claw-like shears was attached to the side of the tractor. This ran along at ground level, unseen in the tall thick grass, cutting everything in its path with mechanical precision. No one took this piece of equipment lightly, and even the rabbits and ground-nesting birds, hearing the clack of the cutter bar, ran for safety out of its path.

Down at the country store, Clarence and Claude had decided to play the Doomsday Boys. They could always tell you forty ways how to fail on anything no matter what you were doing. Now, they and all the other old farmers who came in after work regaled us with horror stories about all the terrible things they had seen happen in the hayfield during a mowing operation. When they ran out of stories they knew, they told us about the ones their fathers had told them, each more awesome than the last, engulfing every possible injury—maiming, mangling, and death.

There was no malice in the telling of these tales, only a delight in watching our horror-stricken faces and letting us know how really terrible things could be. Listening, I was rather reminded of the old ladies who visit pre-op patients in the hospital and tell them about all the possible complications, what the latest mortality rate is on their particular operation, and who they knew who died from it.

Being the new kid on the block, I figured this was the indoctrination course they gave all newcomers, and while I was mindful of all they said, I wasn't too worried because Ewell Early had agreed to bring his son, Goochie, and cut the sixty-acre field. With that commitment, I expected all my troubles in the hayfield to go away, because Ewell had farmed all his life. He did careful, precision work, and was a match in expertise for Clarence and Claude.

They arrived on Ewell's big, red, Massey Ferguson tractor. Ewell would cut with this one, while Goochie cut with our blue tractor. One good look at Goochie and I no longer felt the reassurance I thought I would. At sixteen and six foot four, he towered over his father, and whenever he was spoken to, he raised his hand to his cheek and waved down to whoever was speaking. I ascribed this latent idiocy to retarded maturity and teenage foolishness. It was his eyes that bothered me.

Goochie had carrot-colored hair, a snowfall of freckles, and giddy green eyes that slid around all over the place and gave the impression that he couldn't keep his mind on anything. Whenever Goochie was around, Ewell kept looking around to check on him as though he anticipated trouble at any moment. Although we weren't aware of it then, Goochie had a history of trouble. He had wrecked his father's car, turned over the hay wagon, and set the tractor on fire.

Henrietta's reaction to all of this was, "Boys will be boys."

The one soft spot in her heart was reserved for Goochie. He was her child grown tall, and if he was a little reckless and raced and hot-rodded around on the machinery, and wrecked, broke, and burned a few things, Henrietta figured that was just Goochie's wild hair and a part of growing up. Ewell didn't at all agree with this assessment of the situation, and he tried as best he could to monitor what Goochie did and subdue him whenever possible.

This passive reaction was intended to keep peace at home. Henrietta, as the locals said, wasn't "as big as a bug," but, they admitted, she had the sting of a yellow jacket when riled . . . especially about Goochie. She loved him blindly and without reservation.

The controversy over Goochie swirled about him without his notice. Even when his feet were in the hayfield, his mind was someplace else. Whenever he was not actively involved in a conversation, he was holding his arms up, snapping his fingers in his ears, and twisting in rhythm to the latest dance step. His one asset was that he was big and strong, and though I wouldn't have said he didn't have good sense, he was so irresponsible, he did remind me of an ape with his brains knocked out.

Listening to Ewell's instructions to Goochie as they hooked the eight-foot cutter bar on to the blue tractor, I could tell that Ewell would be aware of and watch everything that Goochie did. This restored some of my original assurance and I decided to lay my concerns to rest and take care of my job, which was to keep everybody out of the field while the mowing operation was going on. Wayne and Billy-Wade had been warned of the danger and weren't even allowed past the gate going to the hayfield. Suzie, our little miniature mongrel cocker, sensed the danger too, and would not let us out of her sight. Everywhere we went, she was underfoot, watching, waiting, and listening.

All day long, Ewell and Goochie drove their tractors in opposite directions round and round the hayfield felling the tall grass with the advancing cutter bars. By the time Larry arrived home from work in the city late that afternoon, great swaths of mown hay lay on the ground ready to be conditioned. Changing to boots and jeans, he went out to the barn and hooked the conditioner with its cleated steel rollers up to the old grey Jubilee to crimp the hay and mash out the moisture.

Before leaving, he took a head count. "Where's Wayne?"

"Off with the school band," I replied, watching him get on the tractor and head for the field.

"See you later," he waved, and Billy-Wade and Suzie and I stood at the gate and watched him drive off, the conditioner's giant steel rollers crushing the moisture from the newly cut hay.

The evening cool had begun to settle on the gently rolling hills, and the light was fading fast from the sky. The odor of the freshly mown hay lay heavy on the land. As Larry approached the gate on his round around the field, he said, "Ewell and Goochie are still cutting down on the far corner, but the light will be gone soon. I think I have time for a couple more rounds. Do you want to go with me to see what's been done?"

I turned to Billy-Wade hanging across the top rail of the gate with his sneakers pushed through the rails. "Don't move from this gate."

"I promise," he grinned.

Climbing up on the tractor with Larry, I rode on the running board. Suzie, never one to be left behind, bounded through the cut grass behind us, her pink tongue panting out the side of her mouth, her curly black ears flopping up and down with every leap over the tumbled grass. As we rounded the corner back to the gate, we noticed that Suzie was no longer behind us.

"Probably," we laughed, "Suzie's so exhausted she's waiting for the next round to catch up."

Larry dropped me off at the gate. "Why don't you go get us a cup of coffee, and I'll make one more round and quit."

I headed for the kitchen and he started his last round. I had just reached for the coffeepot when I heard Billy-Wade screaming, "Mr. Early said come quick!"

My first thought was that Larry had had an accident . . . that the tractor had overturned on the hill . . . that his hand was caught in the cleated rollers of the conditioner . . . that he was crushed. I ran out the kitchen door, past the barn, toward the fields, losing one shoe as I ran.

Ewell Early's son, Goochie, his face frozen and white, was waiting in the field.

"It's the little dog."

One moment was grateful relief that it was not Larry, the next, a stab of pain that something had happened to Suzie.

All the things Suzie was to us ran through my mind as I ran toward her. She had been a member of the family for ten years and the boys' constant companion and playmate since the day they were born. She had patience, tact, and discretion, and she was devoted to total participation. When we were fishing in the pond, she sat in the boat and looked anxiously at the water. When we were out riding the horses in the field, she ran alongside, straining to keep up. When the distance was greater than her endurance, we carried her home across the saddle. She was only fourteen inches high and she was our dearest friend.

As Billy-Wade and Goochie and I ran across the darkening field, we saw her lying in the grass looking back over her shoulder toward us. She made no sound; only her black eyes spoke her cry for help.

"She ran up through the tall grass where I was mowing," Goochie said. "I stopped the tractor as soon as I saw her, but the mower blade had already got her."

She was lying in a pool of blood unable to move. When I lifted her up, three of her legs were gone. I thought, *Oh, Jesus! How do you make a tourniquet for three legs? . . . How do you even make a tourniquet?* Everything I ever knew seemed to leave my head.

The scarf I had worn earlier was still around my neck. Hurriedly, I snatched it off and wrapped it around her bleeding body and ran with her in my arms toward the house. Billy-Wade, retrieving my lost shoe on the way, followed close behind sobbing, "Poor Suzie! Poor Suzie!"

The vet. I had to get the vet. I had no idea where Dr. Caldwell's office was located. I had only seen him once before and that was when he came out to the farm to worm the horses.

Inside, in my hurry, I could find neither my address book nor Dr. Caldwell's listing in the yellow pages. I called the operator. "I have an emergency."

Immediately, I was connected and the doctor's wife was giving me directions for getting there: "Down Center Street . . . past Safeway . . . to the Catholic Church . . . right on Fairview Avenue . . . three-quarters of a mile . . . take the right fork . . . fifth house on left."

I scrawled the directions on the back of an envelope, grabbed a white towel, wrapped Suzie in it, and with Billy-Wade to take care of her in the back seat of the station wagon, raced to the animal hospital in Victorsville seven miles away. The trip was a nightmare of anxiety and uncertainty. . . . the leisurely crawl of evening traffic . . . a landmark unlabeled . . . a street sign down . . . a turn in at the wrong house . . . and time so precious.

At last we were there and Dr. Caldwell was waiting. Mrs. Caldwell took Suzie from us and laid her on the narrow white examining table. Dr. Caldwell, tight-lipped and silent, nodded in our direction and turned on a gooseneck lamp over Suzie to examine her wounds. The right foreleg had been cut off near the chest; the two hind legs, at the first joint.

Sobbing, Billy-Wade buried his face in my side and I was biting back tears. "Can you save her?"

Dr. Caldwell leaned back to look at me over the gooseneck lamp. He was a thin, spare man with glasses and a grey crew cut. His eyes seemed to take our measure. "She will be completely helpless."

"It doesn't matter. We'll take care of her."

"She will require constant nursing," Dr. Caldwell warned.

He explained the operation that would be required to tie off the ligaments and clean the sheared-off bones. He would call us in two hours.

Through it all, Suzie lay there in silent pain. She watched us with eyes full of trust, confident that those who loved her and those who cared would see to her needs and repair her wounds.

Going home, Billy-Wade was huddled in a sad little heap beside me trying to wipe away tears. After the urgency of getting Suzie to the hospital came the realization that something irrevocable had happened. "Things will never be the same . . . ever again," he cried, wiping his eyes on the sleeve of his white sweat shirt.

"Only her legs are gone," I reminded him. "Her heart is just the same."

He brightened for a moment and looked at me with long wet lashes. "Do you really think so?"

I gave his knee a pat. "I'm sure of it."

At home, Larry was waiting. "Goochie told me what happened. Did you have Suzie put to sleep?"

I shook my head. "Dr. Caldwell is operating on her now. He thinks he can save her."

A look of concern crossed his face. "Do you think that's wise?"

I had never considered any other course of action.

"It's all very well to try to save Suzie," he pointed out, "but what about the boys? How are they going to feel once they've recovered from their grief and their first burst of sympathy? How is it going to be for them to see their little friend crippled, mangled, and unable to move?"

How, indeed, would they feel? Repelled by this little fragment of a dog that had been their companion and playmate for ten long years? Bothered by the added burden her care would require? Or, would they truly learn sympathy and compassion for another living thing that needed them now that she was no longer able to care for herself? Was it sensible to risk all their bright, beautiful memories of the past with a constant reminder of tragedy?

"We may have no decision to make," I replied. "Suzie may not survive the operation."

Billy-Wade's single request was that we find Suzie's legs and bury them deep so that nothing else would get them. In the dark, we could only find two of the three legs, and with flashlight, pick, and shovel buried them under earth and stone so that they would remain forever undisturbed.

When Wayne arrived home from his band trip, he listened to the account of Suzie's accident with the masked face a ten-year-old adopts when he feels a situation requires the demeanor of a man. He couldn't give over to tears as Billy-Wade did; he just hurt inside and tried to mask his feelings with a man's face. But his soft brown eyes gave him away.

"Can Dr. Caldwell save her?"

Measured in time by people's lives, Suzie was in her seventies and for the past two years had been subject to epileptic fits which we were able to control with a drug prescribed by the veterinarian. The boys were aware that one day the disease would outdistance the drug, and Suzie would die. They were prepared for that, but not for a mangled death under the mower blade.

When the phone rang, Dr. Caldwell told us that Suzie had survived the operation, and if she lasted through the night, she should be all right.

"Now," Larry said, "you've got a decision to make. It's no longer a question of how can we live without Suzie, but are we going to be able to live with her?"

I hated the position I was in. It was like being chosen to be executioner. I didn't want to call Dr. Caldwell up and say, "Put Suzie to sleep. We may not have the guts to keep her," because I thought we did. Suzie had struggled against colossal odds and survived. She wanted to live. I felt she should have the chance.

"You're gambling," Larry warned, "with other people's emotions and memories."

I was now beset with doubts. What if I ruined everything for everybody? What if what I was doing was nothing more than foolhardiness? I chose to delay what had to be done. I couldn't face the agony of decision. Besides, there might be no decision to make. She might not live till morning.

But Suzie did live till morning, and before the boys came back from school on the yellow school bus, a decision on whether to bring her home or not had to be made. I so wanted someone to tell me how to make the right decision that I called a friend whose dog had family status the same as Suzie.

"What would you do?" I asked.

"Have her put to sleep, for heaven's sake. To keep her now would be cruel to Suzie and a terrible thing for the boys."

Cruel to Suzie? It never occurred to me that such could be so. Had I just misjudged everything? Larry thought so. My friend thought so, maybe Dr. Caldwell thought so, too. I hadn't even asked in my anxiety to save Suzie. I got him on the phone.

"From a medical standpoint, do you consider it a cruelty to keep Suzie alive?"

"Certainly not," he answered instantly. "Suzie has survived. All she needs is care."

His reassurance lasted only a little while, and then the doubts returned. The score was two to one. All I could think was, Can we afford the time, already stretched thin by the demands of a 112-acre farm, to adequately care for an invalid dog who would require constant nursing? Would we find in ourselves the too-human quality of eventually growing irritated by what had become troublesome and burdensome? Too often the good intentions that begin a task do not last until the task is done, particularly if the task is to last forever. If such were so with us, it might be more damaging to the children if we tried and failed than not to try at all.

I had to have an answer—the right answer. I called Kate Cromwell, whose judgment I valued and whose advice I had often sought. She was my other-mother, my own being 500 miles away in Georgia, and I was in need of some mothering.

"Kate, I've got a problem," I told her on the phone.

My voice must have given me away because Kate said, "That bad?"

"That bad."

"Come on up."

When I got there, she was waiting for me. The house was filled with the warm spice of cookies baking, and the teakettle was bubbling. It was such a relief to find a momentary sanctuary from all my problems, to find someone to talk to, that I unaccountably began crying the moment I saw Kate.

"Put your boots back on," Kate said, which was always her way of saying pull yourself together, "and come on back to the kitchen and tell me what happened."

We sat down in our old familiar places across from each other at her kitchen table, and Kate listened, her grey eyes grave as I told her what had happened to Suzie. She had spent many an hour at her kitchen window watching our winter rides on horseback through her pasture with little black Suzie running alongside. Kate knew her well, and knew what Suzie meant to us.

"I'm sorry to hear that," Kate said, with such sincerity that it brought tears to my eyes again.

"What, in my place, would *you* do?" I asked.

Kate paused before replying, looked down at her hands folded on the table, then back at me. "You know I can't answer that. You're the one who has to live with it. Only you can decide."

"Oh, Kate," I wailed. I wanted her to tell me what to do. I wanted her to promise me it would be all right.

Kate reached across the table and patted me on the arm. "Sounds to me as though you've already made up your mind, and you're just looking for reassurances. If that's what you're asking . . . do I think you can do it . . . you know the answer to that . . . I'm sure you can."

Kate's words were comforting, but as I drove back home there still lingered shadows of doubts, because there were no guarantees, and that's what I wanted. No matter how I wished it weren't so, some decision had to be made and some action had to be taken, for I had told Dr. Caldwell that I would call for Suzie at noon, and there was still her third leg to be found and buried.

Back at the farm, with a leaf rake and a disposable plastic bag, I walked out to the hayfield. The temperature had dropped during the night, and it was still cold and chill and grey with morning haze. Sixty acres of hay lay flat on the rolling green hills, and I could no longer remember where or how far I had run to pick Suzie up after the accident. I poked through row after row of the thick, freshly fallen grass and could not find Suzie's leg.

Finally, I saw on the hilltop a little stub of grass still standing. There, beneath the blood-wet grass was Suzie's little black leg with the curly fluff on the foot. That little black leg had run so many long miles beside us . . . every step of the way . . . and now, never again.

I wept to see it. I could stand no more. It was all too painful, too harsh, too much for me. Claude and Clarence were right. It took a special breed to live on the land. It took courage and endurance and dogged persistence just to get the work done, and then it took more to try to cope with the perils inherent to the job. In moving to the farm, I had stepped beyond the safe zone that the suburbs afford, out to the cutting edge where all the predictables I had always known no longer applied. I didn't have the strength for this kind of reality. I couldn't take these kind of losses. If this is what it took to live on the land, I just didn't have it.

Sunk to my knees in the chill grey hayfield, I searched for enough strength just to finish the job I had set out to do. I went through my whole reservoir of aids that could usually be relied upon when trouble outdistanced endurance, but there was nothing left. They had already been used up in the hayfield and at the veterinary hospital with Suzie. I thought about what Kate had said, but I knew now her confidence in me had been misplaced.

I could only sit there in the hayfield and cry for what had been irrevocably done. When I looked up, I saw the blue ridge of the mountains in the distance on the horizon. *I lift up mine eyes unto the hills from whence cometh my strength.*

The words came back, but not the strength. I wished, there in the field, for a thunderbolt to strike me with renewed strength and determination, but it didn't happen, and I just didn't have the heart to do another thing.

Overcome with despair and inertia, I wondered how all the others who had gone before me had managed to survive their losses. The very land my horses now grazed on had been bitterly bought with both Union and Confederate blood in the Civil War. How had the survivors survived? Where did courage come from? How is determination repaired?

The British had managed it in the Battle of Britain. Under siege for forty days and forty nights, they had drawn together the courage, determination, and forbearance to survive the night bombing and each morning face the rubble, clear it away, bury their dead, and brace themselves for yet more of the same the following night. Their losses were epic and their fortitude had always before been a watermark to me. Measuring troubles side by side, I had always figured if the British could do *that*, surely I, with lesser troubles, could cope with whatever disaster faced me. Looking back to their finest hour, this value of the past had always before been a primary aid in generating the renewed effort and the self-imposed determination to get up and try one more time to address myself to whatever challenge faced me.

But now, even this dependable and primary aid seemed of little use as I knelt in the hayfield. The only thing I could do was at least finish the job I had set out to do. The morning chill was fading, the midday sun was rising overhead and warming the land, and Dr. Caldwell would be waiting.

Picking up Suzie's little leg, I put it in the plastic disposable bag. It looked so incongruous packaged there, so out of place and wrong. In this disposable world was this, then, what was to become of Suzie? Her usefulness gone, to be disposed of? Was this the reward for ten years of loyalty and devotion? Was this the example to set for Wayne and Billy-Wade?

I buried the leg with the others and went inside and called Dr. Caldwell. "I'm coming to get Suzie."

That afternoon when the yellow school bus came over the hill and stopped at the gate, Wayne and Billy-Wade ran up the drive with lunch boxes and books and burst through the door.

"Where's Suzie?"

Suzie lay in her dog bed newly lined with a pink bassinet cover, her head on a little pink cushion, her black eyes sad and listless.

"Oh, Suzie!" they cried. "You're going to live!"

For the first time since she came home, Suzie replied with a look of recognition and response. She gave one small thump with her black tail. They knelt down beside Suzie, surrounding her with love and pats and praise. Wayne's eyes were shining with excitement and anticipation.

"I know what! I'll make Suzie an artificial leg with my leather craft set."

Billy-Wade pulled closer. "And, if that doesn't work, I'll make her a skateboard so she can push along on the one leg she has left."

"Yeah, Billy-Wade, and until then, we'll be Suzie's legs . . . right?"

Billy-Wade bobbed his head. "You betcha."

But they had reckoned without Suzie. She had already determined that she would not become the invalid she was destined to be. That very afternoon, as we sat with her in her basket on the front lawn in the warm sunshine, a car drove up. Suzie, having only arrived home from the hospital hours before, rose up on her last remaining leg and barked at the arrival. All of us felt a surge of pride, not unakin to triumph, that this brave little animal would still try to defend us with what she had left. As we showered her with pats and praise, her little black tail swished back and forth as it always did when she heard words of appreciation.

To our great surprise, Clarence and Claude got out of the car. They had come to see about Suzie.

"We heard what happened to your little dog," Clarence said as he lumbered over to take a look. "We know you set a great store by her and we just wanted to tell you we were sorry it happened."

Claude, with his hands held behind him, had ambled up behind Clarence and now held his hand out. "Yeah," Claude said, adding his condolences. "Matthew said he was sorry to hear it too. He had to stay and mind the store, but he told me to give you this for the little dog."

He handed me a can of sardines. Considering how frugal Matthew was, how he never gave anything away, it was a handsome gift. Their concern for what had happened to Suzie made it a splendid offering.

"Thank you for coming, and thank Matthew for sending these."

Clarence bent down and resting his arm on his overall knee, took off his engineer cap and laid it on the grass. "I feel nearly 'bout as bad for pore old Ewell Early. It came close to killin' him when Goochie done this."

Claude stooped down to join Clarence, his thin little legs folded up, his arms wrapped around his knees. "Ain't it the truth! He's been plumb grey-faced ever since it happened."

I put my hand under Suzie's chin and raised it and she looked back with eyes full of promise. "Suzie's going to be all right," I said. "She's managed to survive something that would have killed most anybody."

"Ain't it the truth!" Claude said, using the only phrase he seemed to know. "I thought she was going to look terrible when they told me what happened, but she don't. When she's lying down you can't even tell."

With his thick, coarse hand, Clarence gently patted Suzie on the head. "Beats all I ever seen happen in the hayfield. I seen some bad things happen in my time, and heard worse, but I ain't never seen nothin' survive with three legs gone."

"Me neither," Claude admitted, adding a pat with his own scrawny little hand.

Later, when Claude and Clarence had gone, Ewell Early drove up with Goochie. Ewell's face was drawn and ashen and Goochie's was full of contrition.

"Goochie's got something to say," Ewell said when they got out of the truck.

Goochie looked at the ground instead of at me or Suzie. "I just wanted to say I'm sorry for what happened and wisht it was some way to take it back."

"Henrietta couldn't come," Ewell added, "but she's sorry too."

Their pain was so intense, I could only reply, "It's going to be all right, Goochie. Suzie's going to be able to recover."

And she did. In the days and weeks and months that followed, Suzie had a series of small, sometimes painful successes in her effort to achieve mobility again. She learned to move herself along like a little black caterpillar by pulling with her front leg and pushing with the two back stumps toward whatever destination she chose. The biggest problem was her overcoming depression and despair. We could see it on her little black face and read it in her eyes. She responded to encouragement and never once stopped trying. It took heart, and courage, and determination, but finally she was able to accomplish all her needs with the exception of going up steps and covering great distances, but even on this, she never gave up.

One afternoon the boys and I rode the horses to the back field, leaving Suzie outside under a shady tree. Sometime later, Larry noticed her painfully pulling along on her one leg trying to reach the edge of the pasture where we rode, forty acres away. Picking her up, he brought her out on the tractor, and Wayne carried her across the saddle. All the way home, all we could hear was thump . . . thump . . . thump . . . Suzie's little black tail wagging and hitting the saddle.

We should never have worried about what this little fragment of a dog would do *to* us, for as it turned out, it was what she did *for* us. Despair, and the reason for it, was there, but Suzie chose courage instead. Watching her overcome her difficulty was a thing to make the spirit soar. She became a constant source of inspiration, a living example of how a disability can be borne with dignity and grace, and how a disadvantage can be overcome with dedication and determination.

The boys, ever solicitous, responded with the compassion, love, and care we had hoped for. A tragedy became a triumph, and we never once regretted our decision to save Suzie, for to us, she was a source of pride. In the days that followed, our farm neighbors dropped by regularly to check on her progress and marvel at her accomplishments.

One afternoon, Joe Frost, who had given us the duck named Black Power, rattled up in his broken-down cattle truck with a present for Suzie, a big, raw, red knuckle bone he had saved from a side of beef. When he set it down beside her, Suzie and the knuckle bone were almost the same size. Out of pure politeness and good manners, Suzie gave the bone one delicate lick.

"See there," Joe grinned, enormously pleased, "she likes it."

Later, Maude Hardy, having delivered her school children home, turned in the driveway with the school bus.

"How's the little Lady Dog doing?" she asked, stepping down off the bus and carefully balancing her top-heavy weight on her tiny feet.

"Come see," we told her, pointing to Suzie sitting in the sun, her white jabot fluffed under her chin, her black coat shining with restored health, her eyes bright again.

Maude had just begun her visit when Dr. Caldwell drove up in his jeep with his black bag beside him. "I had a call from out this way, and I thought I'd stop by and see how my little patient is doing," he said, smiling over the top of his glasses.

Maude, as proud of Suzie as we were, told him, "Isn't she a picture?"

Dr. Caldwell looked at Suzie standing on her one leg, saw the dignity and grace and composure in her little black face, and shook his head. "No, not just a picture, I'd say she was a PORTRAIT of courage."

Through it all, despite the trauma of Suzie's tragedy, and as she recovered and got well, the haying operation continued. There was no way to quit.

CHAPTER 10

Eat Fast, Girls, Eat Fast

THERE WAS NOTHING TO DO but keep on keeping on. Every day we got up so tired we could hardly get our clothes on, but every day, it was back to the fields with sixteen sandwiches, two gallons of pink lemonade, five little boys, and whomever we could press into service to run the baler.

Finally, one Sunday afternoon, the end was in sight. We had only one more corner of the field to bale when, of all the outrages in the world, the baler quit. It was out of baling twine, and on Sunday afternoon, in our quiet country community where everyone observed the Lord's Day, there was nowhere in the world at any price to buy baling twine.

Larry, who was helping us by running the baler, said, "Go call Matthew and ask him to open up the store."

I thought I had about as much chance of that as asking him for

the iris out of his left eyeball, but I went in and made the call anyway. When I told him what the problem was and how desperate I
was to have him open the store and let me buy baling twine, he
gasped at this proposed heresy, "It's the Lord's Day."

Calling on St. Luke, I quoted: "The ox is in the ditch."

Matthew seriously considered this awesome circumstance, couched
in biblical terms, that allows enough leeway to get an ox out of a
ditch on Sunday if, as a result of leaving him there, he might be
dead by Monday. After a long and thoughtful silence, he said, "I
tell you what. You wait about fifteen minutes and come down to the
store. I'll set the baling twine outside on the steps and then you can
come and get it. In the morning, I'll write up a receipt and you can
pay for it then."

This seemed to follow the rubric of his prayerbook and satisfy
Matthew's conscience that the sale would not be registered until
Monday, but he made it very clear that I was not to come to the
door to thank him or see him in any way, just pick up the baling
twine that he would leave outside and be gone. I did.

When the work was finally done, we had baled, stacked, and stored
a total of 5,000 bales of hay. Figuring the total poundage, almost
a million pounds of hay had been moved from the field to the barn.
Each bale weighed sixty-five pounds and had required handling
three times: lifting it from the ground where the baler dropped it to
the hay wagon, from the hay wagon to the conveyor, and from
the conveyor to be stacked in the barn.

When the last bale was stacked in the barn and the doors were
closed on our summer's work, we all looked to heaven and said,
"Thank you, Jesus!" As bad as it was, it could have been worse. It
was over and done and nobody had died and I never wanted to hear
the word hay again.

I paid the three Turner boys for their summer's work and drove
them home in the station wagon. They sat there in three tired
little heaps, Timmy and Tad in the back, Tommy up front with me.
On the way, I asked them, "What are you going to do with the money
you've made?"

Timmy, the oldest, answered right away. "I'm gonna buy me a
lawn mower motor and make me a go-cart."

Tad, the youngest, leaned over the back seat, his eyes exploding with anticipation. "You know what I'm gonna do? I'm gonna get me a real bow and arrow and go huntin'."

Tommy, sitting quietly beside me in the front seat, had said nothing.

"How about you, Tommy?" I asked. "What are you going to buy?"

He looked at the roll of bills he held in his grubby hand. "I'm gonna buy Mama two front teeth."

I thought about Mrs. Turner's jack-o-lantern smile and how she always covered her mouth with her fingertips when she talked to hide the fact that her two front teeth were gone.

"How come you gonna do that, Tommy?" Timmy wanted to know.

"Yeah, Tommy," Tad complained. "How come you don't get something we can all share . . . like a rifle. I'd let you use my bow and arrow."

"Cause Mama needs 'em, and, . . ." Tommy's eyes held a threat for the other two, "nobody better tell her what I'm gonna do 'til I get it done."

When I drove into the Turner's yard, Mrs. Turner was again on the porch swing shelling yet another pan of peas with her flock of children around. She flashed her jack-o-lantern smile and said, "Won't you come up and sit for a spell?"

I was still in my jeans with a two-inch coat of dust and hayseeds stuck to the soles of my feet inside my Keds. "Thank you, no. I've got to get back and try to catch up with all the things I neglected in the house while we were out in the hayfield."

Mrs. Turner nodded her head in full acknowledgment. "It do pile up, don't it?"

I thanked her for letting Timmy, Tommy, and Tad come to help in the hayfield, and as I was leaving she said, "Anytime you need anything, let us know. They'll be glad to come."

We were still recovering from all the hayfield's scars, wounds, and bruises, when Mr. Finley, who had been away on the other side of the county for a while, selling and servicing farm equipment, came by and said, "Looks like we're going to have a second cutting."

I wasn't sure what he was talking about. "Second cutting? What do you mean second cutting?"

Mr. Finley's brown eyes beamed, glad to see this season of plenty. "Why, we're going to get to cut hay again."

There was no way in hell anybody was going to get me to cut hay again. I had had it in the hayfield. So had Wayne, Billy-Wade, and Larry. For my part, I never wanted to hear about hay again. I never wanted to see it or touch it, and I, for damn sure, wasn't going to make any more.

I could see that saying this would shatter Mr. Finley's sensibilities. I tried to keep my voice as even as possible and asked, "What do you do if you don't want to make any more hay?"

I had in mind going over to the nearest army installation and borrowing a flame-thrower, enlisting in a course in the Scorched Earth Policy, and setting the fields afire.

Mr. Finley was profoundly shocked, not able to imagine anyone with this attitude. He passed his hand over his mouth and looked up over his glasses. His eyes were serious. "Then you'd better get into cattle business and you'd better get in right away."

"What do you mean . . . cattle business?" I could already imagine what Larry would say.

"You'd better buy some cows to keep that pasture cut down if you don't want to do it," he said.

I had never seen a cow up close, only on a milk carton or out in some farmer's field, but Mr. Finley, who had been farming and raising cattle all his life, said there was nothing to it.

"Just put them out there on that rich pasture and watch them cut grass."

I tried to think of how I could convince Larry of this. "How many do you think I'll need?"

Pausing for thought, Mr. Finley raised his hat, passed his hand across the top of his head, and settled his hat back down on his forehead. "Oh, I'd say about fifty."

"*Fifty!* That's a whole herd."

"It's that or making hay."

"That would take a lot of money."

Mr. Finley shrugged off this problem. "The bank will lend it to you. The cattle will stand as collateral for the loan. A lot of farmers finance that way . . . do it all the time."

When I told Larry of this latest development, his reaction was somewhere close to sustained hysteria. When I told him what the alternative was—making hay again—he lapsed into a comatose state that lasted most of the evening. There was nothing to do but at least try with the cows.

"I'll not be party to that," Larry said. "*You* go to the bank and get them to lend *you* the money for the cows, and if they all die, like they're likely to do, they can take *you* off to debtor's prison."

"All right. Do you want to make hay again?"

"I'd move back to the city and into the ghetto first."

"Then we have no choice."

The bank in Minniesville was a miniature brick colonial with two tiny columns on each side of the entrance. Inside there were two tiny bank officials, a teller, and a loan officer named Mr. Meritt who looked like he had drunk a draft of Alice's Wonderland potion. He was a very small man, barely five feet tall, with small eyes and small hands. He wrote numbers down on a small pad in handwriting so small it was barely legible. When I told him I wanted to borrow five thousand dollars to buy cattle, his lips disappeared into a tight line and he told me it wasn't possible.

"But the cattle will stand for collateral," I protested, parroting Mr. Finley's words.

He drew his lips tighter and drummed his fingers on his desk top. "You've had no experience."

"Maybe not, but my credit rating is unblemished, I've got a hundred acres of good grass, five-strand barbwire fence, and 5,000 bales of hay in the barn."

He shook his head and drummed his fingers again.

"Come out to my place and take a look for yourself," I insisted.

"I have an appointment."

"How about during your lunch hour?"

He opened his mouth to refuse but saw that I was going to persist and decided to humor me instead. "All right. Twelve o'clock."

When he came out, I showed him all the bounty: the fine rich mixture of clover, timothy, and orchard grass in the pasture; the barn, wedged to the roof with bales of hay; the sturdy five-strand barbwire that fenced and cross-fenced the farm. Mr. Meritt was impressed, but he still wouldn't lend me the money.

"The best I can do is let you have this."

He handed me a little one-inch-high glass bottle with a match stem cork. Inside was a newly minted copper penny, outside was an advertisement for the Minniesville Bank. "Save With Us."

It struck me as extremely unfunny. If I didn't get the money, I was going to have to make hay again.

"Mr. Meritt, if this is your idea of a joke. . . ."

He collected himself and managed a chilled, official smile that bore the barest trace of apology. "That's the best my bank can do," he insisted, "but with what you have here, you may get the Federal Land Bank to lend you the money."

The Federal Land Bank was forty miles away in another county, but Mr. Willingham, who managed it, was the diametric opposite of Mr. Meritt in Minniesville. A big man, Mr. Willingham had fed handsomely at the public trough for years with a stomach that overhung his belt to prove it. He was very jovial and affable about handing out public money, unlike some federal officials who acted with the presumption that the money personally belonged to them. He had rough skin, friendly dark eyes, and tufts of short hair that grew in all directions which he kept trying to smooth down with the flat of his hand.

When I told Mr. Willingham what I wanted and what I had to work with, he asked, "Where you gonna get the cows from?"

T. X. Truitt was the name of a trader Mr. Finley had suggested. When I told him, his eyes darkened and he drew his bushy brows together in warning. "You have to watch the traders, they'll skin you."

"Mr. Finley said he'd watch out for me."

"In that case, you'll be all right. Jim Finley knows all there is to know about farming and cattle."

"Then you'll lend me the money?"

Mr. Willingham nodded. "Course it'll cost you something."

"I was expecting that."

The terms were five thousand dollars for ninety days at what amounted to eighteen percent interest by the time membership shares and federal requirements were met. It was the most prohibitive rate for money I had ever heard of, but it was either this or nothing, and between this and nothing, I decided to take this.

Worse than the interest rate was the return of the short-term money in ninety days. This meant *I* had to become a trader—buying low, improving the purchase, and selling higher than what I had paid—all within ninety days. The proposition was fraught with so many perils it was too terrifying to contemplate, but anything was better than making hay, so I signed up for the money and called T. X. Truitt. T. X. was a big, barrel-chested Norwegian somewhere in his fifties, with bright blue eyes and sandy hair swept back and kept in place with pomade. He wore a ring clustered with diamonds that covered the lower joint of his finger and chained his overflowing wallet to his belt so that, he explained, "If they take my wallet, they're gonna have to take my pants too." He carried great amounts of cash and said he wouldn't feel like he had gotten dressed in the morning if he had less than ten thousand dollars on him.

He was right out of P. T. Barnum, assured with the certain knowledge that a sucker is born every minute. He was the finest con man I had ever seen and even when he was cheating, it was done with such finesse that you had to admire the performance.

He was committed to making money and said, "I find some way to do business every day even if it ain't nothin' but swapping pocket knives."

He drove a big car, liked fast horses and little children. He and his wife, who were themselves childless, had adopted twelve, one little girl arriving with nothing more than a toothbrush and a nightgown in a paper bag. And a little boy, named Harry, who later became his strength and helper, was sold to T. X. for a case of beer. All of the children were orphans or castaways that T. X. and his wife brought under their roof and lavished with love and all they could spare from their worldly goods, tending them as though they were their own. I figured a man who would do that couldn't be all bad so I bought the load of Black Angus cows he delivered.

With T. X. you just had to learn fast because it was his nature to cheat, not always out of necessity . . . sometimes out of habit . . . sometimes just for good sport. He liked to live by his wits and if it was a fair deal, it was no fun. The dullest deal in the world to him was where fair money was given for goods received.

T. X. had an excuse or rule exception for everything. When the big cattle truck, called "a possum belly," loaded with mooing black cows and a few small calves in the compartment pouch underneath, pulled up to the loading chute behind the barn and started to unload, I noticed a few painfully thin cows, but T. X. said, "They got on their working clothes. You can't make no money buying pretty cows. You won't have nuthin' to improve."

The bull was blind in one eye. T. X. dismissed this with, "It's better if the bull only sees half what's going on."

One cow was so lame that she walked on three legs and dragged one. To T. X., this was nothing. "You won't have no problem catching her."

Now that I had this herd of cows I began to worry about all the things that Larry said might happen to them, but T. X. radiated smiles and confidence. "Don't worry about a thing. They're safe as if they was in the arms of Jesus."

I was roundly unconvinced, but he grinned and got in his car.

"Just keep the horses out in the fields and them cows penned up in the paddock by the barn tonight so they'll settle down and know where home is. Tomorrow, all you got to do is open the gate and turn them out to pasture. I'll be back from time to time to see how you're doing, and when the ninety days is up, I'll see if I can find a buyer for you."

In a great whirl of dust and gravel, he drove his white Lincoln Continental down the drive, out the gate, and was gone. I went back to the paddock to look at what I had done.

Before this afternoon, I had only had the responsibility of two horses, one pony, one dog, two little boys, and one husband. Now I had fifty black beasts, all of whom would probably get sick, die, or run away by morning. The summer plans to ride, swim, and sit on the upstairs veranda sipping lemonade had been swamped and swept away by this onslaught of nature, this unrelenting, everlasting, goddam grass that grew like a jungle; that, even when cut right to the ground, came back again and again, claiming all our energy and effort. The garden we had planted, neglected by the heavy demands of making hay, was lost in a tangle of weeds that towered taller than the corn. The vision of Currier and Ives had faded so far it was beyond recall. First hay, now cattle.

I sank down on the outside wooden ledge of the water trough which was built into the five-foot white board fence that formed the paddock adjoining the barn. I looked at the cows and they gathered round and looked at me with big black eyes. They seemed as sad and uncertain as I was. I pushed down the handle of the water pump and began filling the trough with cool, fresh water from the well. This seemed to lift their depression and they pushed their way up to the trough for a drink, blinking grateful eyes with lashes so long I was reminded of animals drawn by Disney. As they finished drinking, they tidied up by running their long black tongues up their nostrils to clean their nose. Not my idea of hygiene, but I had already de- cided that this was going to be a live-and-let-live proposition.

Much to my relief, when Larry got home, he was pleased with our paddock full of livestock. Wayne and Billy-Wade were out of their minds with ecstasy, and right away wanted a cow of their own.

"You promised!" Billy-Wade nagged. "I wanted a cow for Christmas and all I got was that plastic one that Santa Claus put in my stocking."

"You can choose one of these," we told him.

With both feet together, he began jumping flat-footed up and down.

"No. I want one with a white face and a pink nose."

"What's he talking about?" Larry asked.

"A Hereford."

"Me, too," Wayne said, jerking at Larry's jacket. "I want one, too."

"Go ahead and get them each a Hereford," Larry said. "If we're going to be overrun with cattle, two more won't matter."

Wayne and Billy-Wade were delighted. Sabre and Brandy were not. They had moseyed up from the pasture to the paddock fence to see what was happening. Right away, Sabre didn't like what he saw. In his nature were all the human frailties, the chief among them, jealousy. He was outraged that a bunch of black beasts, none of whom he had ever before seen in his life, were installed in *his* pad-dock. It was feeding time, and instead of being allowed to come in to his feed box in his stall, he was given a bucket of grain on the ground in the pasture.

As soon as he finished eating, he gave the bucket an indignant kick and began running up and down the fence line, tossing his flaxen mane, swishing his tail, and flashing his dark eyes. He was furious and he didn't want the fact overlooked. Brandy, experienced with life and the way with humans, gave an old man's worldly shrug and wandered off to eat grass. Winchester decided to follow Brandy's wiser lead and dogged after him. Sabre continued his snorting and stomping into the night.

When morning came, I went out to the paddock before Larry had even finished his breakfast. I didn't even stop to dress. I still had on my pink seersucker housecoat, stopping only to switch from slippers to Keds. The cows were anxious to get out and Sabre was anxious to get in. I walked through the mooing mass and opened the gate, expecting an orderly transfer of cows to pasture and horses to paddock.

Sabre held his neck in a marble arch, tail up, and, in a Parade-to-the-Post fashion, trotted into the paddock glaring with all the hos-tility he could muster. The cows nervously edged their way through the gate and into the field. The transition was almost complete when Sabre discovered in *his* stall a cow with a newborn calf, a frail little thing with wobbly legs and big black eyes blinking at all the prob-lems already overcoming him in a harsh world.

Sabre absolutely shuddered with rage and immediately began haughty efforts to evict these unauthorized tenants from his stall. This inflamed the maternal instinct of the mother cow. She turned around, lowered her head, and charged. In the scuffle that followed, the baby calf wobbled out of the stall to witness what was happening.

Sabre, accustomed to a kicking fight, could never throw his hind-quarters around quickly enough to get a good crack at the cow, so he ran over to the little calf and flipped him over with his nose. Un-til then, I had been just an astonished spectator, awed by this horse-and-cow fight. From my perch on the fence, I couldn't think of how to stop it, but when I saw that newborn baby calf crumpled on the ground, blinking dirt from his eyes, I jumped down and joined the fight. I was furious with Sabre. If I had known how to do it, I would have knocked him cold. As it was, I had nothing but my bare hand, so I balled it up in a fist and whacked him hard on the shoulder. He had indulged himself over the edge this time and I would have no more of it.

Stung by this indignity, his eyes flashing with anger and retaliation, Sabre wheeled around and stampeded every last one of the cows through the pasture to Broad Run, a half-mile away. I stood there in my pink housecoat and watched helplessly as everything I owned and owed to the bank stormed out of sight. I had no point of reference on what to do about a stampede. On TV shows, the cowboy jumps on his horse and heads them off at the pass, but I couldn't even do this, because the horse was gone too.

By this time, Larry had left the breakfast table and Wayne and Billy-Wade had come out in their pale blue pajamas. I wanted to cry, but knew I would have to bear up in front of the boys.

I looked at Larry and wailed, "What am I going to do?"

He just shook his head. "I don't know. I've got a nine o'clock appointment in town and I've got to go."

"You're going to leave. . . ."

He didn't even have to reply. I already knew the answer. The job came first. Wayne and Billy-Wade and I stood by the side of the driveway and watched him get in his car and drive off to the city. They turned back to me with eyes asking, "What now?"

"Go get dressed," I told them.

Wayne's soft brown eyes were worried.

"What are we going to do?"

"We're going to form a Graves Registration Squad."

"What's that?"

"That's where you go and count and identify the dead bodies."

"Do you think they're *all* dead?" Billy-Wade asked, clutching the front of his cotton pajamas.

I was beyond caring. "Who knows? Go get dressed and we'll walk to Broad Run and find out."

I expected to go down and find dead bodies everywhere, and I thought I might as well be dressed for the occasion so I pulled on boots and jeans and bitterly considered wearing a black veil. Just as we were leaving the house, Mr. Finley, God love his sweet soul, drove up with a smile and a wave.

"I came to see your new herd of cows you got yesterday."

When he saw the distress on all our faces he asked, "What's the matter?"

As I told him what had happened out in the paddock, my voice broke and I blurted out, "I don't know *what* I'm going to do."

Mr. Finley laid a steadying hand on my shoulder. "There now, child. It's not all that bad. They're just staking out territory. They'll quit all that foolishness in a little while and go back to peaceful grazing . . . just you wait and see."

Those were the first hopeful words I'd heard all day. "Do you really think so?"

"I'm sure of it," Mr. Finley chuckled as though he had witnessed a lot of fuss over nothing more than a trifle. "Go get the halters and lead shanks and a bucket of grain. We'll go down there to Broad Run and get those horses and bring them back to the paddock where they belong."

As we walked through the pasture in the sunshine, I saw in the sky overhead a buzzard winging wide circles over Broad Run. I was seized with fear again.

"Oh, my God," I cried, "I bet they're all dead."

Mr. Finley laughed. "No. Nothing like that, but I can tell you one thing, every good farmer knows to keep his eye on the sky and if you see that buzzard flying, you'd better fly too, straight out to the pasture to find out what's wrong."

"If the cows aren't dead, how come the buzzard's out there flying?" Wayne, who was tagging along with Billy-Wade behind us, wanted to know.

"He senses trouble right off," Mr. Finley explained, "and he hangs around to see if something's going to happen. He's the best early-warning system we farmers have."

Billy-Wade, impressed with this new view of a buzzard, tugged at

Mr. Finley's coat tail. "You mean a buzzard is one of the good guys?"

Mr. Finley reached down and ruffled Billy-Wade's hair with his hand. "After you've been a farming for a while, you'll find that a buzzard is your best friend."

Down at Broad Run, we found Sabre, Brandy, and Winchester all peacefully grazing and the cows hiding out in the strip of woods, peering wide-eyed from behind the trees, afraid to move. True to form, Sabre had let his weakness for grain overcome his intention to cower the cows. With no trouble, we caught him, Brandy, and Winchester and hauled them back to the paddock, and every step of the way I told him about how he would never ever be allowed on the same side of the fence as the cows again.

The cows, having finally recovered from their fright, came out of their hiding places in the woods and began to eat the grass. They worked constantly and conscientiously and never let the pasture grow beyond lawn length. The tractor, conditioner, rake, baler, and hay wagon all sat idle in the barn.

While the farmers all around us labored in the wilting sun making a second cutting of hay, all I had to do was go to the fence and say, "Eat fast, girls, eat fast."

This worked so well with the animals working for us that we got Wayne and Billy-Wade the two white-face Herefords they wanted to add to the herd. Then, Billy-Wade wanted an "outside dog" and Wayne wanted a pig, and after finding a rat had gnawed through the oak boards in the grain room, I wanted a barn cat.

Larry took a liking to the cattle and bought a cowboy hat and a cutting horse named Pride and joined us now on our rides across the green hills and through the deep summer shade of the woods.

With peace in the pasture and harmony in the house, it was as though life had finally righted itself again and our vision of Camelot began to return.

It was the "outside dog" and the princely possession of the Dalmation next door that caused the trouble.

CHAPTER 11

Domino and Sassafrass

DOMINO WAS THE ONLY DOG I ever knew who owned his own automobile. Domino was the princely Dalmation who belonged to the neighbors on the farm next to ours, and from birth, Domino had received treatment befitting royalty. Heywood and Marvella adored him and indulged him in whatever struck his fancy. What he fancied most was sleeping in their car in the afternoon sun while he waited for them to come home from the field.

They indulged this fancy until Domino sat the seat covers off Marvella's new Cadillac and Heywood's custom pickup truck. Then they decided that something had to be done about Domino, but they didn't have the heart to deny him anything. In their house with no children they lavished on him everything he wanted, and he wanted to sleep in the car.

The Cadillac was Marvella's special pride because she had won it at the races, a little at a time. Six days a week she rose before dawn, pulled on boots and blue jeans, climbed on a tractor, and went to the field to work side by side with Heywood. But on Tuesday, the seventh day, which was the way she counted her week, she put on her feather hat, high heels, and her fur stole. With her hair done up in curls and a racing form in her purse, she went off to Ladies' Day at the races and played the horses. She did her home-work on the horses as carefully as she did the bookkeeping on the farm, and by the time she arrived at the track for the first race, she knew the bloodlines of every horse, what his track time was, and how many wins and losses both the horse and the jockey had had.

It had taken a lot of Tuesdays to win enough money to buy that Cadillac and it gave Marvella a lot of pain watching it being ruined, but it gave her just as much pain to deny Domino anything. Fi-nally, it was decided that the only thing to do was to buy Domino his own car. That way he could sleep in it all he pleased and he wouldn't even have to be disturbed when Marvella had to drive her car to the grocery store.

Domino liked to ride, but only before dinner at night. In fact, he had a stomach so delicate that he could only eat boiled chicken breasts, and those only if he had soothed his salivary glands with a ride before table. This presented a grave problem on nights when it snowed and the savage wind blew drifts across the driveway too deep to drive through in the car.

I asked Marvella once, "What do you do then?"

"Why, we bundle Domino up in his hat, scarf, and sweater and take him for a ride on the tractor. The tractor has snow chains, you know." She blushed at her indulgence, and smiled the brave, resigned smile of one who sacrifices for a weaker being. "Domino wouldn't be able to touch a thing without his ride and we'd be up all night worrying about him."

Domino got his car, a red Ford Fairlane that was parked in the drive by the walkway and used to take him on his nightly ride. He became very jealous of his new possession and wanted no one to even touch it. This caused a real problem with the peacocks because they were accustomed to flying around and landing any place they pleased. Though they were billeted in the barn, they liked flying up in the trees, standing on the tractor, and looking through the windshield of the car. They were a curious bunch and anything new attracted their notice. Domino's new red car was the most interesting thing they had seen in a long time. As soon as they saw it, they all flew out of the barn and stood on the hood watching through the windshield as Domino slept on the front seat. They inched closer and closer until the windshield was full of beaks and bulging eyes. Their chattering roused Domino and he came wide awake in a full-blown fury. Domino sprang over the steering wheel, bared his teeth, and barked ferociously. He was incensed that anyone or anything had dared touch his prize possession. The peahens shrank back at this display of violence, but the peacock fanned out his magnificent plumage like battle flags ready to do war.

The little adolescent peacock, seeing his daddy's dramatic display of courage, decided to go him one better and incautiously strutted forward and pecked the windshield where Domino had pressed his angry face. Domino was seized with uncontrollable fury. He jumped through the open window, leaped up on the hood, and grabbed the little peacock by the neck and shook him until he was certain that his neck was irreparably broken. After that, the peacocks gave up standing on Domino's car. Instead, they came over and stood on our cars.

As frayed as the adage is, the first time it happened, I literally could not believe my eyes. We had been living on the farm only a short while, not long enough to know that our next-door neighbors had a flock of peacocks housed in their barn. We had heard these unearthly cries in the middle of the night that sound like a child's scream of direst distress. The first time we heard it, we rushed out in the dark to find whoever was in such critical trouble. Seeing nothing but the dark quiet of the fields and the bare movement of Clarence and Claude's cattle across the road, we attributed it to their new bull who, we decided, must have the shrillest mating cry in the world, not knowing that what we had heard was the cry of peacocks.

My first view of the peacocks was early one Sunday morning. I had gone to the kitchen to make coffee and looked out the window into the still darkness of the paddock beside the barn. There, on the fenceposts, were silhouetted the biggest birds I had ever seen. Perched there with their tails trailing down, they looked like the birds who had accompanied the dinosaurs in Cro-Magnon time. On first encounter it was horrifying to think of birds that big. As dawn edged up over the horizon and the sun painted the board fence pink, I was able to see that this was not an awesome apparition, but peacocks in the paddock. I had never seen peacocks anywhere but in the park. I ran to the bedroom and shook Larry's sleeping shoulder.

"Come here, quick!"

Hearing the urgency, he jumped up. "What's the matter?"

Rushing back to the kitchen and pointing out the window, I said, "Tell me. What do you see?"

"Peacocks."

Relieved, I sank in a kitchen chair. "Whew! I *knew* I didn't have that much wine with dinner last night. I thought I'd finally gone off the edge." I looked up seeking an explanation. "Why do you suppose we have peacocks in the paddock?"

"How do I know?" he grumped, going back to the warmth of the bed covers. "Anything can happen in this crazy place."

The horses were no less startled than we. Seeing the kitchen light from the pasture, and knowing that someone would be coming out with the feed bucket soon, they strolled into the paddock at a nodding gait. Seeing this, the peacock flew down from his perch and confronted them with full-fanned tail. The horses froze, their eyes bulged and widened with fright, and they backed up against the board fence. They had never seen anything so startling. When the peacock stepped forward to challenge them, they wheeled and galloped at a dead run back to Broad Run.

Having overcome such mighty opposition, the peacock and his crew flew back to the barn next door. It was then that we learned that this was where they belonged, but it was by no means the last of their visits.

At the end of the barn by the paddock was a parking shed where we garaged our cars. Since Domino disallowed their sitting on his car, they flew over in the dark of night and sat on ours. This set *our* dog to howling, and the peacocks in turn screamed back, and the night air was filled with fitful noise. Our biggest objection was the big three-pronged footprints they left on the hood of the cars. This was a special annoyance to Larry.

Taking his boss to lunch on a day after a peacock party on the car hood the night before, Larry's boss asked, "What kind of big-footed bird have you got down there on the farm?"

"Peacocks."

"Peacocks!"

Always the astonished response, always the necessity to explain. "Well, you see, this man next door raises peacocks, and they fly over at night. . . ."

By the time we scrubbed all the peacock prints off the car hood, we wished that Domino had gotten them all. There was, however, no denying that when the peacock flew, as he sometimes did, to the top of our three-story barn roof, resting on its very peak, silhouetted black against a blazing red sunset, he was a picture of undiminished magnificence.

We later learned that it wasn't strange at all to see peacocks on a farm. People in the country kept a lot of strange things for pets— foxes, desensitized skunks, orphaned fawns, raccoons that washed everything they ate in their water dish—and one man even bought a buffalo. The buffalo, however, didn't last very long because a sudden thunderstorm got him riled and he took down three miles of fence before his composure returned and he could be corraled again. We had been accustomed to guppies and goldfish, but these were the things that suburbanites owned. In the country, anything was possible.

But for all the pets they owned and for all the things they did for them, no one had the care and indulgence that Domino en-joyed. Every year he had a birthday party where he was the only guest. The table was set with white linen with a centerpiece of red carnations, one for every year of Domino's life. He sat on his haunches in a chair at the table and wore a silver party hat and ate ice cream from a china bowl.

At Christmas, he sent Christmas card pictures of himself in a red

Santa Claus hat with a tassel to the other dogs in the neighborhood and had his own red-trimmed top and toe stocking that was
hung by the chimney with care.

When Domino departed this life, the first call was to the funeral
home and a child's small white satin-lined casket was delivered to
the house to hold Domino's last remains. The florist brought a wreath
of fourteen red carnations marking Domino's life span. This was
attached to the top of the coffin lid where Domino lay in state. A
wake and all-night vigil was held in the living room and when morning came, Domino was buried beside his favorite tree.

There were in our village, as in most others, the self-appointed
monitors of manners and mores who judged harshly all those who did
not fit within the confines of their own narrow concept. To treat a
dog in such a way was to them foolish, wasteful of human resources,
and thereby edging on sin.

What they did not see was the caring and concern, the mutual
love and joy he gave two hardworking people whose productivity
came from the soil. The tunnel vision of those who judged did not
allow them to see that the important thing was the exercise of this
love and compassion, utterly absent in themselves, no matter what its
object.

The controversy among the villagers over Domino's princely possessions was nothing compared to the devastating effect it had on the
other dogs in the neighborhood who were not so endowed. It gave
them all an inferiority complex, particularly our own Sassafrass, a
black and white Border Collie who was one of our new acquisitions
and the "outside dog" Billy-Wade wanted, since Suzie was essentially
a member of the family and an "inside dog."

From the beginning, Sassafrass was painfully shy—actually, downright humiliatingly humble. She constantly wore an apology on her
face as though to excuse the space she took up in the world, and
if anyone approached her, she balled up in the fetal position and
looked up with eyes full of piteous appeal as if she expected heaven
to fall on her head. After months of encouragement and reassurance, we finally got her to stand up and act like a dog, but not
without long and patient work.

We could never figure out why Sassafrass had arrived so psycho-
logically damaged. She was just a baby when we bought her from
T. X. who, as usual, claimed, "She's the pick of the litter." T. X.
didn't bother to explain what category "the pick" was in, but he assured us, as he brought in the little ball of black fluff with a white
fur collar, white feet, and a white tip on the very end of her tail,
that "she's a real cattle dog, knows how to work a herd."

Sassafrass batted baby eyelashes and didn't look very convincing
but T. X., raring back, buttressed his statement. "Hell, these dogs are
so smart they don't need no training. It all comes natural. You won't
have to do nothin'. You can just sit on the porch and watch them
work."

Work wasn't the first problem. The first problem was to get Sassafrass to stand up and act like a dog and stop falling out in the floor
and apologizing for living. We had got her specifically for use as
a watchdog and working the herd. Working the herd was no problem,
for bred into the Border Collie is the ability to herd cattle. It was the
watchdog part that Sassafrass couldn't handle. She had all the
requirements for success: a deep, fierce bark, a ferocious black face,
and a white ruff collar that stood on end indicating an inclination to
attack. Her appearance was such that if a stranger drove up and she
rushed out, they wouldn't even get out of the car. Then, with accomplishment in hand, Sassafrass would go all to pieces and start
wagging her tail and begging forgiveness, and apologizing for what
she had done.

One stranger who drove up and finally got to the back door said,
"What's the matter with that dog? As soon as I got out of my truck
she tried to lick me to death."

The situation worsened when Sassafrass found out about Domino
and all his princely possessions. Instead of regarding this as an indulgence by his owners, she took it to mean that he was worthy of all
those extravagances and excesses and she was not, and this only
deepened her inferiority complex. To make up for what she felt was
lacking in herself, Sassafrass tried even harder to be pleasant and
please.

She had seen Domino, in a moment of play, retrieve a stick. This seemed like such a good idea to Sassafrass that she decided to do that too, only in her mind, more was better. Emulating his actions in hopes of his amount of success, she went out and collected every stick she could find, stacking them all, as an offering, on the back steps. She did this so assiduously that we finally couldn't get in and out the door because of the stack of sticks Sassafrass had collected for us.

One Sunday afternoon, a heavy blanket of heat lay on the land. The cattle had moved out of the pasture and stood soaking in the pond. Sassafrass had joined them. Later, she came running up the hill from the pond with yet another stick, this one black, bigger than usual, and appearing to be rather limp, for it drooped down on each end. Ears back, eyes ingratiating, her black plume tail with the white tip flashing back and forth like a windshield wiper, she tendered her offering.

"Good girl."

As I patted her on the head and took the stick she offered, I found that it wasn't a stick at all, but a cow's tail.

"Sassafrass! Where did you find this?"

She looked enormously pleased and romped off back to the pond. I thought, Fool. She hasn't got a drop of sense, and went off to look for the cow with the missing tail.

Flies were a particular problem with cattle in the summer. They swarmed over them, followed them, and gnawed on them, adding aggravation to the heat. Even with a cattle rub, this annoyance was not eliminated and the cows' tails were in constant motion all day flapping flies away. This was so constant and automatic that they were not mindful of where they were and sometimes, standing by a barbwire fence, they swung their tails too high and got caught on the wire. Unable to untangle, they pulled until they pulled their tail off. This was what I thought had happened.

Out in the pasture, I found the cow with the missing tail. It was "203," the only cow with the signal honor of a number instead of a name. She was the only one with a chain and a metal number hanging on her chest and she was supposed to be my prize. Every time I complained about some deficient or decrepit member of the herd, T. X. always said, "Yeah, but look at '203.' She's a purebred and got a number to prove it. As much as them purebreds cost, she balances out all the rest."

I could never figure out why, if she was a purebred and so valuable, she had been sold off with a grade herd. After I had owned "203" for a while, I realized that she had been culled, and with good purpose. She wasn't just unmindful, she was mindless.

When I found her, she was standing in the pasture with distress on her face, her head straining backward over her shoulder trying to see her torn-off tail. Unlike cats and dogs, cows have no way of caring for their rear quarters when something happens. While other cows gathered to circle around and see what had happened, "203" just stood there looking distraught. The three-inch stub she had left did not have the ragged edges of a tear, but seemed to be a clean-cut, almost sliced off, which led me to think that she had been standing near a very sharp object or wire when she swung her tail. This place would have to be found and remedied.

Sassafrass, having bound off to the pond when I asked her what happened, by now had rejoined me and was all business and ready to do her job. Her all-black face was intent, intelligent, alert, waiting for the order to be given.

"Let's take her back to the barn, Sassie," I said, swinging my hand toward the top of the hill.

Sassafrass seemed to understand the words and know what I meant. Circling the cow, gently snapping at her heels, Sassafrass cut "203" out of the herd and quietly drove her back up to the hill to the barn. There I applied gentian violet to "203"'s wounded stub of a tail and went out to check the fence to find out where she had torn it off. With Sassafrass beside me, I walked the whole three miles of fences and cross-fences but could not find where the accident had happened. When we got back to the house, Sassafrass barked and ran off to the pond again. When I ignored her, she barked again and ran back toward the pond. I could see nothing there but the layers of heat and the shimmering surface of the water, catching golden glints from the now setting sun. Sassafrass continued to bark and run toward the pond, and I thought to myself, She's a born fool, and walked in the house.

Not two days later, "203" was in trouble again. This time missing a part in an even worse place. Fortunately, Flint Blackstone, our new blacksmith in the country was there shoeing the horses. Flint was a tall, lean, muscle-hard man who looked like he had just stepped off the horse in the ad for Marlboro cigarettes. He wore Western boots and a cowboy hat with authenticity and distinction, drove a pickup truck with a rifle in a rifle rack across the back window, and talked to the horses he shod in such honeyed words that he charmed their feet right off the ground and into his hand to prop on his knees covered with a leather apron.

Flint was the most clean-cut cowboy I had ever seen. He didn't smoke, drink, chew, or cuss, at least not around ladies. If a situation required an expletive, Flint said, "By Ding Doggies!" The first time I heard him say it, I thought he was trying to be funny, aping the comic cowboy in the Grade "B" Western. When I saw he wasn't, I was appalled by the epithet but appreciated all the same his deference, even if it was, "By Ding Doggies!"

Brandy, having been on the track earlier in his life, was accustomed to footwork, and when Flint arrived handed his feet over to have his shoes pulled, the nails removed, the hooves trimmed, and new shoes fitted and shaped with the same kind of relaxed leisure that some men have getting a manicure. Sabre was not so inclined. He just naturally hated having his feet handled, even to cleaning the dirt out from around the frog. Worse, he hated getting new shoes, and worst of all he hated blacksmiths. He tried every way possible to kick the one we had back at the stables into eternity, but Flint was his singular exception.

Sabre adored Flint and pushed and shoved to be first in line when he arrived in his pickup truck and swung through the gate with "Hey, Sweet Baby, hand me that pretty foot and let me gaze on perfection." Sabre, smitten with his sweet words, would give him an "Aw, Shucks!" neigh, and hand over his foot for whatever Flint had in mind to do while he listened to Flint's honeyed words.

It was while Flint was doing this that "203," usually so slow-moving, ran up from the pond at a trot, her big udder underneath swinging from side to side. Sassafrass had joined the fray and was running alongside barking with animation and agitation.

I went out to see what was the matter and found "203" in direst distress. One of her teats was almost cut off and was hanging by the barest bit of skin to the udder. Her eyes were full of distress, agony, and pain, imploring me to do something.

"How," I asked, "did this happen?"

Sassafrass was full of explanations, barking, running toward the pond, and carrying on. I turned to her with a scolding look. "I didn't say *where*. I said *how*."

I had heard from the farmers at the country store, who delighted in telling all the things that could go wrong in a herd, that sometimes cows, especially older ones with pendulous udders, missed and stood up on their own teats getting up from a prone position. Sometimes, they said, it would happen in younger cows who were not careful with their feet. "203" fell in this category. She had obviously stood up on her own teat and had nearly torn it off. Until now, because of her chain and the metal number on her chest, she was the only cow in the herd who was designated by number instead of by name.

"You," I told her, "are now going to be known as Mrs. Maladroit."

Flint, hearing all the conversation with the cow, came out of the barn wiping his hands on his leather apron.

"Anything the matter?"

"Flint, I wish you'd look at this. This fool cow has stood up on her own udder and nearly torn her teat off."

"By Ding Doggies if she ain't!" Flint ran his hand over the top of his head, his hair so short it seemed to be shaved. "And that ain't good."

He wasn't telling me something I didn't already know, so I just stood there in grim-lipped silence looking at the torn teat.

"It won't make much difference to her raising a calf," Flint said, "but it ain't easy selling a three-titter."

In addition to working as a blacksmith, Flint also owned a herd of cattle himself and worked on Saturdays at the livestock auction in Mountain View. As knowledgeable as he was, I took what Flint said as gospel.

He bent down to take a closer look at the damaged teat, and then shot back up straight as a branding iron with a shocked look on his face.

"She ain't stood on her tit," Flint announced. "The tit ain't mashed. She's done had it nearly bit off."

I turned my eyes toward heaven and thought, *How can it be?* Here I was standing out in the pasture in the morning sunlight discussing a bit-off tit with the blacksmith. I thought about my poor Southern grandmother, whose standards of modesty and decorum matched those of the Victorian era, and I knew she must surely be dying again in her grave.

I also knew better than to be put off or embarrassed, because Flint was only using the language that cattlemen used every day and it was no more uncomfortable or unusual for him to discuss a bit-off tit than for a clerk in men's wear to discuss a pair of trousers. I knew if I acted embarrassed, it would embarrass him, so I asked, "How do you think she got her tit bit?"

Flint was all action and ready to go. "You got a pond?"

I pointed the way. "Two of them."

"Has she been out wading in the water?"

"Every day."

Flint ran back to his truck and grabbed his rifle off the rifle rack. "Come on," he yelled, "you got a mud turtle."

"Where are we going?"

"To the pond."

"What for?"

"To shoot him."

This was insane. We were going to run off to the pond and shoot a turtle with a rifle. As Flint galloped off over the expanse of green grass and I ran behind him with Sassafrass suddenly come to life again and barking, I yelled, "What's a mud turtle?"

"Bad business." Flint threw the words over his shoulder as he ran. "We gotta get him before he gets another cow . . . or worse yet . . . somebody."

When we got to the pond bank, Sassafrass went into action, barking, jumping, throwing her front feet down in front of the biggest turtle I had ever seen outside a museum. His shell was as big as the lid off a garbage can, crusted with mud, and he was trying to make his way back to the water when we arrived on the scene. Seeing us, he drew his huge head, the size of a man's foot, back inside his shell and Flint couldn't get a shot at him.

"Get him, girl," Flint told Sassafrass, and she went to work barking, snapping, aggravating, coming so close and irritating the turtle so much that he reached out to take a snap at Sassafrass and Flint got him with one shot.

"Good girl," Flint told her, and Sassafrass sort of took a bow and came over to get her head patted.

"Them mud turtles are bad to have," Flint said on our way back up the hill. "They usually lay quiet on the pond bottom in the mud, but they're mean and when they decide they want to come out and sun, they'll attack anything in their way. That's how your cow got her tit bit. That's also what happened to her tail. That mud turtle bit it off."

"Wouldn't you think she would have learned her lesson the first time when she lost her tail?"

Flint shook his head. "Some cows ain't got no sense."

"She's one of them."

A frown creased Flint's suntanned brow as he walked along with long-legged strides. "Looks to me like . . . good as that dog is . . . that she would've told you something."

I looked down at Sassafrass, who was dogging our heels with a satisfied look on her face. She had done a good job and knew it.

"She tried to tell me, Flint," I said, giving her head another pat and remembering all her barking and turns toward the pond. "I just wasn't listening."

I had been so proud of Sassafrass, watching her work with her white collar ruffed and standing on end, her deep growl fierce and fearless, her black face ferocious, taunting the turtle like a toreador tempting a bull. At that moment, in her own element, there was nothing retiring, reticent, or humiliatingly humble about Sassafrass. Social situations might overcome her, but when it came to delivering the goods when it counted, she was a real pro.

I felt it was too bad that Domino's car and princely possessions had given her such an inferiority complex, for she had no cause for that, and I decided that if she wanted a car and it was within my budget, I would buy her one too.

We were so pleased with the work that Sassafrass had done with the cattle, and with the job the cattle were doing in the pasture keeping the grass cut to lawn length, that we decided to experiment further in having the animals work for us. There were 168 panels of white board fence along the road in front of our big white farmhouse. To keep the fence row clipped was impossible because the angle of the embankment by the road defied any piece of machinery, and to clip more than a quarter of a mile by hand was beyond human expectations. It was this problem that led us to the purchase of a goat. Theoretically, it should have worked. In practice, it did not. In fact, it was a disaster.

CHAPTER 12

Dooma Lee Ate the Flag

"WE NEED A GOAT."

There was a long silence on the other end of the phone and then I could hear our livestock dealer, T. X. Truitt, give a deep sigh. "You sure?"

"Yes."

"How much?" T. X. always had to know the price. No matter what a customer ordered, he could manage to go out and find something that he could stuff into the specified price category.

"Ten dollars."

"That ain't gonna be much of a goat."

"Well, it ought to be. They were selling them at the livestock auction last week for four dollars."

"That still ain't much of a goat."

Escalation was T. X.'s intention, so I disregarded what he said and told him, "I want a gentle animal with good conformation and it must be a nice, Confederate grey."

T. X. sighed again. "I'll see what they got at the auction in Minniesville on Saturday."

Late Saturday afternoon he called. "I got your goat. You'd better come down to the livestock barn and pick it up right away."

By the time I got there, everyone was gone, but I had no trouble finding the goat. I followed the bleating sound to the back stall and peered over the high wooden gate.

It was a goat, all right, but there was no trace of gentleness on her irascible face. The good conformation I had requested had been entirely overlooked. She was a lady goat with a Van Dyke beard and two tassels that hung down like misplaced earrings below her ears on her neck. She seemed to be either in the very last stages of advanced pregnancy or the early stages of old age because her guts had dropped and hung hammock fashion between her fore and hind legs. She was, however, a nice Confederate grey, and she was, alas, mine, for all sales at the livestock auction were irredeemable and final.

I decided right then to name her Dooma Lee for a human disaster I once knew, and I put her in the tailgate of the station wagon, to take her home. This did not seem to suit her. As we drove along, she stepped over into the backseat and sat catlike on her haunches, her forelegs drawn primly together, looking from side to side and tossing her beard with satisfaction. When we pulled up at the farm, I opened the rear door for her and she grandly got out and tested the country air with a sniff of her black, heart-shaped nose, and curled her thin black lips into a smile of approval. She liked what she saw, and this seemed to be a good beginning.

"Come along, Dooma Lee."

Waiting for her were the 168 panels of white board fence, down by the road front. Her job was to nibble the grass around the fenceposts and under the fence, progressively working her way to the end, at which time she could begin over again.

Her teeth looked good, but I didn't like the cunning look in her yellow gold eyes. It was also disconcerting to see that her pupils lay in black horizontal bars and shifted from side to side like the carriage of a typewriter. Maybe she wasn't American. Maybe she was Eurasian. She certainly didn't look like the lovable darling that Heidi shared her milk and cheese with, but she was smiling, enigmatic though it was, and something absolutely had to be done about the grass around the fenceposts. I went to the barn and got a collar and chain and took her out to the front fence to put her to work immediately.

The grass was rich, soft, and green. Right away, she trimmed the first fencepost with the precision of a manicurist. Satisfied with her efficiency, I went back to the house. I did regret that her conformation was so poor and hated for my neighbors to see such a godawful goat out on my front fence, but the tack shop sold horse blankets. Maybe they had goat blankets too, and if I covered her up, she might not look so bad.

Almost immediately, I found that that wouldn't be necessary. I had no sooner got in the house than I heard a horrible noise. It rivaled even the cry of the peacocks next door, and I had thought nothing was worse than that. This was.

Rushing outside, I found Dooma Lee standing on her hind legs, her forelegs propped on the top rail of the white fence, her head thrown back, not bleating, not crying, but screaming. This caused a near-stampede from the fields to the barn. The horses and cows rushed up to the paddock fence to see who was being massacred. Trouble of any kind distressed and frightened them, and at the first signal they would rush to the sanctuary of the barn.

From where she hung over the fence rail, Dooma Lee had a clear view of this gathering. She threw her head back and screamed all the louder. She was, I learned, unhurt, unmolested, only lonely. She wanted to be taken to join the company of the other animals. Ill-advised as it is to give over to an animal who stubbornly wants its way, I took her before somebody called the sheriff about the public nuisance tied to my front fence.

Already, the cows in the field across the road had gathered at the fence to see what was going on at our place, and Claude and

Clarence were no longer shaking their heads, they were shaking their fists at this disturbance that had upset their herd.

"What's going on over there?" Clarence yelled.

"My new goat," I explained.

"Better put her in a pen till she gets used to being there," he said, with ill-concealed irritation.

Pen? I wanted to put her in jail for causing all this commotion and embarrassing me in front of these seasoned farmers who thought "city folks don't have no sense no way."

I gave up on trimming the fenceposts as a bad job and a regrettable idea. In theory it should have worked; in practice it did not.

I took Dooma Lee and put her in the barnyard paddock, but she wouldn't stay there either. With her delicate, long legs, she stepped through the slats of the board fence and was gone, eating the roses so lovingly grown by the neighbor next door, and scaring the living daylights out of her peacocks, who all began to scream at high pitch and in unison. This time I thought *I* might be arrested. My neighbor's soft cheeks turned purple and trembled with rage as she shouted her indignation at this unspeakable outrage and trespass.

I took Dooma Lee home and shut her up in the passageway of the barn between the first stall and the grain room. It amused her for a while to stand on her hind legs and peer over the partition to watch the cows eating hay. The cows weren't amused, but Dooma Lee liked it. What she liked even more was the grain we gave her when we fed the horses. She insisted on having more and when we refused, that cunning look came back into her eyes.

The next morning, Wayne and I found her lying, very nearly dead, on the barn floor, her head resting limply against the stairs to the loft, her golden eyes glazed, their horizontal pupils shifting from side to side.

"Poor Dooma Lee looks done for," Wayne said, cradling her head in his arms trying to restore some life.

I ran to the phone to call Dr. Caldwell. "Come quick. We have an emergency. Our goat is dying."

During the night, Dooma Lee had broken open the grain room

and eaten twenty-five pounds of horse crunch and an undetermined amount of grain and cardboard boxes. Fortunately for Dooma Lee, Dr. Caldwell arrived and pumped her stomach before the pressure of so much corn, oats, sorghum, and assorted foodstuffs killed her. By the time he finished, she was no longer our ten-dollar goat, she was our forty-dollar goat, and as goats go, that's a sizeable investment.

I lectured to Dooma Lee about her excesses and indiscretions, but she just looked at me with her long, stupid face and shifted her horizontal eyes from side to side. I let her know that it was neither an easy matter nor an inexpensive service to get a busy veterinarian to leave an office full of yowling-cat and barking-dog patients to come administer to a sick goat; that next time, he might not get there in time. But Dooma Lee just smiled and showed me her small, even teeth. She didn't care. She liked to eat. Anything.

Dooma Lee was especially fond of paper bags. This I learned too late. Coming home from grocery shopping one day, I left a too heavy bag on the ground beside the car. When I returned for it, cans of coffee, soup, peanut butter, and soap powder were scattered all over the lawn. Dooma Lee, smiling contentedly, was munching the last remains of the grocery bag.

Since she had such a penchant for paper, I decided to make her channel it into something useful, like picking up and eating bits and pieces of paper blown into the yard. This didn't appeal to Dooma Lee. Her preferences ran to the big stuff, like the Monday morning wash.

One summer morning, having tired of eating grass, she decided to lunch on the laundry hanging on the line. With her grass-stained teeth, she gnawed little green holes in everything. Finding at last what suited her most, she completely consumed all the sleeves on Larry's shirts, right up to the shoulder seam. Thereafter, he referred to her only as "Damned old Dooma Lee," which I thought was really too harsh a judgment until the morning she made a snack out of my bridle and saddle.

Grooming Sabre for a morning ride, I had tied him up at the paddock fence, the bridle and saddle across the top rail nearby.

Dooma Lee, always anxious to join in any social activity in the barn-yard, ambled up on the other side of the fence.

I looked up from what I was doing.

"Good morning, Dooma Lee."

Dooma Lee smiled, showing me her small, even teeth.

Busy brushing the horse, I said no more to her until I turned back to pick up my reins. The fine, soft leather had been chewed into a saliva-soaked tassel, the saddle gnawed so badly it looked like it had been edged with pinking shears. They were both completely ruined. I was furious.

"Dooma Lee," I shouted. "You dumb goat! Look what you've done."

Dooma Lee was dumb only in the sense that she had no discre-tion. She did, however, have a marvelous streak of keen animal cun-ning. Realizing that this time she was really in trouble, she decided to fake it. Her face was a mask of innocence, her golden eyes honor-bright, an appealing smile curled her lips.

Such impudence only further enraged me. I bolted over the fence after her. "I'm going to kill you! I'm going to hang you from the barn rafter. I'm going to tar and feather you!"

Alarmed by more than the usual amount of threats, Dooma Lee curled her tail into a tight little knot and began to run round and round the house, strafing the shrubbery, flowers, and rosebushes. Either through nervousness or the notion that this might truly be her last meal before execution, she whacked off a mouthful everytime she passed a flower, bush, or shrub, chewing it as she ran.

To look at Dooma Lee standing in the barnyard, she seemed very awkward, but once free and frightened, she had the speed and agil-ity of a gazelle. For thirty maddening minutes she ran, whacking and chewing. By the time I finally caught her, only little black stubs bordered the house where the shrubbery and flowers had stood be-fore. The tender rosebushes were gone, right down to the ground.

When I thought of all the time and effort, all the plant food and water that had gone into landscaping and growing those pretty things, how the big white two-story house had begun to look like a Hallmark card—and now it was gone!—I was ready to demolish

Dooma Lee. I wondered what kind of sentence the S.P.C.A. could bring down on someone who murdered a goat and whether the American Civil Liberties Union would defend her or me. Whatever it might be seemed worth it at the moment.

Other farmers had goats. *Their* goats grazed contentedly in the open field with the cows and horses and deported themselves with decorum. Dooma Lee was an uncontrollable outcast.

There was nothing to do but keep her chained to a tree, fence-post, pole, or anything permanently fixed that would hold her fast and not allow her to run free. For Dooma Lee, this was not a solution, but a challenge. When strength and sheer cussedness wouldn't work in freeing herself from the tree she had been chained to, Dooma Lee decided to try something dramatic, like an unsuccessful attempt at hanging herself. She ran round and round the tree she was chained to until she stressed the chain to its very limit and was obviously choking.

When I saw her, she was slumped against the tree with her yellow gold eyes bulging and her tongue falling out the side of her mouth. She looked like she was dying, and I thought, "That's no bad idea."

I was sorely tempted to leave her there to die of her own doing, but then guilt and fear of the S.P.C.A. got the better of me, and I unwrapped her from around the tree, slowly enough so that Dooma Lee decided not to try that number again.

Instead of trying to redeem her disgraceful conduct, Dooma Lee turned herself to other efforts and sat around figuring out ways of escape. She became more accomplished than any outlaw of the Old West. One unguarded moment, and she was gone.

This necessitated a sentry system so that one of us was always watching to make sure she didn't do something else destructive. What started out as a firm resolution eventually became a sometime thing. With all the duties a day on the farm demands, no one could afford to be full-time watchman for a delinquent goat. But the worst was yet to come.

True to her established pattern, Dooma Lee chose an unguarded moment to strike again. It was the Fourth of July. A flag fluttered on the front lawn. Friends from the city had driven out to the farm to join us for a picnic under the trees in the backyard.

Suddenly, there was a scream. "Come quick!"

We all ran around to the front. There stood Dooma Lee. This time she had really done it! *This time she ate the flag!* Fortunately, she had not finished all of it, only twenty stars and the top two bars.

With stricken faces, our friends from the city gasped, "Isn't that awful!"

Dooma Lee was a disgrace. No longer a private disgrace, but a national disgrace. This time Dooma Lee had desecrated the flag. Unquestionably, something would have to be done about her, but what?

We couldn't give her away. How in good conscience could we foist off such a derelict on a friend or an unsuspecting stranger?

We couldn't sell her. She was notorious throughout the county as an unmanageable maverick. No one in his right mind would willingly buy trouble. She was incorrigible and it seemed that nothing short of exorcism would cure her deviltry, but where was there ever a goat exorcist?

The hard truth was that Dooma Lee was ours and we were stuck with her until some better idea came along. We put her in the maximum security stall—the solid board bull pen, eight feet high—in solitary confinement with no possibility of parole. We thought and thought of what we could do with Dooma Lee, but no solution surfaced. She was like a problem child who couldn't adapt herself to the discipline of daily living. When I suggested this to Larry, he snorted, "Problem child, hell! She's a damn psychotic and needs to be shot."

It was true that Dooma Lee seemed to suffer from several psychotic symptoms and severe personality disorders. The general suggestion for rehabilitation from those who knew about such things was to find something the psychotic was interested in and encourage them to do that. What Dooma Lee was interested in, we couldn't allow.

Weeks passed. August had come and it was time for the County Fair. All the other animals were being groomed and schooled to compete for the blue ribbons. Dooma Lee, of course, couldn't go. There was no entry in the sideshows for a goat. She was full of remorse. Her shoulders sagged, her long ears hung down like drain spouts, her eyes always on the ground. She was very sad.

Montaigne once said, "Everything has its season, even the best." He might have also said, "even the worst," for Dooma Lee finally had hers.

The young members of the Future Farmers of America decided to operate a Mini-Barn at the County Fair. Baby animals of all sorts —chickens, ducks, pigs, calves, colts, dogs, and donkeys . . . even a pair of chocolate-colored baby goats—were to be displayed in small stalls for the children to pet.

As a member of the F.F.A., Billy-Wade had duty at the Mini-Barn during the fair. After the first day, he came home with a problem. The baby goats had been withdrawn by the woman who owned them. The tiny-tot visitors, it seemed, had shared with the little goats whatever they were eating: popcorn, cotton candy, paper plates, and pop.

"The owner got very angry," Billy-Wade reported. "The little goats got sick and she said they couldn't *ever* come back. Now we have an empty stall at the Mini-Barn, and my instructor Mr. Ellman, said it would be all right if I brought Dooma Lee. Can she go?"

Dooma Lee went to the fair, and she was a sensation. For sheer size of crowd, she outdrew the Fat Lady, the Sword Swallower, and the Ape Man. People from miles around brought their children to feed the goat who would eat anything. She consumed candy and cartons and chewing gum. She ate boxes, balloons, and old tennis shoes, carefully spitting out the metal eyelets lest they give her indigestion.

Now, standing at center stage, she gave it a little theater and did it all with dash and style and finesse. What had been a curse became a crowning achievement. She ate absolutely everything. No matter what the offering might be, challenge lit her horizontal eyes, a swagger curled her thin lips, and with showmanship and a smile she chewed up everything with her small even teeth.

When it was all over, Dooma Lee had become a celebrity—barrel-bellied, but a celebrity nonetheless—who had heard the cheers of the crowd and experienced adoration from those who appreciate an expert in the field. On leaving, we felt considerable relief and a certain amount of pride that Dooma Lee had finally found a destiny and fulfillment for what had formerly been a failing. Sensing this sensation, as we led her down the crowded fairway, Dooma Lee leaned over and lopped the top off a little girl's pink ice-cream cone.

"Dooma Lee!" we cried. "How *could* you?"

Dooma Lee's golden eyes glistened with mischief and she smiled, letting us know that complacency had no part in her nature and that her old ways, though forsaken, had not been forgotten.

But Dooma Lee was not the least of our troubles. We were shortly joined by a bunch of bandits who should have been shot the moment they arrived.

CHAPTER 13

Effie's Chickens

WE HEARD ABOUT THE SHOOTING on the radio on Saturday night, but we didn't know until Sunday morning that the man who did the shooting was the tenant on our neighbor's farm. We were dressing for church when we heard an insistent knock on the back door. Larry was busy tying a four-in-hand tie around Wayne's neck and Billy-Wade was impatiently awaiting his turn.

Larry nodded toward the direction of the knocking. "Can you get that?"

When I opened the door, a small, elderly black woman with a rim of white hair, run-over shoes, and a flowered apron was standing on the back steps.

"I'm Effie," she told me from the bottom step. "I lives over at Dr. Grawson's place. It was my Jake what shot that man last night."

She paused, waiting for a reaction.

[158]

"I'm sorry to hear that."

She worried with her apron. "I got to call my daughter in Washington. Would you let me use your phone . . . I'll call collect."

She followed me inside and even though I left her in the kitchen to make the call, we could clearly hear the conversation.

"Carmel? This is Mama. Jake killed a man last night . . . yeah . . . they got him in jail, but that ain't what I'm callin' you about. Dr. Grawson say we got to leave . . . say he don't want no tenants what go around killin' . . . yeah . . . right away. You got a place for me? Okay, honey. I'll be there soon as I can . . . you'll meet the bus? I'll let you know when."

She left the phone wringing her hands under her apron. "Lawd, I don't know what I'm gonna do."

"What do you mean, Effie?"

"I gotta move . . . right away . . . and I gotta get rid of my livestock and chickens. Dr. Grawson say he ain't never had no trouble and don't want nobody that's got none."

This immediately aroused our sympathy. We certainly did not need any more livestock, the fields were full already, but we didn't have any chickens. We could at least help Effie by taking the chickens. I spoke to Larry and he, too, was sympathetic to Effie's plight.

"How many chickens do you have?" I asked.

Effie screwed her mouth up in an off-center knot and looked at the ceiling as she figured. "I reckon about twenty."

"How much do you want for them?"

Effie tested the water tentatively. "Would twenty dollars be too much?"

With chickens selling for nineteen cents per pound, twenty dollars was a lot, but since Effie was in distress circumstances, I told her, "We'll take them."

Effie looked down at the floor, flapping her apron in a helpless gesture. "I ain't got nobody to help me catch them."

Wayne and Billy-Wade sprang to life. "We will!" they said gleefully.

Effie smiled, showing snuff-stained teeth. "You boys ever caught chickens before?"

"No, but we can do it," they chimed.

Now that Effie had unloaded her chickens and arranged for us to catch them, she edged her way to the door. "Okay. Come over to my house after dark and bring a crocker sack to put the chickens in."

Wayne and Billy-Wade could barely sit through church imagining the adventure that lay ahead that night. All day they planned what they would do, and after dinner, they sat on the steps with burlap bags waiting for it to get dark. Only the anticipation of Christmas had put such a shine in their eyes.

Effie's idea of catching chickens was to go out to the chicken house, a small wooden structure about the size of an outhouse, close the door, and grab. It was insane. It was like being in a bat cave in the midst of a fly-over. Chickens were squalling like scalded pigs and flying everywhere. Everybody was grabbing everything . . . a foot here, a wing there, a neck someplace else. In thirty-five years I had never witnessed such hysteria.

We would catch a chicken, stuff it in the burlap bag, and before we could get another in, the first would be gone. When we finally got them all, we walked back to our station wagon with two writhing sacks full of hysteria. Effie was carrying the rooster, a splendid red cock with a mane of green and gold feathers curling down his neck.

"This," Effie said, holding him up with pride, "is Joe Louis. You want to carry him separate so's nothin' will happen to his fine feathers."

This created a problem. Wayne and Billy-Wade already had one sack of chickens each to hold until we got home and they clearly had their hands full, so I held the rooster while I drove, one hand on the steering wheel and one hand holding the rooster's legs, careful to keep his feet pressed to the car seat so that in his outrage he did not slash me with his long, sharp spurs.

I had never seen a living thing so angry and indignant. He flapped his wings and tried to free his feet, and when he couldn't, he dropped little grey balls of dung all over me and the front seat. It didn't take long to become disenchanted with the idea of owning chickens.

When we got home, Wayne and Billy-Wade wanted to know, "Where are we going to put them?"

We had no chicken house, and after catching chickens all night, I was in no mood to figure out where to billet them.

"Turn them out in the yard and we'll try to think of something tomorrow."

The chickens went screaming in all directions and disappeared in the dark. We went inside and got in the bathtub. We were a mess, covered with dirt, dung, mud, and feathers, but Wayne and Billy-Wade could hardly wait till morning to go out and gather eggs. They ran to their closets and began rummaging around for old Easter baskets.

When morning came, we got a good look at what we had brought home. I had never before seen such a ragged assortment of chickens . . . black and white, green and tan, orange and red, speckled, striped, and spotted . . . all of indeterminate breed. They looked like the motley crew that old sea captains used to hijack off to sea. They roamed about the yard like a bunch of ruffians, digging for worms and snatching them away from each other. What was needed was to impose some order and discipline on them.

We began by building nests in the barn, shaping hay into little indented circles in a nice, orderly row so that all they had to do was deposit their eggs for us to gather. These efforts were not only ignored, they were completely scorned. They were utterly undisciplined and intended to stay that way. They roosted in the trees, on top of the car, and under the tractor. They laid eggs wherever the notion struck them: in the driveway, on the doorstep, inside an old tractor tire. To expect eggs for breakfast was beyond reason. It was like going on an Easter egg hunt every morning. It took hours of looking into every crack, corner, and cranny. Wayne and Billy-Wade finally put their baskets back in their closets. Hunting eggs for hours every morning wasn't their idea of fun.

The chickens were even more imaginative when it came time to "set." They chose every absurd and inconvenient place possible to lay their eggs and raise their chicks. Larry didn't laugh at all when he found one had filled up his toolbox with a dozen eggs and screamed her head off every time he tried to get a hammer or screwdriver. Worse than that was the one who laid her eggs under the hayrack in the barn where the cows came in to feed, and when the baby chicks hatched was forever trying to keep them out from under the cows' feet.

Periodically, Wayne and Billy-Wade would go peer under the hayrack to see the progress of the hen and her family. One night they ran in from the barn wild-eyed. "One of the baby chickens has a blue leg." We went out to the barn, and sure enough, a cow's hoof had squashed it flat.

Billy-Wade tugged at my skirt. "Call the doctor."

Wayne elbowed him in the ribs. "Dummy. There's no chicken doctor."

"Then call the horse doctor," he insisted.

I wasn't about to call the vet to come see about a blue chicken leg, but from childhood, I remembered my mother swabbing Vicks Salve on everything, from chest colds to bruises.

"Go get the Vicks Salve," I told them, and when they returned with the blue bottle of aromatic salve, I took the chicken's frail little blue foot and swabbed it good. The odor offended the others and they immediately ostracized the one that had been medicated. The foot didn't fall off as I had expected. It was permanently impaired, but improved enough so that she eventually could make limited use of it, and walk with a limp. This is how she came by the name of "Limpy Louise," and when she grew up, she had better sense about raising babies than her mother had.

The one who had no sense at all was a black bantam hen with orange eyes whom we called Miss Droopy Drawers because of her feather pantaloons. She was never able to raise a family because she never laid her eggs in the same place twice. The confusion of trying to remember where they were was too much, and she gave up raising children as a bad job, and just walked around the barnyard looking addled.

The disorderly fashion in which the chickens conducted their business was not the only problem. Having bought the chickens sight unseen, we did not realize until we got them home that we had purchased nine roosters and eleven hens, an imbalance that caused the hens constant hysteria since almost any place they looked, there was another rooster. Larry said something would simply have to be done.

I called up our livestock dealer, T. X. Truitt, and told him I had some livestock to sell. He arrived the next day in his big white Lincoln ready to deal. The smile slid off his face and all his affability left him when I told him I wanted to sell him eight roosters and a hen. Larry insisted that the one who was inhabiting his toolbox be taken away.

T. X. mustered all the reluctance and excuses he could think of but didn't dare outright refuse after I had bought fifty-two cows, a horse, and a goat from him.

"I just don't know what I'll do with eight roosters," T. X. said, still trying for an out. "The hen's all right, but them eight roosters. . . ."

I insisted and he put the eight roosters and the hen in the trunk of his white Lincoln and took them home. Two days later he was back. His face was flushed, like the aftermath of a fight.

"I just wanted to tell you what happened," he said, his blue eyes angry with remembering. "I took those chickens home and turned them out. The next day, when I got home, the top of my cherry tree was gone."

I was appalled. "You mean they ate it?"

T. X. gnawed the end off a big, black cigar and spat it on the ground with what seemed a good deal of venom. "Hell, no. My wife shot the top off."

"The cherry tree?"

The cherry tree was something T. X. cherished. He had nurtured it and diligently tended it and finally was about to be able to pick cherries from it. On arrival, the eight roosters and the hen vandalized his wife's tomato plants. She was so enraged by this that she took the shotgun to them and they all flew into his cherry tree. Unfortunately for T. X., she missed the roosters and shot out the top of his cherry tree.

"I just want to tell you," T. X. said, revving up his motor to go, "that not under any circumstances *whatsoever* am I gonna buy any more chickens from you."

He drove off in a storm of dust, but I could not find it in my heart to feel remorse about T. X.'s cherry tree. I felt that the chickens I had sold him, in some measure, made up for the goat he had sold me.

Sassafrass shared T. X.'s sentiments about the chickens. She just hated the hell out of them. Her feelings of inadequacy toward everything and everybody stopped when it came to the chickens. Here, she drew the line. Servility turned into surliness. All the submerged, pent-up emotions, the hurt and grief over what she perceived as her own inadequacies and unworthiness, Domino's princely possessions, and the unfairness of things, held in check before, were released now in full-flown fury.

Joe Louis, the one rooster we had left, paraded around the lawn as though the land belonged to him. He stood on the fencepost in the paddock and yelled "cock-a-doodle-doo" from daybreak until sunup, much louder and more often than was necessary.

After the first few mornings of being awakened bleary-eyed to this early morning call, it began to lose its charm for us, but for Sassafrass it was much worse. It was intolerable. It shredded her nerves. She just naturally hated the chickens, and what she hated most of all was their standing around on the back steps when she was lying across the top step trying to sleep in the sun. One day, she had had enough of their crowding around while she was taking her nap, and she snapped at them. One chicken had little enough sense to peck back, and Sassafrass snapped her head off. This started her taste for blood, and after that, it was downhill all the way.

Claude and Clarence, at the farm across the road, had a Border Collie, too, named Frances. They claimed Frances was so smart that they could say "Frances, go cut that dry cow out of the herd," and Frances, out of a field full of cows, could go cut out the very one they sent her for.

I never saw Frances do that, but they claimed she could, and with that much expertise, I decided to consult them about my problem. When I told them about our trouble with Sassafrass killing the chickens, they shook their heads gloomily.

"Ain't no way to stop it, once they get a taste of blood."

We had a clear choice between the chickens and Sassafrass, and we all voted for Sassafrass. The only trouble was that ours weren't the only chickens around. All farmers had chickens, and if she got in *their* chicken houses, not only would *she* be in trouble, *we* would be in trouble. Farmers thereabouts just didn't take kindly to anyone or anything messing with their chickens or in their chicken houses. It got them riled, and only rustling cattle was worse. I thought it absolutely singular how strongly they felt about chicken thieves because it was true to God, they'd shoot first and find out who they shot later.

Down at the country store, they told all kinds of stories about what farmers did when someone tried to break into their chicken houses. The one they laughed about the most was the old farmer who was awakened in the middle of the night by screams from his chickens. He ran outside in his bare feet and nightshirt, taking his shotgun and dog with him. Seeing no one, he walked inside the dark chicken house to listen for the dog, fox, or ground-hog that might be lurking there. His dog eased in behind him and laid a cold nose on his bare leg, startling him so goddam bad that he let go with the shotgun and killed forty chickens. He spent the rest of the night plucking feathers and dressing chickens so they all wouldn't go to waste.

They laughed so hard about this, I figured it was the perennial joke they told newcomers, but it was no joke about stealing chickens. It got them so riled, they regularly shot off a groundhog's head, shattered a fox, or blew away a dog. If they *caught* a chicken thief, they hauled him into town and expected the sheriff to hang him.

Sad as it was, Sassafrass would just have to go. Before she did, however, we tried everything to break her of her bad habit—scolding her, whapping her hard with a rolled-up newspaper, and pushing her nose into the bloody mess she had made of the chicken. Nothing worked. Sassafrass hated the chickens worse than she dreaded the punishment, and she continued, unabated, getting progressively worse until she was not only killing the chickens in anger but eating them with relish. Now, Sassafrass was not only a criminal, she was a cannibal, because in the farm family she was eating one of its own members and this was untenable.

It did, however, give Larry an idea on how we might train Sassafrass not to touch the chickens. The top strand of barbwire near the barn was electrified to keep the cattle from rushing the fence and breaking out. All of us took precaution not to come in contact with the electric fence because the jolt was such that it would shake your teeth loose. The very next time that Sassafrass got a chicken, Larry took it and ran a section of electric wire through it. When Sassafrass sank her teeth into it, it literally curled her hair. I thought it was a genius idea, but all it did was make Sassafrass think something had gone wrong with our chickens, and at night, she would slip down the road and get somebody else's.

Claude and Clarence shook their heads. "You better shoot her," they predicted darkly, "before somebody comes and shoots you."

It gave me considerable pain, but the only solution left was to look for another home for Sassafrass. We found it with the butcher who worked down at the rendering plant in town. He had decided to branch out on his own and raise and butcher his own beef. He had found a piece of land to rent; way out in the country, with no neighbors for miles around. He didn't plan to have any chickens but he did need a cattle dog to help protect and round up the steers he planned to raise.

He was a tall, spare man named Aaron, with a smiling moon-faced wife named Annalee and two little cherub children. He said he and his wife and children loved animals and he promised to give Sassafrass a good home. He came one Saturday afternoon in his pickup truck to take her away. Sassafrass knew what was happening. She sat on the front seat beside him with her shoulders slumped and her head hanging down and cried bitter tears. We cried, too, because we had failed in our effort to help Sassafrass overcome her failing for killing chickens.

A black gloom settled over the house and Wayne and Billy-Wade decided that they hated the chickens and wouldn't eat any more of their eggs. We tried to persuade them that what had happened to

Sassafrass was not the chickens' fault, that Sassafrass was incorrigible and therefore had to be got rid of.

They sucked in their breath and shot a worried look at each other.

"What's incorrigible?" Billy-Wade asked.

"It means she couldn't change her bad habits."

A cloud of concern settled on Wayne's smooth face. "You mean if we aren't good you might get rid of us?"

I pulled them together in a bear hug. "Certainly not. I won't *let* you be incorrigible."

Billy-Wade's face brightened. "Then can we have another dog?"

"What about Suzie?"

Hearing her name mentioned, Suzie, always the soul of tolerance and patience, looked up from where she was stretched by the fireplace.

"Suzie is an inside dog. We need another outside dog."

From the time he and Wayne were old enough to watch TV, every Sunday night had been reserved for Lassie. They would sit side by side on a sofa cushion on the floor, completely engrossed with Lassie's adventures, to the final fade-out when they waved "Goodbye, Lassie. Goodbye, Lassie."

Billy-Wade's memory was indelibly marked and he would not be satisfied until we found a collie just like Lassie. His name was Chief, and he was a glory of red gold hair, with a plumed tail and a white ruff collar that he wore like a monarch's mantle. Together, he and Billy-Wade reenacted every scene Lassie had ever played. They roamed the green hills and ran through the hot-gold sunlight in the pasture. They swam in the pond together and when we rode the horses, Chief took the point, fanning out in the field in front of us, lifting coveys of quail that soared skyward and out of the way.

Chief had no problem with the chickens. He would dash through a congregation of them out scratching for worms and scatter them like a motorboat cutting a wake in the water. Chief's problem was helping to herd the cows. Not bred for cattle as the Border Collie is, Chief just joined in the activity for fun. Driving the cows up to the paddock, he was helpful in not letting a stray turn the herd back, but once they got to the gate opening onto the paddock, he would go into a barking fit, not letting a single cow through the gate. The cows, upset with this reception, would then turn back and race through the pasture all the way back to Broad Run. This meant going through the whole thing again: driving them up, not letting a stray turn back, and getting to the gate only to have Chief do the same thing again.

One afternoon in August, T. X. Truitt brought a customer to look at the herd of cows that would soon have to be sold. On the lush summer pasture they had grown sleek and fat, and T. X. wanted to walk them quietly to the paddock so that the customer could see what a nice, quiet herd they were. We had just gotten them to the gate when Chief did it again. The same thing the second time. On the third try, T. X. took me aside.

His face was hot and flushed; perspiration was pouring down behind his ears and dropping off the end of his nose. "How about selling me that dog?"

"What for—"

"Just sell me the dog."

"I don't want—"

He was reaching in his back pocket for his bulging brown leather wallet. He fanned out four hundred-dollar bills. "I'll give you four hundred dollars."

"What do you want Chief for?"

His eyes were livid. "I want to shoot him and it's worth four hundred dollars to do it," T. X. said, his eyes on the customer now getting restless as he waited in the sun to see the cows who had disappeared again over the hill.

I gathered Chief up in a protective embrace. "Shame on you, T. X. Truitt, for saying such a thing. I'll put him in the house with Suzie, but damn if anybody's going to start shooting dogs in my paddock, especially if they're mine."

T. X. snatched his handkerchief out of his back pocket and tried to wipe the aggravation off his face. "When a customer is standing there with the cash money in his pocket. . . ."

But I wasn't listening. I took Chief to the house and left him, much to his grave indignation, with Suzie. He barked and yapped about the indignity of being made an inside dog, and pressed his nose to the windowpane to get a closer look at what he had been cut off from on the outside.

The chickens were laughing. Having witnessed what had happened, and seeing Chief secured on the inside, they sashayed back and forth in front of the window in an "I-told-you-so" manner.

Redemption had finally come. They had endured having their numbers reduced by Sassafrass' slaughter, but Sassafrass was gone. They had lived through the humiliation of having Chief scatter them like autumn leaves, but Chief was now shut up inside the house. At last, they had the outside to themselves. For the moment, they had won. *But only for the moment.*

Growing up in the yard outside was a new warden, a self-appointed peace officer named Puttie, who wouldn't put up with them or their foolishness, and their days of decadence were numbered.

CHAPTER 14

Puttie

PUTTIE HAD NOTHING going for her, at least, nothing you could see at first glance. She was Mrs. Carmichael's daughter and the Cinderella child. Her two elegant, aloof brothers were perfectly splendid. Joe Willie, named for football's Namath because of his exquisite eyes, wore a dawn-grey coat of finest fur. The other brother, Pretty Boy Floyd, was dressed in a silken black tuxedo with white tie, vest, and spats on all four feet. Puttie was dressed in calico rags from the kitchen—black, white, brown, orange, and red—in a pattern so careless that she looked as though her coat had been put together by an uncaring seamstress.

"There's no excuse," Larry said, pointing to Puttie crouched on the kitchen floor, "in a cat as ugly as that being allowed to live. Why doesn't somebody drown her?"

It was true that she was the homeliest cat we had ever seen. Her mother, Mrs. Carmichael, was a big, gorgeous, grey barn cat, and her father, a tiger red, was from the farm down the way. With lineage like that, it was a mystery to us how Puttie's genes got so mixed up that she ended up looking like the kind of cats seen in alleys on dark streets looking for fishbones in garbage cans.

An off-center white flame ran down Puttie's forehead, dividing her face into two unequal parts. A black smudge covered one eye like mascara hurriedly and badly applied. She wore white slippers on her front feet with one brown toe poking through, and stockings on the back with one sliding down lower than the other. Around her middle, she wore a white fur apron that covered her knees when she sat. No matter how we tried to improve Puttie's appearance with bowls of cream and choice bits from the table, she remained as thin as a fence rail and carried her hindquarters higher than her head, like a wheelbarrow in use, with her tail held straight up and slightly tipped at the top like an unhealthy weed.

"Plenty of disasters happen around here," Larry said. "Why doesn't one happen to her?"

Puttie purred when she heard the words. Her outside dressings might be poor, but inside resided a thoroughbred spirit and a loving heart. Puttie's purpose was to win hearts, not admiring glances, and she set out to capture them one by one. She had not inherited her mother's attitude.

Mrs. Carmichael took poorly to being a barn cat. She did her job but sat outside the kitchen window and complained about it in such a loud and persistent voice that when she first arrived at the farm, not knowing that she was female, we had named her Stokely Carmichael for the political activist who was at that time giving voice to everything in the streets. After her first litter of kittens, we had to change her name to *Mrs.* Carmichael.

Puttie's two splendid brothers, Joe Willie and Pretty Boy Floyd, disdained the other farm animals and tiptoed around on silken feet, aloof, arrogant, and annoyed, that these other lowly creatures shared the world with them. Puttie, by contrast, had the heart of a little homemaker and not only loved them all but cared for them all. She wanted home to be a haven and worked at it.

Dooma Lee was Puttie's first conquest. When Dooma Lee cried for company, Puttie stopped what she was doing to go out and baby-sit Dooma Lee. When Chief waited outside the kitchen window to be fed, Puttie slept between his paws. Before dinner every night, she washed his face with quick little licks of her pink tongue, and when she had finished that she stood on her back legs, took his head between her paws, and cleaned his ears. When the cows came up to the barn to be fed, Puttie ran to the paddock and sat on her haunches on the fencepost, her white fur apron spread over her knees, her front feet drawn primly together, her tail trailing down the post. She studied each cow with interest and in order to get a good look at them all, walked the fence rail from post to post until she had made the complete circuit of the paddock and was satisfied that they were all all right and accounted for.

She kept an eye on the chickens and ducks to see that all went well, and if they decided to obstruct the back steps by sleeping there, Puttie ran them away, scolding them with a hard-eyed look and a flick of her tail.

On golden afternoons when we saddled the horses and rode out in the field, Puttie tried to come along too, paddling through the tall grass like a swimmer trying to make it across the English Channel. When she tired and couldn't keep up, she would climb up to a treetop and watch from there until we and the horses were home safe and she could follow us back to the barn, glad the ordeal was over.

The single holdout and the one who did not enjoy Puttie's extravagant attention at all was Suzie. Suzie was, and knew herself to be, the Queen of Hearts. All of us loved Suzie the most, and Suzie didn't want Puttie to get any idea that she might impose herself on that position or her prerogatives. Puttie's goal was one hundred percent, so she put her mind on, if not winning Suzie's approval, at least gaining her tolerance.

It was Suzie's habit after lunch to go to the living room and sleep in the circle of sun that fell through the window on the floor. Taking note of this, Puttie strolled into the living room and tried to cozy up to Suzie. Suzie stiffened at this impertinence, showed her teeth, snarled, and would have none of it, but Puttie persisted. She liked and wanted to share all of Suzie's favorite spots . . . beside the heat register opposite the gold sofa, under the marble-top coffee table, and the special spot of sunlight that fell in a rectangle through the living room window on the green rug in front of the fireplace. But more than that, Puttie liked Suzie and wanted Suzie to like her.

Old and disabled, with three legs gone, Suzie feared that Puttie's freely given love would displace her in our affections, and Puttie set out to reassure her that it was only friendship she was after. When Suzie wouldn't allow her in her circle of sunshine, Puttie sat on the edge in the shadows to watch Suzie sleep. Suzie closed her eyes and tried to ignore Puttie, but knowing that she was being watched, barely opened one eyelid. Seeing Puttie still there, she gave an exasperated sigh and closed her eyes tighter.

Puttie simply wore Suzie's resistance away. Every day she eased an inch closer until finally she had an edge of the sunshine. Suzie, at last, was persuaded to share her special spot with Puttie, but only if Puttie slept behind her so that she couldn't see that she was there.

Puttie had the household running smoothly and everything pretty much in hand until a little field mouse decided to move in and join us. He gained passage through the cellar and under the kitchen floor into the pantry. Night after night he feasted like a king, gnawing the corners off cracker boxes and scattering crumbs all over the floor, trying out packages of spaghetti and spilling the contents on the shelf, and liberally eating his way through packages of cake mix.

He timed his raids to coincide with Puttie's absence when she was outside attending to other chores, or during night patrol, which was one of her self-imposed duties. She was aware of his presence and his plundering and was set upon ridding her household of this predator. She would sit for hours in front of the pantry, impatiently tapping her tail on the polished white kitchen floor just waiting for him to show his impertinent face, but the mouse knew better than to tempt Puttie. He stayed safe in his hiding place until she was out the door and gone.

Lulled by his successes, the mouse misjudged Puttie. As time went on and he was able to continue without being caught, he risked daylight raids for a quick afternoon snack with Puttie in the house. Puttie was in a near-rage about this, leaping from the floor onto the shelf to catch him, but he was through the floor and gone. His expertise in evading Puttie made him bold. He had concluded that Puttie wasn't clever enough or agile enough to catch him, and he chanced ever more daring attempts. Puttie watched it all with glazed green eyes, patiently waiting for the day that he made one maladroit move.

It came. Bold and brazen now, he tripped out on the pantry shelf for a late afternoon snack, got himself trapped in front of a can of apricots, and Puttie was on him in a second.

All the animal fury, the frustration and delay in catching him, was now indulged. Puttie's expression was one of pure satisfaction. Her purr, usually so gentle, was a satisfied roar. She crouched on all fours with the little grey mouse in front of her. She looked up when I came in but there was only an eyelash-flick of recognition. She turned her attention back to the business at hand. With the mouse between her paws, she batted him back and forth in a game of solitary soccer. After a while, she sat down again and studied her prize. The mouse, pretending to be dead, lay stretched out in front of her with his eyes closed, not daring to move.

Witnessing this, I, for a moment, felt a sympathy for the little grey mouse who had dared and lost, but I was in no way prepared to intervene in nature's laws or an animal contest. The mouse, I decided, must surely have known the risk he took, and Puttie had patiently awaited her opportunity to end this intruder's brazen raids.

She watched him for a long contemplative moment, the fur on her back standing up, her tail noiselessly drumming the kitchen floor. The mouse, thinking he had a reprieve, decided to make a run for it, and dashed toward the pantry door. Puttie snatched him up and began a virtuoso performance. She batted him around and under the table, up one leg of the chair, and down again. It became a game that grew ever more skillful. She stood on her hind legs and tossed him from side to side, catching him in one paw and throwing him back to the other until she lost her balance and fell backward.

It so angered Puttie that she had made this maladroit move and ended her virtuosity, that she snatched him up and crunched his head with her teeth.

"Puttie!" She had reached the ultimate in what I could endure. I opened the kitchen door and tried to coax her outside, but she wasn't interested in leaving. I got a Kleenex, picked the mouse up by the tail, threw him on the back steps, and came back for Puttie. By the time I got her outside, Chief had run up, snatched up Puttie's mouse, taken it to the barn, and eaten it. Poor Puttie was not able to dine on her prize, so I gave her a plate of cream as consolation. She ate it without much relish because what she had her taste buds set for was the fat little mouse, and it left her unsatisfied.

After that, she took to stalking the front field for field mice before they ever entertained the thought of setting up camp in her house. In the tall grass, frail little Puttie was a tiger stalking game, alert, waiting, ready to pounce. As she caught them, she brought them to the back steps and laid them out in a row so that her day's work could be seen and admired. Chief finally got tired of stealing her booty and got his fill of field mice and we had to stop Puttie from stacking up so many mice on the back steps.

Then she turned her attention to the barn swallows, which she hated more than the field mice. The barn swallows richly returned her feeling. They hated her even more because she was a danger, not only to them, but to the brood of babies they were trying to raise under the eaves of the barn. There was a constant war between them, and when they saw Puttie outside, the alarm was sounded and they flew out of their stations under the eaves of the barn and dive-bombed and strafed Puttie. Puttie fought off their attack and planned an offensive of her own.

There was a slight sink-hole in the backyard lawn between the house and the barn that was big enough for Puttie to bury her body in. Thinking she was concealed, she would lie in her foxhole and wait for the barn swallows to fly over. When they did, she would spring like a panther from her hiding place and catch them in mid-air between her paws, smash them to the ground, and promptly gnaw off their heads, so that they did not disturb the good peace and quiet of her walk to the barn and the duty of her patrol.

What Puttie liked best was when her goal of harmony and happiness reached achievement on summer afternoons when we sat in the lawn chairs under the oak tree on the back lawn and all the animals gathered round in company and companionship. The ducks waddled up from the pond and settled themselves in the grass, the chickens scratched and plucked bugs nearby, the horses hung their heads over the fence, the cows moved up from the pasture, Dooma Lee strained her chain to get as close as possible, and when Puttie was certain that everyone was there and accounted for, she would settle between Chief's paws and take a nap.

These moments of peace didn't last too long, because Chief began going farther and farther afield, and sometimes, late at night, he still had not come home. Puttie always reported this by coming to my study window and tapping on the pane with her little pink paw. One night he didn't come at all, and the next day he was still gone. We began a systematic search, going from farm to farm, but no one had seen him. He had simply disappeared.

Some weeks later, Mr. Finley, who had been away working on the other side of the county, came by.

"I know where your collie is," he reported. "Clear across the county down in some deep woods, chained to a tree. The people who have got him are right mean folks. I'd be careful going to get him."

Larry drove us there and when we arrived Chief barked and whined and tried to break away from the tree he was chained to. He was ragged and dirty and underfed.

Three mean-looking men in undershirts and khaki work pants were sitting inside on a bench in the dining room under a shotgun hanging on the wall. They claimed that Chief had walked twenty miles down the road and five miles into the woods and arrived at their place and he was now their dog.

The older man said, "My grandbaby allus wanted one of them collie dogs and I aim for him to have this one."

Larry tried to explain that Chief was a registered collie and we held the registration, that by law he was ours, but the man refused to release him. It was a real dilemma. We couldn't very well ask to use his phone to call the sheriff to arrest him and we knew that if we left to go get the sheriff Chief would not be there when we returned.

"What will it take to get him back?" we asked.

"Replace him with another collie dog."

"That's absurd. You leave us no choice but to go and get the sheriff."

He rubbed his whiskered chin. "What you willin' to pay?"

"We're not *willing* to pay anything. What will it cost to get him?"

"Well, the least you could do is pay for the food I give him."

"How much is that?"

"Fifty dollars."

It was an outrage. He couldn't have fed Chief more than fifty cents worth of food, considering the condition he was in, but it was clear that if we wanted him, we would have to ransom him. We paid the money and took him home and then went by to see the sheriff.

I had only seen the sheriff twice before, both times with warrants for arrest—once for me and once for three of my cows. On the first occasion, I had only recently arrived in the country. I had been to the grocery store in town and had driven into the drive and parked my station wagon at the back walkway to the kitchen. As I looked up, I saw in my rearview mirror the sheriff's brown patrol car with the blue bubble light flashing pulled up behind me. I couldn't imagine what was the matter. I hadn't run any stoplights, I hadn't been speeding, I hadn't made any reckless left-hand turns. I hadn't done *anything*.

When I got out of my station wagon, he was standing beside his patrol car waiting for me, adjusting the Sam Brown belt that crossed the tailored brown jacket of his uniform. The big five-point silver star with SHERIFF emblazoned across it glistened in the sunlight, as did the gold stripe down his trouser leg. He was a stocky man about the size of a middle-weight wrestler, with a four-inch scar across his cheek where he had, barefisted, overpowered the armed gunmen who tried to rob the Minniesville bank. Beneath his Smokey Bear hat that he wore squarely on his head, his brilliant blue eyes were like laser beams.

I was so overcome by all this solemn authority that I fairly shrieked, "What's the matter?"

His smooth-shaven face never moved a muscle. With the laser beams fastened on my face to detect any dead-giveaway guilt, he said, "I have a warrant for your arrest."

"Warrant for my arrest! What for?"

"Your part in that numbers racket in town."

For a moment I thought he was joking. I expected his dead-serious look to turn into a grin. Maybe this was a new kind of country joke. Not very funny, but maybe. . . . I could see from the stance he had taken, both feet planted in the ground, and the no-nonsense look on his face that he wasn't joking. He was standing there waiting for me to confess.

"Numbers racket!" I cried. I didn't even know what a numbers racket was. "Look, Sheriff, you've got the wrong person."

He looked bored and took a folded white official paper out of his pocket. "That's what they all say." He glanced down at the statistics on the warrant and began calling them out: "White female . . . five foot five . . . 120 pounds . . . approximately thirty-three years old . . . brown eyes . . . reddish brown hair. . . ." He looked back at me. "That's you all right."

I was just horrified. I had read of instances of mistaken identity where people were hauled off to prison and left there for years before proof of error could be brought to court. Worse than that, Wayne and Billy-Wade would be coming home on the school bus soon and it would traumatize them forever if, in full view of all their class-mates aboard the bus, they saw their mother arrested and hauled off by the sheriff, right in our own front yard.

The sheriff was putting the paper back in his pocket and squint-ing his eyes in a cunning way. "Yes, ma'am, that's you all right."

"No, it's not," I protested.

He looked really annoyed that I was denying a physical descrip-tion that was so obviously true.

"I mean. . . ." I was afraid I was going to start stuttering and then it was going to seem that I was guilty even though I didn't know anything about a numbers racket. I only knew that this was no sheriff to fool around with. We had been in the country only a matter of days when the big story on the local radio station was about the sheriff arresting the engineer on the Southern Railroad train.

Where we lived in Forksville, the railroad cut the one artery of the village with Matthew's store on one side and the one-room post office on the other. There never was much traffic on this line of the railroad and the engineer decided one day to park the train here, for whatever reason, blocking the railroad crossing so that farmers couldn't get back and forth across the road to their fields. When forty-five minutes had passed and the engineer was still blocking the crossing, the farmers called the sheriff and he came out and arrested the engineer. When the engineer protested, the sheriff grabbed him up by the collar of his blue denim jacket, hauled him into town, and threw him in jail. It took an official from the Southern Railroad to come bail him out.

I wasn't taking any chances on provoking this sheriff. I tried to say, ever so politely, "I mean, I'm not the one you're looking for."

He quirked his mouth down at the side and gave his head a knowing nod. He'd heard it all before and he didn't want to hear it again. "Isn't your name Eloise Adams?"

I thought, oh, thank God, I've got something I can really deny. "No. No, I'm not Eloise Adams."

When I told him who I was, he said, "Let me see your driver's license."

I turned my purse upside down on the hood of his patrol car and tore through the contents to find my driver's license. In so doing, I scattered lipstick, comb, and compact, and accidentally broke a little bottle of pink hand lotion that began to slide down the side of his shining clean patrol car. I could see this was a bad move, but I found my driver's license.

"See! See!" I held up the driver's license with the picture right next to my face so that there would be no mistake.

He took the license from me, looked at it, then at me, then handed it back.

"Be damned," the sheriff said, "I could of swore you were Eloise."

It turned out that Eloise was hiding out on a farm about a half-mile from me and when the sheriff saw me in town shopping, he thought I was Eloise.

The next time the sheriff came, it was with a warrant for three of my cows. When I opened the door, he was standing on the back steps with the warrant in his hand.

"I hope you're not looking for Eloise again," I told him when I opened the door.

He didn't think that was funny. He didn't like to be wrong. "I got a warrant for three of your black cows . . . one long-legged one with white markings, and two short fat ones."

I thought he was kidding. I couldn't believe he was going to arrest my cows. "What for?" I asked.

"Unauthorized entry."

Jesus. He meant it. "Unauthorized entry into what?"

"The landing field over yonder across Broad Run. Them fellows can't get their planes down till you get your cows out of the way."

Across Broad Run, the stream that bordered our pasture, and through a field, was a small landing strip where the men with money in Victorsville kept lightweight hobby planes. The three cows, managing to step through the five-strand barbwire, had waded the stream and ventured onto the landing strip and were presently wide eyed with the new world they had discovered.

"Look, Sheriff," I propositioned, "if I get the cows off the landing strip, will you drop charges?"

The sheriff, a part-time farmer himself, with cows of his own and an understanding of how unmanageable they can be, said, "I reckon we could manage that."

Pressing my luck, I added, "And would you help me go get them?"

There was a good-humored twinkle in the sheriff's eyes. "I reckon I could manage that."

On the way over to the airstrip in his patrol car, I decided to make light of the whole thing and said, "Where were you going to put my cows, Sheriff, if you arrested them? In the bull pen?" meaning the general lock-up in the jail. He didn't appreciate my double entendre.

His face resumed its solemn, official look. "Don't get smart with me, young lady, or I'll put you in jail and your cows, too. Just remember, anything your animals do, you're responsible for."

When we got to the airstrip, there they were. They were mine all right, the tall long-legged one leading the way, the two short fat ones following, their heads in the clouds looking around like three tourists ogling the sights in New York City. Two little planes were flying round and round the airstrip waiting to land; the official on the ground, red-faced, and shaking his fist. The sheriff and I got them off the strip, through the field, across Broad Run, and back in my pasture. After that, I put up nine-strand barbwire. When it was done, I shook hands with the sheriff and thanked him. "Much obliged, Sheriff."

He tipped his hat and smiled. "Stay out of trouble."

Now I was back wanting him to do something about the backwoodsmen who had shanghaied Chief, but when I told him what had happened, the sheriff just leaned back in his swivel chair, propped one boot on top of his desk, and said, "You've removed the evidence. All they'd do is deny it. We've had trouble with those folks before. They lure a dog off the road into their pickup truck and take him down to their place in the woods. I'll *try* to catch them, but if I were you, I wouldn't let that dog go wandering anymore."

Puttie was so glad to see Chief that all that mattered was that he was at home. She spent all day giving him a bath, cleaning his ears and straightening out his tangled mane. But we couldn't stop Chief from roaming and ranging across the open fields, and one night, as he was crossing the road, a car swept over the hill and hit him. Puttie was back at my windowpane tapping with her little pink paw. Thinking this was just another of her anxieties, I ignored it and continued to work. Puttie was housemother to the world and couldn't sleep until everyone was home in bed. But I couldn't ignore it. Puttie persisted and kept pat, pat, patting at the windowpane until finally, I went outside to see what troubled her so. With her tail straight up in the air, she ran down the driveway, and there on the edge of the road lay Chief with all his life's breath gone.

We buried him in Boot Hill and grieved, but none so much as Puttie. For Billy-Wade, it was a special loss, but for Puttie, it was a heartache. Someone in her household was missing.

Not long thereafter, she had a new assignment. The butcher named Aaron who had taken Sassafrass home with him returned one Saturday afternoon in his pickup truck with Sassafrass sitting beside him.

"I thought I'd better see if you wanted your dog back," he said.

The land he had leased had been sold and he and his family were having to move back to town and into an apartment where there was no place for Sassafrass.

He patted her on the head. "She's a good dog. Gentle with the cows. I thought maybe you might want her back."

I didn't really. After all the trouble with the chickens, I would like to have declined the offer, but here was Sassafrass, homeless, and besides that, she was pregnant. There was nothing to do but take her in and take care of her.

Puttie went right to work, taking up the duty and care that had formerly been designated for Chief. She welcomed Sassafrass and made her feel right at home again, and Sassafrass, having been away, must have learned something in her absence, because she went out of her way to be pleasant and pleasing and never chased chickens again. In fact, she spent most of her time on her back, belly up, with all four feet in the air like a renegade cowboy with both hands up in surrender.

In all the time of Puttie's life, she never did anything dramatically heroic, no single event set her life apart, but there was a special kind of heroism in her homemaking, her caring, her constancy, and her concern for those she loved and those who lived there. Her life was set apart by the endless, ordinary deeds of duty and devotion strung all in a row like beads on a string. It was this that made up the mosaic of Puttie's life.

She may have been Mrs. Carmichael's Cinderella child and the homeliest cat we ever saw, but to see Puttie sitting on the porch in the sunlight, her white fur apron over her knees, her face full of care and concern for her family, I was always reminded of my mother's words: "It's not what you see in the mirror that counts, it's what you look like turned inside out." Turned inside out, Puttie had a sterling quality and a lasting beauty that neither of her two elegant brothers could begin to match because Puttie wasn't interested in admiring glances, only in winning hearts, and before it was over, she had won them all.

The intervals of tranquility and peace that Puttie provided were island oases in the turbulence and trials going on elsewhere on the farm. These intervals were necessary and vital, for they nourished us and gave us strength to meet the next challenge.

The Federal Land Bank's ninety-day note was due. A customer would have to be found and the cattle would have to be sold to repay the five-thousand-dollar loan.

It was time to put on the trading hat.

CHAPTER 15

Powder Puff

TRUE TO HIS WORD, for once in his life, T. X. did just as he promised. He found a buyer who purchased the herd of cattle I had bought. There was money enough to pay off the Federal Land Bank's principal and interest, T. X.'s ten-percent commission, with a seventeen-hundred-dollar profit besides.

I became suspicious. Things went well dealing with T. X. only when he had an ulterior motive. I thought it likely that he had something else in mind and a way to get the money I had earned away from me.

Meanwhile, I took the check to the bank in Minniesville and asked Mr. Meritt, who had refused to lend me money, for my change. Impressed with the profit I had made, he was now willing to extend me a loan.

"No, thank you!" I sniffed. "I don't need it now. My pasture grass is almost gone, my fields are clipped, and the barn is full of hay. I plan to sit back and enjoy the fall and winter."

T. X. thought this was a bad idea. "What are you going to do with all them 5,000 bales of hay?"

"They're going to feed the horses forever. I'm never going to have to make hay again. Even if they live to be forty years old, I'll still have hay left in the barn."

T. X. looked down at his big diamond ring and studied its rainbow rays of red, lavender, and green. "Won't be no good."

"What do you mean . . . no good?"

"Second-season hay ain't fit for feeding . . . lost all its value. Only thing it's good for then is bedding."

I figured this was just one of T. X.'s trading techniques to scare me into something I didn't want to do. It was. Because his next suggestion was that I either sell off most of the hay or else buy another herd of cattle to feed it to over the winter.

"I already got a herd spotted," T. X. said. "You can buy 'em cheap and sell 'em high next spring when the farmers are looking for something to put out on pasture."

I didn't want to feed cows over the winter and slush through rain, cold, and snow looking for stray calves. I wanted to sit by the fire and read, and drink hot tea from china teacups, and look out over tranquil landscapes at the peace and quiet of the country, a condition I had not known since spring began and the grass began to grow.

I shook my head at T. X.'s suggestion. "No. I moved from the city to enjoy the peace and quiet of the country."

"There ain't none. That's some idea city folks get from looking at pictures on them seed store calendars. If your gonna live in the country, you gotta work at it. You just sit here and look out the window and you know what'll happen?"

This was going to be a good one. I could tell. T. X.'s blue eyes were alive with opportunity and exaggeration, and on his lips, dire predictions.

"Them fields you see out yonder,"—his hand swept over the panoramic view that took in everything including the horizon—"will start sprouting spruce trees, and the grass will start growing again, and next thing you know, nature will have done took back all the land it took so much trouble to clear and seed to pasture, and the next thing you know. . . ."

T. X. paused for dramatic effect. His technique was to begin with a grain of truth for credibility, then weave it into a fantasy of frightening proportions so that the only solution possible was what he had suggested in the first place.

"And the next thing you know," T. X.'s eyes danced with satisfaction at the picture he had painted, "you'll be sitting here not able to get out the door for the overgrowth."

Even T. X. had to laugh at the extravagance of this exaggeration. I considered what he had said with mock seriousness. "You really think so?"

"I seen it happen."

I was just not going to be persuaded. I wanted time enough to enjoy what had taken us so long to find out in the country. When I told T. X. this, he shook his head over my breach of judgment.

"Suit yourself, but you'll find you either gonna have to buy cows or sell hay. That hay ain't gonna hold for another season and those horses won't be able to do nothing but sit on it."

I figured T. X. was probably lying because he had another herd he wanted to unload, so I decided to ask my neighbor, Ewell Early, who told me, "It's true. All the nutrients will be gone by next year. The seeds will drop off and all you'll have left is straw. Your best bet is to buy cattle or sell hay."

Remembering all the unrelenting work, trouble, and aggravation the hay had caused, fair market I felt should be somewhere around five dollars a bale. Nowhere, outside the deserts of Arabia, could such a price be got, because the current going rate was fifty cents a bale. I couldn't see selling all our hard work that cheap because, figuring labor, maintenance, and supplies, it meant we had worked for something like sixteen cents an hour. My only recourse was to buy another herd of cattle. I wasn't ready to make that kind of commitment, and when T. X. came by again, he asked, "What you gonna do?"

"I haven't decided yet," I told him. I wanted to at least enjoy the end of summer. The fields were empty now except for the horses and Ida Belle and Maggie Mae, the two white-face Herefords that we had bought for Wayne and Billy-Wade to raise. They frolicked in the pasture like two fat girls on a diet of delicacies. Their summer on grass had bulged their bellies, round as barrel stays. This token amount of cattle was enough for me. I didn't want all the work that went into caring for a herd of beef cattle. I just wanted to play farmer like Larry did.

Every morning he got up, put on his Brooks Brothers suit, and with his briefcase and furled umbrella, drove out of the country into the city to pore over purely intellectual problems over a martini lunch in a swank French restaurant carefully overseen by a maître d'. In the evening he returned, put on his cowboy hat, boots, and jeans, and went outside to "look over the farm." Weekends meant a tractor ride and work when he was available. He liked driving the big farm machines and cutting a cow out of the herd with his quarter horse, but he didn't care at all for building fence and making hay. It seemed to me that he had the best of both worlds and I wanted a piece of that pie, but I couldn't figure how to slice it. Somebody had to assume the responsibility for all that work, and I was elected.

T. X. and I were standing in the hot sunshine by the paddock fence. "I just don't want to winter cows," I told him.

T. X. propped one foot on the bottom rail and leaned on the paddock fence. "There ain't nothin' to it," he said, brushing aside this objection as though it were only a trifle. "All you got to do is drop a few bales of hay down that chute in the barn to feed them, and they'll do the rest. Besides," his eyes lit up with dollar marks, "this herd I got spotted has all been bred and this time next year, you'll have a hundred head instead of just fifty. Ever' one of them cows oughta calve by spring."

"Calve! I don't know anything about calving."

"Don't have to. Them cows know their business. You just leave 'em to it. The onliest thing you gotta do is count 'em to make sure one of 'em doesn't get lost, strayed, or stole."

Before, I had just been grazing cows; now, I would be breeding cows. The idea was awesome. T. X. tried to make it sound like nothing at all; I knew better. I would end up being midwife to a cow, and that was a job description I didn't choose to have at all.

This resolution had no sooner been made than Maggie Mae, much to our surprise, began to calve, with the disastrous results of her ending up paralyzed. After the trauma of that awful day, her recovery, and our delight in having saved her, wintering cows who would calve by spring didn't seem so bad. We had been initiated. If we could survive that, we could survive anything because we had seen the worst. With the choice narrowed to selling hay or buying cows, we decided to buy the herd of cows that T. X. had spotted.

"Spotting" was part of what T. X. did for a living. He rode about the countryside in his big white Lincoln until he found farmers with cattle to sell, and arranged a sale by talking them out of sending their livestock to the weekly auction where a per-head yardage fee was charged.

"Ain't no use giving them money when you can put it in your own pocket," T. X. would reason.

Before any money changed hands, however, T. X. would find a buyer and broker the cattle so that when the transaction was made, T. X. had collected a commission for buying, a commission for selling, and a slice on the side. This was done by telling the farmer, after he had agreed to sell his cattle, how many things he had wrong with his herd that would hurt him at auction. All the things that T. X. scoffed at when he delivered a herd to a buyer now became a matter of serious importance when he was buying.

The thin cow who "had on her working clothes" earlier would now, according to T. X., probably die on the truck being delivered. The one-eyed bull's lack of vision would damage his disposition and make him mean from not being able to see where he was going, and the lame cow . . . , "Hell, she ain't got but three legs."

I had seen it all, and the first time, bought it all, but now I had gotten street-wise. Before I bought this herd, I had T. X. take me over to look at them first. When we got there the farmer was gone and the gate was locked.

T. X. sighed. "Too bad we can't get in, but you can look at them from here."

The cattle were on a hill about a mile away, and T. X.'s customary method of showing a prospective buyer a herd of cows was to drive through the fields in his big white Lincoln and let them look from the air-conditioned comfort of his automobile.

I opened the car door. "I don't mind walking."

"Hot as it is today?"

"It's not that hot."

His face stiffened as he made the unpleasant suggestion, "You'll have to climb through barbwire fences."

"I'm used to that."

From what I saw standing out in the pasture, the herd looked all right, but I couldn't be sure until I had them home in my own paddock to study them for defects. I agreed to buy them on the contingency that if he delivered any cows that didn't suit they could be returned or replaced.

The expression on T. X.'s face soured. "You ain't buying dresses from the department store, you know."

I ignored his put-down. "No, these cows cost a whole lot more."

"Things just ain't done that way. You see 'em, you buy 'em, you own 'em."

I walked back to the car. "I didn't want to winter cattle anyway."

By the time we got back home, T. X. had agreed to the return or replacement of any cow he delivered. "But you ain't gonna want to return any because I'm gonna check ever' one of 'em for soundness myself." He was wearing his country fox look.

Late the next afternoon, the big silver possum-belly cattle truck ground its sixteen wheels up the driveway and around the barn to the cattle chute. Black noses and tails were hanging out the slats in the side of the truck and the mooing had reached an awful roar. I watched each one as they pushed and shoved down the ramp into the back paddock. They didn't at all look like the cows I had seen in the field the day before. Even to my inexperienced eye they looked a good hundred pounds lighter. I told T. X. this, but he sopped the perspiration off his brow with his handkerchief and said, "They've had a rough ride. Hauling in all this heat is bound to make 'em lose a little weight."

"Not that much."

By the time I got them in the barnyard paddock and had time to study them, I decided to take only thirty of the fifty Black Angus he had delivered. The other twenty would have to go.

Immediately, T. X. began making excuses.

"I ain't got no place to put 'em down for tonight, and it's too late to go look for one. Just let 'em stay here till morning and I'll come back and get the ones you don't want."

I knew that would probably be the last I'd ever see of T. X., but I agreed and wrote him out a check for thirty cows.

"This ain't the right amount of money." T. X. held the check in one hand and hit it with the other.

"That's the right amount for thirty cows. The other twenty belong to you, and if you aren't here by morning to get them, I'll have to charge you for hay and pasture."

I could see that T. X. didn't like me anymore, but he had marvelous restraint, and the certain knowledge that he'd be able to think of something before tomorrow. That's what worried me.

He managed a smile and said, "T. X. Truitt is a man of his word. You pick out the ones you don't want and I'll be back in the morning with some of the boys to help load and take them out of here."

I knew then that T. X. planned to do. He would bring a bunch of helpers, get out in the paddock, and get the cattle all stirred up so that we would not be able to tell one cow from another. With his skill and expertise, he would end up with twenty good cows and I'd be stuck with the twenty bad ones he was trying to unload.

"I'll just get a little paint can and dab a spot on the ones I don't want." This was what was done at the sales barn where the livestock auction was held every Saturday, to help distinguish one man's cattle from another's.

"No," T. X. yelled. "Don't do that. You'll get 'em all messed up and then I can't sell 'em. Just pick out the ones you don't want and me and my boys will do the rest."

I worried all night. I knew what was going to happen. I *had* to figure some way to mark them without leaving a mark. By morning, I was in despair. To lift my spirits a little I decided on treating myself to a bubble bath. It was in toweling off afterwards and dusting with bath powder that I got the idea, and it was a triumphant idea: bath powder! White powder on black cows! I jumped in my boots and jeans and ran to the barn and started dragging out bales of hay, cutting the bales and strewing hay along the inside fence rail of the paddock. The cows, grateful for this morning snack, all lined up at the fence and began eating. They stood quietly with their heads to the fence rail and their hindquarters toward me. This way it was easy to see those whose flanks were hollowed with age, those who had full udders, and those who stood on only three legs.

I ran back to the bathroom and got my box of bath powder, took out the fluffy pale green powder puff with the pink rose on top, and began going up and down the line of cows.

"This one . . . this one . . . this one . . . and this one."

Each time I chose one to eliminate, I gave the hindquarters a little pat of powder until I had marked the twenty I did not want.

Right on schedule, T. X. drove up with his bunch of helpers, five hard-eyed men who looked as though they'd steal the wedding ring off their mother's hand. T. X. grinned broadly and rubbed his hands together briskly. "Well, me and my boys are here to get them cattle. You want to point them out?"

I was pleased to say, "That won't be necessary. I've already marked them."

"I told you I couldn't sell them cattle in a private sale with paint on them."

"Not paint, T. X., powder."

He furrowed his brows together, not understanding what I meant. "Come on. I'll show you."

We walked to the paddock where the cows were still peacefully eating the hay strewn against the fence. "There's a white powder puff mark on the backside of every cow I want taken out of here. All you've got to do is get your men to load those on the truck."

T. X. propped by hands on his hips. He looked at the cows as though he were seeing them for the first time. "I'll just be god-damned," he muttered. "I'll be a sonofabitch if I ever seen the likes of that." He had no choice but to take the ones I had chosen to eliminate.

He threw both hands in the air and walked back to where his motley crew was waiting to load the cows. "Hey, boys," he beckoned to them, and when they came up, he draped an arm confidentially around their shoulders. "You ain't gonna believe this, but what we got to do is pick up the cows with the powdered asses."

One thing you had to give T. X., he never gave up trying. When they had loaded the cows, he came back to the paddock briskly rubbing his hands together again. "Now, what you need is a bull, so you can breed those cows back when they come fresh. That way you got a three-in-one package . . . a cow with one on the ground and one on the way. Now I know where there's a bull. . . ."

I held up my hand to stop him. "I don't want any more one-eyed bulls. This time, I'm going to pick my own."

First, T. X. tried to look hurt, as though his efforts to help a friend had been rudely refused. Then, his eyes saddened at my reckless folly. "No more experience than you got, you'll like end up with a baloney bull."

"Baloney bull?"

"That's one of them that ain't no good for nothing but sending to the rendering plant to make baloney out of."

He was trying to scare me again, but I held fast. "Maybe, but I want to pick him myself."

I was tired of having a disgrace out in the pasture that was so blind he kept walking into the side of the barn, and I was done doing business with T. X. He was a caution to watch and the best performer in conartistry I had ever seen, but it took too much time, effort, and energy trying to figure out what pitfall he had prepared next.

It was in looking for the bull that we found Luther Stokes.

Luther had what country people call "a sunny disposition." His face was round and as full of light as the sun itself and his eyes were a guileless blue. He was from a family of twelve children, and when his father died, the family's 120-acre farm was equally divided so that each child got a ten-acre slice. This was, for Luther, too big to live on and not enough to farm so he sold his share and bought himself a tractor to make a living.

He worked for hire cutting and baling hay in the summer, and when the grass was gone and winter came, he cut mulch, the marshy, weed-choked grass in untended areas that was baled and sold to a Pennsylvania company for their mushroom caves. Working in the fields cutting and baling year-round had developed in Luther a calm and patience that Job himself would have admired. Absolutely nothing got him upset. No matter how many things went wrong, he would set his smooth-faced lantern jaw and work at it until he wore the problem out. Trouble was something he was accustomed to, and he took it as a challenge. It was not in his nature to say "I can't," "It won't work," or "There's nothing I can do." Once challenged, he had a bulldog's tenacity and couldn't leave the problem alone even if it took all day, all night, all week, or all month to solve it.

I wasn't aware of this when he answered my ad in the local newspaper for a bull to breed my herd of Angus cows. I had talked with some of the other cattlemen in the area and they were breeding the French Charolais bull to Angus cows and getting a bigger calf that put on poundage faster and brought a higher market price than grade Angus. Since I could not afford to buy a foundation herd of purebred Angus on short-term money, I decided to try breeding the Charolais to the Angus.

Luther had a young bull he had raised himself, a splendid white beast weighing 2,000 pounds, with a brass ring in his nose. Raised gently, his disposition and conformation seemed good, so I bought him and had Luther deliver him. It was a golden autumn day when Luther drove up with him on the truck, and as the sun glistened on that fine white bull, I was reminded of Pericles, who brought the Golden Age to Athens. Right away, I decided that he would be called Pericles, too, because what I hoped for was that he would bring the Golden Age to my pasture.

He gave every evidence that this might happen because he jumped off the truck, ran to the first hill in the pasture, and threw out his massive chest and roared. The cows, all grazing under the trees by Broad Run, a half-mile away, heard the trumpeting sound. In cow language, it must have sounded like Tarzan's jungle call, because they all stopped what they were doing and thundered through the pasture and up to the hill to greet him, glassy-eyed with excitement.

CHAPTER 16

The Perils of Claudine

PERICLES, BIG AND HANDSOME as a Greek, was an instant sensation. Our cows weren't the only ones who were glad to see him. When the herd that belonged to Clarence and Claude in the field across the road heard that he was in the neighborhood, they all crowded up and hung their heads over the fence and began to moo "yoo-hoo" and bat their big, daisy eyes. Virile as he was, he wasn't about to let his public go unattended, so he decided to make the rounds of the neighborhood.

I wasn't aware of this until the next morning when I was walking from the bedroom through the living room on the way to the kitchen to make breakfast, I looked through the bay windows and saw that Clarence and Claude had a new bull that they had put with their herd. Squinting farther, he seemed to be an exact match of Pericles in size and color.

"That's really something," I muttered to myself in way of congratulation. "I must have managed to get a really good bull for them to go out and buy one exactly like mine."

I was still musing over what a watermark this was and handing myself accolades over the bacon and eggs when the telephone rang. It was Heywood Mason, our neighbor who lived at the farm next to ours.

"I saw your light come on in the kitchen, and I thought I better tell you that I saw your bull come by a while ago."

"My bull? It couldn't be."

"I'm most sure of it. I was sitting at my breakfast table and he came barreling down my driveway right past my window headed for Claude and Clarence's field."

I knew it was true as soon as he said it. I ran outside and sure enough there was the eight-foot aluminum paddock gate lying like a pretzel on the ground. Pericles had just started walking toward the herd of cows across the road and walked right through the gate.

I was trying to figure out what I could say to Claude and Clarence and how I could get Pericles back when the phone rang again.

"D'ja know your bull was out?" It was Clarence.

I would like to have lied and said no, that I didn't know anything about a bull, that I didn't even own one, but Pericles was too big to deny.

"Heywood just called me. I'll have to find where he went through your fence and figure some way to get him back."

"That's all right. Me and Claude'll bring him back. We don't want him jumping no more fences."

"You mean he jumped the fence?"

"Shore did. He didn't go through it . . . he went over it . . . clean as a huntin' horse."

Pericles wasn't a bit pleased when Claude and Clarence interrupted his visiting, and he had no inclination to leave this bevy of beauties that he had just found. He was even less pleased when they had to drive him five miles through their fields to the loading chute to get him on a truck to bring him home.

I felt just awful about what had happened. Claude and Clarence had purposely taken their bull out of the pasture so that their cows wouldn't be bred until the scheduled time, and damned old Pericles had gone and undone everything they had done. I wanted to wring his golden neck and when they brought him back I apologized for his waywardness and tried to pay them for their trouble.

Clarence refused my offer, holding his hand out at arm's length. "Oh, no you don't. We don't take money for bringing animals home."

"Why not?" I insisted. "It took your time and effort and a half-day to get him back."

"Because." Claude began vigorously bobbing his head to Clarence's explanation. "If I was to charge you and then my bull busted out and got in your field, think about what you'd charge me."

They saw this as a breeding ground for a vendetta and could not be persuaded otherwise. I could clearly see that argument would do no good, that I was up against local and country mores, so I thanked them profusely and went inside to call Ewell Early to come repair the crumpled gate that Pericles had crunched down.

When there was no answer to my phone call, I got my keys and drove down to Ewell's farm, figuring he was likely out at his barn working.

Ewell's two-story white farmhouse stood back from the road under a brace of oak trees. The sloping green tin roof wore its black patch in the middle as a badge of brave effort to hold things together. Evidence of effort was everywhere, in the clean-kept yard, the mended fence, and the painted green tin buckets that held a tumble of red, pink, and purple petunias on each side of the front steps.

Behind the house were the farm buildings, the equipment shed, Henrietta's chicken houses, and two barns, one painted red. The red barn held all the collected scraps and pieces of useful things that Ewell had gathered over a lifetime—odd pieces of lumber, old tires, tire rims, bent nails, remnants of barbwire, discarded railroad ties, rusted coat hangers, and broken pieces of equipment from which he cannibalized still usable parts. This was Ewell's workshop, where he could most likely be found working or repairing when not out in the field.

Growing up on a farm during the Depression, Ewell was land-wise and had learned all the ways of using ingenuity to mend and repair instead of buying expensive replacements. Bred into him during those early years struggling for survival was the necessity for the productive use of everything, and "making do" or making repairs with whatever he had available at hand.

This necessity was still upon him, and in addition to his own extra work in the fields of others, Henrietta sold eggs from the chickens they raised. This, somehow, was an indignity for her that she never quite got over.

With regularity, she verbally gave Ewell the back of her hand for his financial failures, holding her eighty-year-old father up as the example he should follow. Ewell bore this, as he did his lack of prosperity, with patience and resignation, for he was painfully honest and he had no heart for trading. He wouldn't cheat a man by so much as a blade of grass. The hay he sold was all good and full measure. If anything at all was wrong with a cow he had for sale, he felt obliged to point it out to the buyer.

A farmer driving a pickup truck was pulling out of Ewell's drive just as I turned in. As I parked on the side of the house by the barn, a flock of dogs ran up to bark a welcome, and a bunch of cats pussyfooted from under the house with their tails held up in a shepherd's crook to see who had arrived. A couple of ducks ran back toward the pond, quacking at this disturbance of their nap in the cool dirt under the trees.

I heard Ewell's voice coming from the red barn and walked in that direction, arriving just as Henrietta, her hands propped on her hips and her neck stuck out, shouted at Ewell, "You didn't have to tell him that! If he'd bought that cow down at the auction barn, he wouldn't have known any better." She paused and glared at him. "You just had to run your mouth and ruin the sale, didn't you?"

When I heard what was going on, I tried to step back out of the doorway and go back home. I didn't want to witness his humiliation, but Ewell, had already seen me walk in. "I'll be with you in a minute," he said.

Brushing past me, Henrietta stalked off in a wrath back to the house and slammed the kitchen door. Her father, standing on the kitchen steps listening, was wearing the same disapproving and wrathful face as Henrietta, only his was older.

"You mustn't mind Henrietta," Ewell said, trying for a smile in an attempt to gloss things over. "She just gets a little upset sometimes." He was still holding the rope tied to the cow he had just shown. "You need some help?"

When I told him what had happened, he said, "I got to go put this cow back in the pasture and fix Henrietta's car so she can deliver the eggs. I can't cut loose now. Just shut the gate to your back pasture so the cows can't get out and I'll be up first thing in the morning."

An apricot sun was rising above the blue Virginia woodline at the foot of the pasture when Ewell drove up the next morning. By the time I got out to the barn, he was lifting a spider's intricate octagonal web from the tangled gate he had come to repair. Woven the night before, the web, studded now with dewdrops, glistened in the rays of the rising sun.

"I hate to disturb another man's work," Ewell said, admiring the intricate effort and gently setting it aside with a work-hardened hand.

"Now," he said, turning back to the crumpled gate, "what have we got here?"

It was then that he noticed Claudine standing in the barnyard rubbing her feet together. Claudine was a small, white, nervous chicken of indeterminate breed. Her feathers were worn out and frayed from fretting. Had she come equipped with a pair of hands, she would have been forever wringing them. As it was, she relieved her nervousness by standing in the barnyard and taking one yellow foot and rubbing it on top of the other. Whenever Claudine did this, I knew she had something on her mind.

Lately, she had been doing this quite a bit, standing apart from the other chickens and rubbing her feet together, her anxious orange eyes darting one way and then the other. I supposed that her anxiety came from comparison to the other hens. They had hatched their eggs and now strode about the barnyard with a fluffy flock of yellow chicks flying at their heels. All but Claudine.

As she saw me and Ewell head for the barn, she gave a hysterical scream and flew back to her nest, tucked behind a board nailed to a two-by-four on the side of the barn wall, about three feet off the ground.

Seeing her settle on the side of the wall, Ewell shook his head. "That's no fit place for a nest."

I agreed. "But at least it keeps her up and out from under the cow's feet."

I already had one bad experience with the baby chick who went astray and got its frail little foot mashed flat by a cow's hoof.

"How long has she been sitting on those eggs?" Ewell asked.

"Couple of months, I guess."

"They won't hatch."

"Maybe not, but they keep her occupied."

Ewell frowned. "It'll make her crazy waiting and waiting and nothing happening." His eyes were full of serious concern. "Most people forget . . . animals and chickens and all living things have feelings and problems, maybe not like mine and yours, but feelings and problems all the same. Most times, they'll tell you what's wrong just from looking."

He looked back at Claudine hovering anxiously over her nest. "You'd better get her some more eggs."

"Where'll I get more eggs? All the other hens have hatched theirs."

"I think I can get some for you."

When Ewell returned the next day, I was busy inside the house baking a cake. "I got you some more eggs. I'll just slip these under that hen and take the others away."

Relieved to have this problem taken care of, I thanked him and returned to my task in the kitchen. Later, I looked at Claudine nesting on the side of the barn. She seemed to have trouble covering all the eggs. Like a fat lady with a too short dress, she kept tugging at one side and then the other to cover all the exposed areas.

Thinking Ewell may have replaced more eggs than she had laid, I tried to lift her up to take a look. Her orange eyes grew indignant. Her scolding cluck let me know that lifting up a lady chicken and inspecting her underneath feathers was an indecency that she would not tolerate. She snapped her beak sharply several times indicating that she would brook no more such nonsense, and since she was so insistent, I left her to her business of shifting from side to side trying to cover the eggs to her satisfaction.

Fall was on its way and Claudine's problem was crowded out of my mind by the many necessities that a change of season brings. Primary among the problems was checking the three miles of barbwire fence to determine where fenceposts would have to be replaced, and where new strands of barbwire would have to be stretched before the winter storms began.

In order to readily relocate the trouble spots, I stuffed a piece of old sheet in my pocket, and as I found a place to be repaired, ripped off a ribbon of sheet and tied it to the fence. The strips fluttered frantically in the autumn wind like the last strands of icicles on a discarded Christmas tree.

Completing the task and climbing the hill back toward the barn, I could hear loud and hysterical cackling coming from inside the barn. Before I arrived, I recognized Claudine's shrill tone. Something was dreadfully the matter. Hurrying along, I got there just as Claudine flew down from her nest. She threw her head back and screamed. She lifted her white wings and beat her breast. She jumped up and down on her thin, yellow feet. She was positively having a fit.

I looked down at her frenzied protest. "What on earth is the matter?"

In response, she went through the whole act again. She screamed. She beat her breast. She jumped up and down.

I looked in her nest to see if something had harmed her eggs. Then I found the cause of Claudine's hysteria. The nest was full of broken eggs, and amidst the shells stood four brand-new fluffs of yellow just opening their round dark eyes onto the world. The trouble was, they had bills instead of beaks and webbed feet instead of toes. The eggs Ewell had substituted were duck eggs and Claudine, not recognizing another breed, was beside herself with despair. They didn't look like chickens, they didn't act like chickens, but they must be chickens because she had hatched them herself. To her mind, she had hatched four freaks. No chicken ever looked like that. It was beyond her comprehension how she could have so patiently sat on those eggs all that time and ended up with *that*.

I lifted the little ducklings down to the barn floor so that Claudine could have a better look. They, assuming that this was mama, cuddled up close to Claudine's thin, yellow legs. With one last hysterical scream, Claudine ran out of the barn and across the barnyard, the four little ducklings following in flat-footed pursuit.

Back at the house, I got Ewell on the phone.

"Those eggs you put under Claudine were duck eggs!"

There was no surprise in his voice. "I know. I didn't have any hen eggs, but my Peking duck had enough to spare so I figured she may as well sit on duck eggs. That way she'd at least have something for her trouble. Did they hatch?"

I described Claudine's hysteria and rejection.

"She'll settle down soon enough and raise four fine ducks."

Ewell figured without Claudine's temperament. For days she ran around the barnyard trying to escape the four fluffy ducklings, but they paddled after her in determined pursuit. Claudine's only escape was to fly up to her nest on the side of the barn. Directly below on the barn floor, the four ducklings huddled in a shivering cluster and waited for her to come down. Claudine, in the nest, would look down, see them there, and sigh with exasperation. There was no escape. Finally, out of conscience or defeat, she decided to accept what was so definitely hers. She fluttered down from the nest, gave them a "Come on" cluck, and took them to the barnyard.

Here, she instinctively gave them the instruction that small chicks should have. Clucking out the details, she demonstrated how they should scratch the soil loose to find the little edibles they needed. Heads cocked to one side, the little yellow ducklings listened attentively to Claudine's directions, but were patently unable to carry out her instructions. They flapped at the ground with their flat webbed feet, but could in no way do what Claudine had demonstrated. She scolded them, arched her foot and showed them her toenails, then clawed the earth and uncovered an edible. Snapping it in her beak, she gulped it down. Turning a hard eye on the four fluffy ducklings, her eyes flamed the message: "See this! Now do it!" She waited for them to follow suit.

Obediently, they flapped at the hard ground, but this try was as unsuccessful as the last. Exasperated, Claudine stalked out of the barnyard, under the fence, and into the soft expanse of green grass that bordered the barn. Here, the little ducklings came into their own, snapping at insects and bugs along the grass blades. No more urging was necessary; the little ducklings flew from one interesting patch to another, snapping, gulping, running on again across the carpet of grass that covered the pasture and rolled down the hill to the pond beyond.

Claudine's problem of showing them how to feed themselves had been solved, but another emerged: the discipline of staying together. The other hens clucked calmly and their baby chicks followed their mother's lead with obedient cheep-cheeps. Claudine clucked and clucked in her most authoritative manner but the little ducklings ran about at will, chasing bugs, flies, and insects. Despite the indignity of it, she had to resort to herding them up, running from one to the other and chasing them back to the group; but by then another had broken loose and Claudine was off again.

To Claudine's clear embarrassment, the other hens looked on in frank amazement at her efforts to enforce discipline on her brood, but Claudine, committed to doing her duty to what was hers, continued her efforts until her feathers were frayed and her orange eyes bleary with fatigue.

The only compensating factor was that the ducklings were genuinely fond of her, occasionally rushing back to tell her of some triumph that had happened in the tall grass, and when night fell, clustering around her for comfort in an awkward heap. None of the things that Claudine knew how to do seemed to work out. The other hens were able to fluff their feathers and cover their chicks with a warm blanket of feathers against the chill night air. Claudine, unusually small for her size, and the ducks, unusually large, was not able to do this, so she did what she could. When they clustered into a nest on the barn floor, she climbed up and sat on their heads.

They ended up in an awkward pile with a beak sticking out here, a tail there, and a feathered wing somewhere else. Accepting this as the cross she had to bear, Claudine unsteadily sat on their heads throughout the night.

But the worst was yet to come. With the renewed energy of autumn's cool days, the ducklings ran farther and farther afield until finally they found their way to the pond at the foot of the hill. Claudine, acting as warden of her brood, tried to warn them of the dangers that the water held for chickens. She clucked and cautioned, "Don't go near the water!"

But the ducklings didn't hear. In a headlong rush, they ran out into the water and paddled away. This was more than Claudine's small mind could bear. No chicken had *ever* done such a thing, but unbelievably, right before her own eyes, hers had done the clearly impossible. She stood for a moment nervously rubbing one thin yellow foot on top of the other. She clucked and called out to them, but in vain. The ducklings, finding their own element at last, swam blissfully away, not heeding her last hysterical cry.

When I saw Ewell again, he asked about Claudine. "What happened to that chicken that was raising ducks?"

I described the agonies Claudine had endured. "When they got to the pond and she saw her "chickens" swim away, it just blew her mind. If ever anybody needed psychiatric rehabilitation, it's poor Claudine."

Ewell squinted into the distance toward the pond. "She'll get over it," he predicted, "and the ducks won't forget who their mama was."

And they didn't forget. Periodically, they waddled up the hill to the barnyard, sought Claudine out, and settled down for a visit. With much nuzzling and quiet, contented quacking they told her about their adventures on the pond, and Claudine, her orange eyes darting from one to the other, listened with unrestrained pride. The other hens had only raised chickens who grew up and went off on their own, but she had raised four snow-white ducks who came back to visit. Their contact continued, and sometimes in the late afternoon, Claudine strolled down to the water's edge and gave a cluck.

Recognizing their mother's voice, the ducks quacked joyously and paddled across the pond to the water's edge for another reunion.

We were happy to see Claudine find a happy issue out of all her afflictions and wished that such had been the case with the cows.

Claudine and her problems were little league compared to the herd of cattle. Their problems were bigger, more unmanageable, and more complex, and when they had nothing else to do, they walked around looking for a way to die.

CHAPTER 17

Looking for a Way to Die

As it turned out, T. X. was not only a cheat, he was a liar. He said there was "nothing to breeding and birthing cows." He said they knew their business and just naturally did what they were supposed to do. The bunch he had left with me apparently had not been so informed.

While we were busy building fence and repairing gates, they sat around in the pasture thinking up ways to escape, be derelict in their duty, or die.

The first fool was named Norma Nell. I had been advised by the old-time farmers down at the country store to immediately name all the cows so that I could identify them and their problems. Otherwise, it was necessary to remember markings. Norma Nell made herself known right off. She was a beef and dairy half-breed with the Angus' head and solid black hide, and the long, lanky legs and bony back of the Holstein. The dead giveaway was the big white udder seen only in milk cows. This was an advantage in raising a calf, and since the object was production and not purebred conformation, Norma Nell's ungainly appearance was not what mattered.

The trouble with Norma Nell was that she had a wandering foot. She would stand out in the pasture and graze and get to chewing grass and looking out at the blue hills beyond the fence line. While she was doing this her attention was drawn to a cluster of golden butterflies traveling around together, and she decided to do some traveling of her own.

Most cows with escape on their minds look for a soft place in the fence where a post is down or the wire is loose and they only have to step across to be gone. Norma Nell decided to leave in style. She had watched with studied interest as we rode the horses in the fields and jumped the fences, taking them clean and galloping off. She decided she would too.

I had no idea that Norma Nell entertained such plans. She gave every impression of the contented cow when I drove out in the pasture to take a head count. This was one thing of value that I learned from T. X.—using the air-conditioned comfort of the automobile on hot summer afternoons when it was too humid to ride the horses to go out and check the herd.

Whenever I did this, Norma Nell was always the first one to run up to the car and press her big black nose against the glass, blinking her long, black lashes. Then she would stretch her neck out and lift her head up and make a big display of showing me that she was chewing the grass she had in her mouth. I thought this was one of those busy acts that office workers pull when the boss comes around. She was giving me the contented-cow bit and I bought it and paid no more attention to her.

The cows were always interested when I drove the car to the fields, stopping what they were doing to come over and take a look at me while I looked at them. Sometimes, when they gathered round, they pressed so against the car that it was impossible to see anything but a windshield full of black noses and long lashes, and I would have to get out and stand on the hood of the car to get an accurate count.

Other times, when they were strung out across the fields, I found it easier to take the field glasses and stand on the hood to take a count. The binoculars were also good for scanning the fields from the kitchen window during the daytime if there seemed to be trouble in the pasture.

It was on one such occasion in the kitchen that I noticed a great gathering of cows down in the far corner of the field near the gate at Broad Run. Looking at them through the binoculars, it seemed that they were all just standing there looking at the corner of the field, but I was not able to see through the great wall of flesh what they were looking at. I went upstairs to the outside spiral staircase to get a better view. I could not be sure, but it looked as though one of the cows was hanging over the fence. I threw a bridle on Sabre and rode out to see if what I thought I had seen through the field glasses was really so. It was.

Norma Nell, with flight on her mind, had decided to sail across the back gate and had not made it. She hung there like the Monday wash with her long front legs on one side, her bony back legs on the other, and her face humiliated and hurt by failure.

It took everybody up and down the road to come help get Norma Nell off the gate, and when we did, I marched her back up to the barn and penned her up in the paddock. She slumped around, saddened and depressed, and I thought she was repenting her wayward ways. Actually, she was just waiting to recover from a sore belly and sore ribs from hanging on the fence in her unsuccessful attempt to sail over. Two days later, I looked out the kitchen window and there she was again—this time, across the paddock gate.

This time, no one was home, no one but me, and I wasn't about to try to get her off the gate by myself. Ewell Early was off cutting hay in Mr. Matthews' field, Clarence and Claude had gone to the feed store, Wayne and Billy-Wade were in school. It was hardly worth a try, but considering the circumstances, I decided to call Larry in Washington.

"I've got a crisis," I told him. "I've got a cow hanging over the gate and . . ."

"YOU'VE got a crisis!" he yelled. "Don't you know we're right in the middle of the elections in Rhodesia, and . . ."

I was tired of his global concerns and the grand generalities that affected world governments. I gave up patience and understanding as a bad idea and shouted:

"I don't give a damn about Rhodesia! I don't care if France just fell or Russia has turned Republican. I have a cow who has a good chance of dying if I don't get her down."

He used his office voice. "I'll talk to you about it when I get home," he said, and hung up.

I kicked the wall, slammed up the phone, and went out to take another look at Norma Nell.

"You just got outranked by Rhodesia," I told her, "and you're going to have to hang there until somebody gets home."

She looked dismayed by the decision, but there was nothing else I could do. T. X. always said if they weren't bleeding too near the heart, they'd be all right. Norma Nell wasn't bleeding at all, except maybe from a broken heart. She took her failure very badly because she drooped in all directions, and kept her eyes cast down so that I couldn't see her crying.

After hanging there all afternoon until help arrived home, Norma Nell gave up jumping fences and just wistfully watched the thoroughbreds after that. We had no sooner finished with Norma Nell and her problems than Miss America began with hers.

T. X. had left me with the impression that all the cows he had sold me had been bred to calve in the spring. This was as far from the truth as most things T. X. said. I had some idea of spring flowers and the return of warm gentle breezes after winter's cold and cows dropping little calves like golf balls out in the pasture and their frolicking around their mothers' heels over the rolling green hills.

Done properly, that's what should have happened, and the optimum time for cows to calve is in spring or fall. In my ignorance of animal husbandry, I had thought that cows, like cats and dogs, came into season twice a year and breeding was instinctively programmed on that schedule. From the cattlemen down at the country store, I learned that this was not so. Cows come into season every twenty-eight days.

"If you want spring calves," they told me, "you gotta put the bull in the pasture nine months ahead of time. After he's serviced all the cows, you gotta pen him up."

If the bull were allowed free range, to breed whenever the notion struck him, they said, calving would be a year-round thing, with newborns trying to survive the intense summer heat or the bitter winter cold. Summer calves didn't gain weight properly, they said, and winter calves were apt to get sick and die.

In the herd of Angus that T. X. sold me, the cows had obviously gotten together with a free-ranging bull and had chosen the breeding time themselves, because just weeks after they were delivered, in killing summer heat and humidity, Miss America had a little bull calf.

Miss America was the prettiest cow we had. She had precious little curls hanging down behind her ears, liquid eyes, and lashes so long they looked false. She used them for sweeping, suggestive glances at the bull, and she had the wide-eyed vacuous look of a beauty queen. With all these pinup qualities going for her, she wasn't interested in motherhood. After she gave birth to the baby bull, she walked off and left him by the fence where he was born.

I did not realize that this had happened until I looked out the kitchen window and saw the buzzard flying in wide, lazy arcs over the pasture. I flew outside, following his course until I came to the fence where the little calf, already half-dead, lay. We had already had one bad experience with a cow in the summer heat and I knew I had to get him to shade. I tried to pick him up to move him under a tree but his hundred pounds of dead weight, his lolling head, and long, limp legs were more than I could manage. I went back to the house to get Wayne and Billy-Wade. And overhead, the buzzard kept patrolling.

The two boys sprang into action and we got the little calf under a tree some distance from where he had been left. Wayne then was concerned that the mother cow would not be able to find him, and Billy-Wade thought it would be a good idea to stand beside him and moo until the mother located him again.

They began a chorus of moos that continued until Miss America strolled over, gave us all a bored look, shrugged indifferently, and went back to eating grass in the pasture.

The boys were shocked, and so was I, as Miss America's attitude was completely unexpected. We had assumed that she would do her duty by her own once she saw what the situation was.

Wayne's face was pale and anguished. *"She doesn't even care!"*

Appalled by this aberration of mother love that is supposed to be instinctive and last forever, Billy-Wade turned up worried eyes. "Why doesn't she like him?"

I looked at the little heap of black legs, head, and body, dehydrating in the sun, struggling to stay alive, and felt a flash of fury at Miss America for neglecting her duty and at the buzzard overhead for waiting to do his. The baby calf was trying so hard to live, giving little weak moos, and asking for help.

"I don't know," I told Billy-Wade, "but we're going to drive Miss America to the barn and lock her up in a stall and put this baby in there with her. With no other choices, maybe she'll do her duty."

Miss America did her best to resist our attempt to drive her out of the pasture and into the barn, skittering from one side of the field to the other, tossing her pretty head. But, like basketball guards flapping their arms, we would not let her through the half-moon circle we formed behind her. When we had finally penned her up, I drove the station wagon to the field and we gently lifted the little calf into the tailgate and delivered him to his mother in the barn.

Miss America stomped around the stall indignantly. She took one annoyed look at her baby calf and nosed him down in the dirt. With this, she became a challenge.

The barn, having once been used for dairy cows, still had the stanchions with head locks. With a bucket of grain, we got her head through the stanchion and snapped the headlock in place. While she ate, we held the little calf up so that he might get the milk he so desperately needed, but Miss America foiled every attempt we made by swishing her hindquarters from side to side, making it impossible for the calf to nurse. She made it clear that she meant to have nothing to do with the baby she had deserted and that there was nothing we could do to get her to cooperate.

T. X.'s advice had always been, "If a cow's just looking for a free lunch" (the definition here being unproductive, uncooperative, or incorrigible) "it's time to send her on down the road." That, I decided, was precisely what was going to happen to Miss America, pretty curls and all. We got her out of the stall and into the loading pen behind the barn where a gate led onto a loading chute. There we left her until arrangements could be made to haul her off.

Meanwhile, the little calf's condition was critical. Our first thought was to find a mother cow who had lost her calf, as sometimes happens, and match the two, so that our orphan would have a mother. Asking around at the country store in an effort to locate such a cow, Claude and Clarence shook their heads.

"Won't work. Angus ain't like dairy cows. Angus will accept only their own calf."

There was nothing to do but bottle-feed him ourselves. The calf was now too weak to stand, and Wayne held his head in his lap while Billy-Wade held the warmed bottle of milk to his mouth.

"What are we going to name him?" Wayne asked.

"Black Moses." This seemed the most appropriate name because he was black and because he had been set adrift in the world.

We took turns feeding Black Moses and checking on him during the night, and for a while it seemed it might work. He was able to stand, but the bottle-fed milk didn't seem to give him the strength he needed, and we went to the feed store and got a special formula for newborn calves. Black Moses didn't much care for this and would ooze it out of his mouth as soon as the taste touched his tongue. Less than a week after he was born he developed scours, a disease common to young calves, which is an intestinal disorder like diarrhea, debilitating and weakening.

Medicine from the vet improved him only a little. Black Moses now lay on a fresh bed of straw on the barn floor with his head in our lap to be fed, his long black lashes blinking over his sad, dark eyes. Between gulps of milk, he still cried for his mother. Shortly thereafter, he developed pneumonia, and would take nothing at all. Penicillin and care could not alter the course that had been set for him. On the afternoon Black Moses died, he was still calling for the mother who abandoned him.

Billy-Wade, with tears running down his cheeks, seized him by the shoulders and shook him. "Don't die, Black Moses. Don't die."

Wayne thrust his hands in his jeans pockets, hunched his shoulders, and turned away trying manfully to hide his tears, but there was no hiding it. We were all crying and all heartbroken that the little life we had tried to save was gone.

We buried Black Moses in Boot Hill, a special burying ground we had not far from the barn for those we loved and those who were meaningful to us.

There was never much time for grief on the farm because one crisis would scarcely have ended when another would have begun. It was a late August afternoon on a day that had been so humid and hot it was like walking through molasses. The cows had come up out of the pasture and over the hill to the pond early in the afternoon and had stood shoulder-deep in the water trying to keep cool. The ducks floated listlessly on the other side, making no effort to swim. It was too hot to move.

The storm came suddenly. The hot blue sky, drained of color, was white in the east and black in the west with angry clouds rolling in. A gentle breeze blowing the heat away became a wild wind, bending the trees and rattling the tin roof of the barn. Thunder rumbled out of the west and as darkness descended over the afternoon sky, angry streaks of lightning split the blackness overhead with brilliant jagged edges.

The chickens, plucking bugs from grass blades on the lawn, scurried to the barn like frightened schoolgirls. The horses, with manes and tails flying, galloped back to the paddock and shivered in their stalls. The ducks swam to shore and sheltered themselves on the bank, but the cows were too slow-moving and too far out to make it out of the pond and through the pasture to the barn before the storm broke. They sought shelter instead under the trees at Broad Run.

The greatest worry in an electrical storm so severe as this was always the danger of their being struck by lightning, since they invariably chose to stand under a tree or beside a barbwire fence. For this reason, I, along with the other farmers, carried fire and lightning insurance. So far, I had been lucky. Others around me had lost cows in electrical storms; I had not.

Wayne and Billy-Wade and I hurried to move the lawn chairs and to secure what things we could before dashing back to the house. Inside, with little black Suzie hovering at our heels, we watched the fury of the storm continue, the rain driving down the kitchen windowpane in gushes, obscuring the pasture beyond. The wind lashed the sides of the house and jagged bolts of lightning lit the sky. A fiery streak, a deafening crack, and the pear tree, heavy with fruit, fell to the ground in the yard outside. A trash barrel, torn from its place beside the barn, tumbled across the yard, releasing its contents and scattering paper like confetti in the wind.

"Is God mad at somebody?" Billy-Wade asked.

Wayne screwed his face up in disgust. "Billy-Wade, you are so dumb. God doesn't throw lightning bolts."

They both edged in closer so that we stood in a tight little knot by the window. Billy-Wade jutted his chin out. "How do *you* know?"

With no conclusive answers, Wayne gave him a dark look that precluded any response, and Billy-Wade gathered up Suzie, now having a shivering attack of nerves, and held her in his arms for comfort.

After more than an hour, the storm was over. I pulled on rubber boots and an old army field jacket and headed for the pasture and Broad Run.

"Stay here," I told them. "I've got to check the herd."

The rain had turned the paddock into a slush of mud and manure. Beyond the gate, little rivulets of water ran down the hills of the pasture in the drainage ditch in the bottom. A brilliant sun was edging out from behind the clouds as I reached the stand of woods by Broad Run. The cows, wet from rain, their backs covered with black ringlets, had begun to nose again through the grass. As I looked them over, everything seemed in order. The worst of the storm had only broken branches and torn leaves from tree limbs. I began a head count to see if they were all there.

"Counting cows," Harshaw had said long ago, "is so hard a job, I have to hire someone to do it."

On first hearing this, I thought it seemed not only extravagant but downright decadent. I no longer thought it extravagant or decadent, for counting cows, I had learned, was no easy task. They move, shift, shove each other, and halfway through the count it's hard to be certain whether the count is twenty-six or twenty-seven. When I finished the first count, I had one more cow than I should have had. The second count gave me one less. The third count gave me the number that were supposed to be there, and I decided to settle for that. Outside of scattered limbs, leaves, and debris, it seemed that the pear tree was the only casualty.

Early the next morning, my mother called long-distance from Georgia. As we visited on the phone, I saw through the kitchen window that the buzzard was circling the field and had come to rest on a fencepost.

"Mother, I've got to get off the phone . . . *right now.*"

"What on earth is the matter?"

"My buzzard is telling me something."

There was a pained silence and in a patient voice she said, "You know, dear, I really wish you wouldn't say things like that. *I* understand, of course, but someone else might not."

How could I tell her how important that buzzard was to me? When everyone else was at work, school, or play, the buzzard never left his post in the sky. He was the only full-time help I had and for that I counted him as my best friend, but there was no time to persuade her of this.

"I'll have to call you back. I really must go."

Her tone was stricken. "Very well, dear."

By the time I got outside, the buzzard was in the sky again gliding overhead in wide circles, his beak pointed down, his wings arched in a span. I strained to see what the buzzard saw, but from my distance there was only the cross-fence in the field with the line of trees and bushes that grew beside it.

With a graceful glide, the buzzard swooped down and settled on a fencepost beside a tree. I knew then where to look. Hurrying through the field to the spot, I found a cow lying beside the barb-wire fence on her back, all four feet in the air, her mouth open, her tongue hanging loose to the side. The singed hair and blackened tongue were evidence that she had been struck by lightning in yesterday's storm, but my estimate of this would not be enough. It was the insurance man who would have to verify what had happened before the cow could be moved and a claim honored.

I hurried back to the house to get the insurance agent on the phone. It was Friday and I was afraid he would be gone for the weekend.

"Let me speak to Mr. Lewis. It's urgent."

"Mr. Lewis is gone for the day and won't be back till tomorrow," the secretary said in a high singsong voice.

"I have a cow that was struck by lightning yesterday and I need to see him right away."

"That's where he's at now," his secretary explained. "A lot of cows in the county got killed in that storm yesterday."

"Would you ask him to call me first thing in the morning?"

"I'll tell him," the secretary singsonged.

The rush to see the insurance agent had to do with the disposal of the dead cow. If a cow was "fresh dead" and not diseased in any way, the Hunt Club would come and collect the cow on something that looked like a large, wide sled, haul it back to the kennels, and render it for feed for the fox hounds.

In response to any call about a dead cow, the kennel master, a tall man with watery blue eyes and rough hands, always specified: "Remember now, it's got to be *fresh* dead."

By the time the insurance man got there the cow would no longer be "fresh dead"; she would be very dead and starting to disintegrate. This meant *we* would have to bury her. As I looked at the size of her, I tried to imagine the hole that would have to be dug in the hard, sun-baked soil, and how to get it done.

She certainly couldn't fit into Boot Hill, nor did she merit it. Neither could she be buried in the front field where she had been struck. She would have to be hauled, somehow, to the edge of the back pasture and put under there.

This would be a problem too because, unlike the Hunt Club, we had no sled nor anything for lifting her onto a wagon. It would mean putting a chain around her neck and dragging her with the tractor. Even this wouldn't be possible if the insurance agent delayed his inspection trip much longer. The sun was already high and hot and the cow had been lying where she was struck for two days.

The next day I rang the insurance office again. "Is Mr. Lewis in?"

"He'll be gone for the rest of the day."

"But I have this dead cow. . . ."

"I told him about it and he said he'd try to get to your place first thing in the morning."

"In the morning! That cow will be completely decomposed!"

"I'm sorry. Mr. Lewis said it was the best he could do."

The buzzard continued to swoop and sweep the sky over the dead cow but never descended to where she lay. At the country store, I asked Claude and Clarence about this.

"Buzzards don't eat nothin' that's been lightning-struck." Clarence said.

"Snake-bit either," Claude added. "That buzzard will keep swoopin' and sweepin' around, but you won't never see him lay his tongue on nothin' that's lightning-struck."

I was sorry to hear that. I thought the buzzard might do me a very great service if he were to bring in all his friends and consume it after the insurance agent had made his check.

When Mr. Lewis arrived the next morning, we walked through the dew-wet fields to where the cow lay swollen and baked by the sun and untouched by the buzzard. Mr. Lewis was a heavyset man with tired eyes and an ulcer that he seemed to try to soothe by rubbing his stomach.

Taking his notebook out of his shirt pocket, he marked down a few notations. "She was lightning-struck all right. Must have been standing right next to the barbwire fence."

"Then she's covered by the lightning insurance?"

"Yep. All you gotta do now is bury her."

I dreaded the dismal task. "That's the problem."

"Won't be easy," Mr. Lewis said, shaking his head. "Good luck to you." And he was off to the next farm.

The next four hours will live in infamy in our memories forever. Fortunately, for once, Larry was home to help, it being Sunday. With the tractor and chain, we rode off to the field to dispose of the dead cow, putrid now from lying in the sun. With the chain fastened around her neck, we began dragging her through the fields to the back pasture for burial. As we eased along we could feel her head give way, and there was the horrible possibility of what we would have to do if her head came off. Mercifully, it did not. We got her to the back pasture and began digging a hole with the scoop on the tractor.

The hole for burying a 900-pound cow has to be enormous. Unfortunately, the hole Larry dug was not enormous enough. When we got her in and covered her over, one leg was still hanging out. We simply could not unbury her and dig the hole deeper and bury her again. Larry had already used the last shred of his patience.

"Damn if I'm going to spend all weekend being undertaker for a cow." He stomped off and got a great big rock and put it on top of her leg, but as the body bloated, she kept knocking the rock off and Larry kept putting it back. It was a nightmare that never seemed to end. We thought it was terrible, Claude and Clarence thought it was fine.

Our efforts and experience had earned us a new currency at the country store. We had entered the comradeship of those who lived on the land and worked it and struggled to survive.

Clarence smiled approvingly as though the dead cow was the initiation fee. "You ain't never done no real farming till you go out in the pasture and find one with all four feet in the air."

"Yes," I agreed gloomily. "They just sit around and look for a way to die."

Claude cackled and nudged Clarence's big expanse of belly with his thin little elbow. "She done spoke the truth."

With the misery of this latest experience, we became "one of the boys," which earned us the right to tell our stories of turmoil and trial around the stove at the country store.

But who would ever believe what happened to Desdemona?

CHAPTER 18

Desdemona

IF WOMEN'S LIB had ever opened up for ducks, Desdemona would have been a charter member. She was the diametric opposite of Puttie, and part of the pair of Muscovies that our neighbor, Ewell Early, had given us in the spring to replace Billy-Wade's ducks eaten by the foxes.

Independence developed in Desdemona. She didn't start out that way. From the beginning, she followed her mate, Othello, at a respectful distance, some three or four duck paces to the rear, and listened patiently while he quacked away about anything that crossed his mind. Desdemona limited her responses to quiet quacks of agreement or concession and never once raised her voice in dissent.

Unlike their Shakespearean namesakes, Desdemona was the Black Moor, with little white wing tips. Othello had the splendid expanse of white chest feathers over which he wore a black frock coat. One tiny black curl topped his tail feathers, and his face, even when he wasn't quacking, was the rough red of a turkey gobbler's. Desdemona was demure, Othello, authoritative.

Their relative roles were clear. They went everywhere together and Othello called all the shots. He was forever harranging Desdemona about the bugs she ate, the way she ate them and the ones she chose. To improve her choice, he felt obliged to point out which bug to bite, how to bite it, and he constantly counseled her on the best way that this should be done. Desdemona always complied. It was easier than arguing with Othello.

They spent every day gliding across the glass surface of the pond, watching their own reflections and the reflection of the blue sky overhead with its white cottonball clouds. Sometimes, they dived for fish, their heads and bodies all the way under the water, leaving only a pair of orange feet and a curled-up tail on the pond surface. Before evening, they walked pigeon-toed up the grass hill to the backyard where they settled themselves comfortably on the back steps, and, if Puttie wasn't looking, fluffed their feathers and waited for the grain that they would be fed at feeding time.

All spring and summer and then into fall, they followed this pattern, with Desdemona trailing the required distance behind Othello, and he occasionally looking back and quacking impatiently for her to keep up. Without a word, Desdemona did what she was told, leaning forward into the effort, trying to match Othello's stride.

Othello loved her dearly and admired her fine black feathers that shone blue in the sunlight, and though it wasn't necessary to quack at Desdemona, he felt that he should, so that she would remember that he was boss. He was the one who made the decisions: at what moment they would leave the pond, where they would sit on the steps, and which bug to snap at while they waited.

It all worked very well for Othello until one hot afternoon when he decided to come to the house earlier than usual. Since Puttie was there and wouldn't permit him to sit on the back steps, he chose to settle himself and Desdemona under the forsythia bush by the corner of the house. Desdemona just couldn't get herself comfortable that day no matter how she burrowed in the dirt beside the roots and fluffed her feathers. Without so much as a by-your-leave to Othello, she got up and walked to the water pail under the outdoor spigot, used for watering the small animals. She dipped her orange beak in, lifted her head, and gargled down the cool water. This was so pleasing to Desdemona that she did it again. Satisfied even further, she decided to get into the water bucket.

Upset by this unauthorized behavior, Othello jumped up from his resting place under the forsythia bush and began to quack and fuss at Desdemona floating in the bucket, but Desdemona was comfortable and content and wasn't about to get out of the cool water. Othello was really annoyed. He began walking round and round the bucket, tugging and plucking at Desdemona's feathers, but Desdemona would not move. He continued his tirade until feeding time, when Desdemona decided she would get out to eat. All through dinner, Othello quacked and fussed between each mouthful of grain, but Desdemona's only response was to regard him without a word, shutting her upside-down eyelids, that closed like a car window, against the sound of his voice. What she had done for her own comfort pleased her and she wasn't going to listen anymore.

Othello was in a huff for days, stomping up and down the hill to the pond, quacking at Desdemona every step of the way, but Desdemona was looking into other pleasures. All her life, all she had ever done was follow lockstep behind Othello, and now that she had lifted her eyes from the ground she had been walking on, she began to see the indulgences other fowl enjoyed.

When the peacocks flew over from the farm next door and landed on the paddock posts in a great swoop, Desdemona watched with envy and awe the splendid wingspan of their brilliant feathers against the glistening sun, the grace of their sapphire blue bodies as they glided past, and the hauteur with which they balanced their majestic heads on their long, slender necks. The peacock who decided to sit on the eight-foot-long aluminum gate that opened onto the paddock beside the barn was of special interest to Desdemona. She waddled across the green lawn and squatted at the gate, gazing up with longing and admiration at the trailing tail feathers with golden eyes on the end, folded into a fan and dangling down the gate.

Othello was alarmed by traffic with such large birds and scurried over to where Desdemona sat to scold her away. She had no business sitting over there by the peacocks in the paddock, being dazzled by their fine feathers when she was supposed to sit where he told her. But Desdemona was beyond persuasion or admonition. She had seen something wonderful and wanted to try it herself.

When the peacocks expanded their splendid wings and flew up and away and back to the farm next door, Desdemona decided to try a little gate-sitting herself. She had learned the ecstasy of indulgence and independence that Othello had always known and she wanted the same for herself.

After several attempts to get her heavy-breasted body airborne, by beginning with a running start, she was able to fly up to a perch on the aluminum gate, but this presented a difficulty she had not anticipated. Her big, wide, webbed feet would not permit her to grasp the rail as the peacocks had done to maintain their balance. All she could do was rock precariously back and forth on the top rail, but this accomplishment seemed to please her and she refused to get down even when we swung open the gate to walk through.

On the ground, Othello ranted and raged about the impropriety of this spectacle, but Desdemona turned her head away and wouldn't listen to a single quack. She had always done just as he wanted her to do, and now she wanted to do some things of her own. She had seen the peacocks come to rest and preen themselves on the tops of the cars parked under the shed by the barn, and Desdemona decided to try this too.

This new view of the world suited her so much that instead of going back to the pond that night, she slept on top of the car. Othello scolded her until he lost his voice and his bill just clapped together noiselessly, but Desdemona wouldn't budge, and he finally stalked off to the pond, his anger unspent, and left Desdemona to her own caprices.

When morning came and Larry was ready to back his car out to drive into the city, Desdemona refused to get down. Flinging his hand, he growled at Desdemona, "Will you get the hell off the top of my car?"

Desdemona just gave him a glazed look and continued to sit. Larry backed the car out and swung around the circle in the driveway, thinking the fast movement would make her fly down. Instead, Desdemona crouched down like a hobo riding the rails atop a freight car, and clung to the roof of the car.

Larry blew his horn and yelled to me, "Come do something with this damn duck. I can't drive down the freeway with her on top of my car."

I had a damp dishcloth in my hand and went out and gave her legs a smart snap with the end of it. Desdemona's response was black annoyance. She fluttered down indignantly and stomped off to the pond in a huff, looking back over her shoulder and muttering angrily about the discrimination against ducks. The peacocks had sat on top of the car, why couldn't she?

Her indulgences accelerated and continued, but there was little time to keep account of them because fall had come with a riot of red, gold, and burnt orange leaves. The yellow school bus was coming over the hill again to pick Wayne and Billy-Wade up at the entrance gate, and on moonlit nights when the air was clear and cold with a feeling of frost in the air, off in the distance, in the woods across the way, could be heard the bellowing and barking of hounds giving chase to a fox.

Soon, the front fields were black and alive with birds arriving with a great fluttering swoop, settling on the pasture to feed on the grass and sit on the telephone wires like hundreds of clothespins clipped to the line. The fall migration had begun and all the visitors who had stopped by in the spring on their way north were stopping by again on their way south for the winter. With ill-concealed envy, Desdemona sat on the pond bank looking at the sky and watching them arrive—the wild geese, the wild swans, the wild mallards—led in by their leader flying the arrow point, splashing down on the pond feet first, gliding across the water, grand and glorious.

Desdemona was awed by the robust and massive white geese, impressed by the beauty of the swans, but it was the wild mallards that she envied and most wanted to emulate. They were ducks the same as she, and she terribly wanted to fly up in the blue and join the traffic with the others. For days, she sat on the pond studying flight and how it was accomplished. Seeing the freedom and the far skies that the others flew into, she meant to try it herself even if it killed her. And it did.

The flight plan that the mallards used was to fly off the pond, up the hill to the house, turn right, then up and off toward the sun. They did this every day during their stopover at our pond, visiting other farmers' fields and the surrounding area, and coming back to our pond at night.

As they prepared to continue their trip south and leave the final time, Desdemona, done with studying the aspects of flight, determined to try it herself and find out what lay on the other side of the blue mountains and how it felt to float free in the air, decided to join them. She managed to get herself airborne and fly up the hill with the others, but when they got to the house to turn right, Desdemona, inept and inexperienced with maneuvering, misjudged the turn and flew right into the side of the house, hitting it with such force that she broke her neck. The others didn't even notice that Desdemona had not made it as they flew away into an apricot sun. Only Othello saw. He rushed up the hill to where she lay, her wings still stretched out in flight, her fine black feathers shining blue in the sun. He grieved and cried and wept and was inconsolable. But Desdemona, for whatever it cost her, had apparently died at peace and in a moment of triumph. There was a smile on her face. Even though she had ultimately failed, she had known this fleeting moment of success, soaring with the rest.

Puttie, never one to leave a loss alone, took up tending to Othello. He was so disconsolate over Desdemona's death that he plodded up the hill from the pond, no longer interested in all the bugs along the way. He sat outside the back door in the sun, listless and no longer caring to fluff his feathers under the forsythia bush. Seeing this, Puttie would go out and sit beside him to keep him company.

After he had eaten his grain at night, she washed his face and feathers with her little pink tongue and got him all cleaned up again. And when nothing else would do, she allowed him her greatest indulgence, sitting on the back steps where none of the others were allowed. After a while, Othello came to depend on Puttie's companionship so much that if she wasn't sitting outside when he came up from the pond, he would stand on the back steps and quack until she did.

As Othello's situation eased, another came into focus. With all the care and concern demanded by the other animals, little attention had been paid to Oink Anderson, the pig Wayne had bought to raise when we first moved to the farm. His quarters were separate and apart from the other animals, and his requirements were minimal: plenty of food and plenty of water; he asked nothing more from anybody. He had grown from a little pink piglet with a corkscrew tail to a now huge hog that lumbered around slurping up enormous amounts of food. With frost coming, we had a decision to make: butcher him for our own use or send him to market at the Saturday livestock auction in Minniesville.

"Better slaughter him yourself," Claude and Clarence advised when I saw them at the country store. "When you raise your own, then you know what you're eating."

The thought of eating Oink Anderson was just too grim to contemplate, and I could see from Claude and Clarence's expression that we lost some of our farmer points, when Wayne, beside me, blurted out, "Yeah, but then you know *who* you're eating."

For all our experiences with animals on the farm, we still had too much suburban sentimentality about everything we owned. The other farmers were practical. They raised something, killed it, cooked it, and ate it, or they took it to market and sold it with no more remorse than they'd feel selling a bale of hay they had made in the field. The idea was so appalling to Wayne that a suggestion of cannibalism could not have been worse.

"Butcher him! You mean *eat* Oink Anderson?"

We sat down on the kitchen steps outside and watched a brilliant orange sun dying in the west under a cover of dark blue clouds.

"You see, darling, farm animals aren't pets. They are raised for a purpose. They all have to produce something . . . eggs, beef, pork. . . ."

He slumped over, resting his elbows on his knees, facing a fact of life he had been ill-prepared for. "Could *you* do that?" His eyes were troubled, expecting something better from parents who were supposed to do the right thing. "Could *you* eat Oink Anderson?"

I really couldn't, nor would I be able to cook him after watching him grow up from a little piglet, but the pig was Wayne's and the choice was Wayne's.

"Couldn't we just keep him for a pet?"

I hated saying no, but I shook my head.

Protest and persuasion were on his lips. "But Mrs. Marietta has a steer that's eighteen years old."

This was an eccentric old lady renowned in the country for buying a young steer to raise for beef and becoming so attached to him that eighteen years later she was still feeding him and unable to give him up.

"That's not what farmers do. If we're going to be farmers. . . ."

His eyes were full of hurt and the answer was an agony. I wanted to say we'd keep Oink Anderson forever, but this was beyond sense or reason.

He pressed his lips together so that his chin came up. "I'll take him to market."

We made arrangements to take Oink Anderson to the livestock auction on Saturday and called Luther Stokes to come haul him there in his pickup truck, but we had figured without Oink Anderson and the weight he had gained since putting him in the pigpen as a little piglet. When it came time to load him, we couldn't get him through the gate of the pigpen.

Oink Anderson had by far the best accommodations of any pig in the county. The structure that we had selected for his use had been built by the former owner to house his pair of fox hounds. Oink Anderson's pig palace was about the size of a large dollhouse, five feet high, painted white, with a green shingled roof, standing in a large yard surrounded by an eight-foot chain link fence. A three-foot gate hung on sturdy oak four-by-fours planted firmly in the ground. When Saturday came and Luther arrived, we all went out to load Oink Anderson on the truck—Wayne, Billy-Wade, Larry and I, Luther and his two young sons whom he called "Honey" and "Sonny," aged four and six. The problem was that we could not get Oink Anderson through the gate. During his stay, he had grown to 290 pounds and was too wide to wedge himself through the four-by-four gate posts. We divided up into one in front and one behind Oink Anderson, we tried pushing and pulling, tugging and shoving, but we could not get Oink Anderson through the gate and he protested our efforts with loud squeals that became shrieks. First of all, he didn't want to be touched and second of all, he didn't want his flesh pressed through that gate.

There were few other choices. We could not lift him up and over the fence, he was too heavy; and even if we had been able to manage that, if he had wriggled out of our grasp going over the sharp edges of the chain link fence, he would have ended up as bacon strips before we ever got him to market. It would have been foolhardy to cut down the gate posts and ruin a perfectly good farm building. So, like it or not, Oink Anderson had to go through that gate.

Luther, who never despaired no matter how difficult the problem, went to the barn and brought back heavy strips of plastic and a can of thick, black tractor grease. Nailing the plastic to the gate posts, he then swabbed it down with big wads of tractor grease.

"You going to put that on Oink Anderson, too?" Wayne asked.

Luther grinned. "Can't use tractor grease. That'll mess him all up for the auction and he won't be pretty enough to bring a good price. Go to the kitchen and bring me back some salad oil."

By the time Luther finished, Oink Anderson was oily as an anchovy, and hard to herd toward the gate because he was so slick he would slip right past us since there was no way to grab a hold. Luther had parked his pickup truck with a loading ramp right up to the pig-house gate, and when we finally got Oink Anderson in position and pushed, he popped right through like a cork out of a bottle.

The auction was an experience in itself. The building, built off the edge of the highway with an unpaved expanse out front for parking cattle trucks, pickup trucks, and horse vans, was a two-story wooden structure with two loading docks on the ground floor where farmers backed in to unload the livestock they had for sale. Here, the animals were weighed, numbered, and tagged on the ear, then shunted through a maze of rough oak gates to a holding pen until their number was called by the auctioneer. When this happened, they were run into the auction ring by handlers carrying canes, who sometimes found it necessary to climb a fence or jump a gate to get out of the way when a bull, cow, or horse became crazy or cross with unfamiliar handling or unfamiliar surroundings.

For farmers with livestock for sale, there are two breathtaking moments: when the animal is weighed and when it is run into the ring for auction. Both moments mean money. It's the end, at last, of all the time, effort, care, and concern that has gone into raising an animal to maturity for market. It's all the nights spent in the barn nursing them through sickness. It's all the days spent in the hot sun building fence so they won't get out. It's all the icy mornings carrying buckets of water to a water trough whose pump handle is frozen. It's all the evenings slogging through mud, muck, and rain to take them their grain at feeding time. Finally, and at last, it's payday.

For the farmer who earns his living on the land from the livestock he raises, how the animal weighs out on the scales and how the buyers bid means whether or not there's money to pay the feed bill, replace barn tools, buy a new dress for his wife, or afford a store-bought treat for his kids at the hamburger stand in the sales barn.

Though not this critical for us, the weigh-in was momentous all the same. Oink Anderson slid off the truck and onto the scales in the weighing room, an area the size of a freight elevator enclosed by folding steel doors. From the adjoining office, we watched the scales' hand on the circular dial tremble between pounds as Oink Anderson, unnerved by all this activity, ran around the weighing room floor looking for a way to root himself out.

"That's right at 290 pounds," the scales master told us, handing us a number and a ticket. "The auction begins upstairs in fifteen minutes."

As we climbed the stairs, we heard a handler say, "Watch out for that hog. He's slick as a whistle. Better put him back there in that boarded-up stall, else he'll slide out from under the bottom rail and be gone."

The last we heard were a few frolicsome grunts from Oink Anderson and the sound of the handler's feet running after him.

Inside the auction barn, the air was heavy with the odor of hamburger and onions being fried by an elderly woman in a flowered apron at the hamburger stand on the second floor. Truck drivers and children were lined up waiting for the wad of meat, dripping with grease, to be sopped onto a cold bun and doused with mustard and catsup from bottle necks whose tops were crusted brown.

The rough wooden benches in the amphitheater where the auction would be held were already filled with buyers, sellers, and spectators who had come to see what the market was bringing on livestock that day. There were the traders, like T. X., who had come to buy cheap and sell high somewhere else; the packinghouse buyers, wearing windbreakers and carrying clipboards on which they wrote precise numbers in neat columns; ruddy-faced dairymen with a crowd of baby calves to be sold for veal; and dirt farmers with their wives and children beside them waiting to see what the day would bring for their year of work.

Wayne leaned across his seat to caution Billy-Wade again.

"Now, remember, Billy-Wade," Wayne said intently for the tenth time, parroting the advice that he had once heard T. X. give. "Don't go scratching your head or pulling at your ear, or the auctioneer will think you've made a bid, and the next thing you know, you'll have bought something you didn't even want."

To prevent such a disaster, Billy-Wade ran his hands under the seat of his blue jeans and sat on them. The possibility of inadvertently buying something was, of course, a gross exaggeration, as was everything T. X. said, but it was true that the auctioneer searched the faces of the audience for the slightest motion to make a bid and pointed the person out and shouted from his perch above the dirt ring where the animal was displayed:

"Will you give me . . . fifty? Will you make it fifty-five?"

Until, sometimes, the weak and timid, embarrassed by being singled out of the crowd, acquiesced and agreed to the bid the auctioneer made.

The traders and packinghouse representatives, professional buyers who regularly attended the weekly auction, all had individual and cavalier ways of indicating their bids. Since this was regular fare for them, instead of raising their hand to show they were bidding, one chose to pull his earlobe, another winked his eye at the auctioneer, and another flicked the pencil he held between his fingers. With these casual motions, hundreds, sometimes thousands of dollars went on the tab.

The exhibit ring had an entrance door, like a theater wing, on one side that the animal was run through and penned in while the auctioneer rattled off numbers that were almost unintelligible. When the sale was made, the animal was run through the exit door on the opposite side to a holding pen where he was kept until the buyer picked him up. Wayne and Billy-Wade squirmed impatiently waiting for Oink Anderson's turn. While we waited, we watched baby calves, old bulls, and what T. X. called "ruint cows" sold by the pound for slaughter.

When it came Oink Anderson's turn, he gave it a little theater by coming in, taking one shocked look at the amphitheater of people, and running right back through the door he had come in. Trying to prevent this, the handler grabbed him, and Oink Anderson slipped right through his hands, leaving the handler sprawled on the dirt floor and Oink Anderson off and gone. The act was a sure crowd pleaser and the spectators roared at the handler's efforts to handle Oink Anderson. When he was finally corraled and brought before the auctioneer, he had won the attention and affection of the crowd. This was old hat for the professional traders and packinghouse representatives, who had heard and seen everything, but it won the notice of a farmer in the audience who liked Oink Anderson's lively nature and bought him for a breeder.

We went down to the holding pen to say good-bye to Oink Anderson, but he looked at us without a trace of recognition. He was not interested in us, only in where his next meal was coming from, and that was good, because if he had cried, we might have cried, too. This way, Wayne was able to realize that we had not sold one of the family, but one of the farm animals.

Wayne went upstairs to the office to collect his money, a long green check with a stub that gave Oink Anderson's weight, price per pound, the commission fee, and the yardage cost for use of the sales barn. A shirt-sleeved agent looked over the counter at the pride on Wayne's face.

"Well, young fellow, you got a good price on that hog. What are you going to do with all that money? Buy another one to raise?"

Wayne shook his head. "I'm going to buy me another cow."

Billy-Wade, expecting to see something like a four-foot stack of money, looked at the check Wayne clutched so proudly in his hand.

"Is *that* all you got for Oink Anderson? A piece of green paper?"

Wayne raked Billy-Wade with a look of utter disdain and turned to me, "You know, he's nothing but a kid."

Wayne, of course, considered himself a man of the world, a farmer, experienced now in going to market to sell his livestock.

He almost grinned himself to death going into the bank in Minniesville on Monday morning to get his check cashed, and when it came time to endorse it, he couldn't have taken greater or more deliberate pains had he been carving the endorsement in marble. Once the money was in the bank, buying the cow that Wayne wanted was a problem because there wasn't enough money from the sale of Oink Anderson to buy a whole cow, only enough for half a cow.

If we put up the money for the other half, we would get into unending escalation because if we bought Wayne half a cow, Billy-Wade would want us to buy him half a cow too. This, of course, wasn't possible since Billy-Wade didn't have the money for the first half in the first place and then we would be into one of those "Oh hell, how do we stop this?" situations. The best thing was not to begin the unequal distribution of moneys in the first place.

"You don't have enough money for a cow," we told Wayne.

"I'll earn it."

"How?"

"I'll sell my pumpkins out of the garden."

The garden, planted in the spring and neglected all summer because of the heavy demands in the hayfield, was a tangled, ten-foot wilderness. Only God knew what grew in there because from looking at it, there was no way to tell.

Wayne's suggestion of selling pumpkins to buy the other half of the cow sent Larry's eyeballs right to the back of his head so that only the whites showed.

"Can I?" Wayne insisted.

There was no way in the world that he could find enough pumpkins in that patch to pay for half a cow, but, never ones to discourage resourcefulness and free enterprise, we told him, "You can try."

There began weeks of foraging in the tangled mess that the garden had become to pull out pumpkins, load them in the wheelbarrow, and take them to the roadside stand to sell. Even when all the pumpkins had been found and sold, there was nowhere near enough revenue raised to buy the other half of the cow . . . maybe a foot . . . but that was all.

Wayne sold his baseball cards to Billy-Wade, and polished his daddy's shoes, and vacuumed the floor for me. He had his heart set on having his own herd, and buying this second cow was really important to him. He already owned Ida Belle, the Hereford that we had bought him when we first moved to the farm, and the sister to Billy-Wade's Hereford, Maggie Mae. This gave him the idea of using Ida Belle as collateral to borrow the money to buy the other half of the cow he wanted.

I was shocked by the proposition. "Collateral? What do you know about collateral?"

"Well, I heard you . . ."

"Don't say a word," Larry interrupted. "He comes by it naturally." We drew up a contract that would allow him to pay off the lien against Ida Belle with the sale of his first calf. This successful transaction set in motion a long series of loans against Ida Belle, so many that had she been merchandise put on the counter, she would have been the most shopworn cow in the world.

In the meantime, we called Luther to find the cow Wayne wanted to buy, and two days later, he drove up in his pickup truck with a fine little fat Angus, heavy with calf. Wayne decided to name her Geraldine after a golden-haired little girl who was his current favorite in the classroom at school.

We soon learned that Geraldine was even more assertive and set in her ways than Oink Anderson.

CHAPTER 19

The Counterfeit Calf

GERALDINE, Wayne's new Angus cow, was not only a personality, she was a presence who had arrived. With her bulging bullfrog eyes, topknot tuft of hair, broad nose, and steady stare, she walked off the truck like a sturdy little woman with her sleeves rolled up and ready to work.

She shot one perfunctory look at us, decided we would do, and headed off to the pasture to pace off her new surroundings. The first order of business was to walk the fence line to determine the length and breadth of her new surroundings. She tested the texture and quality of the grass, inspected the barn, checked out the stalls and the hayracks, then headed for Broad Run, where the herd was lazing under autumn trees in the warm October sunshine, watching fallen leaves, that were like gold sovereigns, floating on the glass surface of the water.

Geraldine stood on the edge of the crowd facing them with a

hands-on-hips attitude and took their measure. She dismissed Ida Belle and Maggie Mae, the two Herefords, without so much as a glance. They weren't even Angus. With her big, bullfrog eyes, she sized up the white Charolais bull and decided she had no objections to him. She looked over the other cows in the herd and the calves they had, and even though they were bigger than she, Geraldine knew they would be no competition for her. Small as she was, she always managed to have the biggest and finest calf in any pasture she had ever been in.

The only one who struck her fancy was a thin, crippled cow called Hopalong, after the cowboy named Cassidy. Hopalong, as always, stood off away from the herd, allowed only to watch at a distance what the others were doing. The other Angus didn't like her very much because her crippled leg made her slow and she couldn't keep up, but Hopalong's pride was her little black calf with the white face mask, named Halloween.

Geraldine went over for introductions, and Hopalong, usually ignored by the others, seemed downright grateful, welcoming Geraldine to the cow community and willing to show her around. This, of course, wasn't necessary, because Geraldine had attended to business first and had already checked out everything before becoming involved in social pleasures.

With the pleasantries over, Geraldine went right to work doing all the things a cow is supposed to do, eating grass and getting fat. One morning, with no assistance from anyone, Geraldine gave birth to a fine bull calf. As she had anticipated, he was the best in the pasture. With motherhood upon her, Geraldine gave her devoted and undivided attention to raising and tending to her new baby.

Beyond question, he was the cleanest calf in the pasture. Every morning and every evening and at every opportunity in between Geraldine gave him a spit bath with her long black tongue until she was satisfied that the gleam and glisten of his coat was better than that of any calf in the pasture. She nuzzled him with her head and love was mirrored in her eyes, and no matter what she had on her mind to do, if her calf was hungry, she would stop in mid-stride to nurse him.

Miss America, the cow from the earlier herd who had deserted her baby and let him die, could have taken a page from Geraldine's notebook. Geraldine's watchword was eternal vigilance. Sassafrass was chased as much as a half-mile through the pasture to Broad Run just for being in the same world with Geraldine's baby. Othello was stampeded and frightened into flight because he waddled past the water trough when Geraldine's baby came up for a drink.

The only ones allowed an audience with Geraldine's new offspring were the other members of the herd, and even at that, Geraldine was very selective about whom she allowed to come up and take a sniff. It had always been common practice, with this herd and every other, that when a new calf was born, all the other cows came by to take a look and a sniff at their newest citizen while the mother cow stood proud and admired her latest addition. Geraldine stood proud all right, but everyone was not allowed an audience. Some cows were allowed only a look and others were allowed a sniff. Geraldine decided, and stood by to make sure her decision was carried out.

Unquestionably, the cow community was impressed with Geraldine's progeny, for she had won the pasture prize hands-down. Hers was the biggest, strongest, healthiest calf in the herd.

There was one problem, however. Geraldine's new baby had one failing. He was terribly, incurably, exasperatingly lazy, and very slow to mind what she told him to do. For this, he was named Black Molasses, and his laziness brought Geraldine no end of trouble.

When she wanted to exhibit him to the others, he was stretched out snoozing in the sun. When she wanted to walk to the pond, it took her half the day to get him up. When it was time to return to the barn in the evening, he was still asleep. But once awake, Black Molasses shot around the pasture like a black bullet, running circles around the other calves and showing off the physical prowess he had when he chose to use it.

Geraldine did her best to correct his inherent laziness, cautioning and scolding him with a variety of mother-cow moos and bellows; but Black Molasses just loved lying around sleeping, and no matter how Geraldine tried to alter this failing and discipline her young calf, Black Molasses simply would not listen, and this was a fatal mistake.

October's brilliant blue skies and burgundy leaves were gone, and grey November, overcast with clouds, had moved in with trees stripped bare and days damp with chill hanging in the air. Out in the pasture, the cows herded together, gathering companionship and warmth against the increasing cold, but Black Molasses, unwilling to admit that the sun and the summertime fun was over, still lay snoozing in the drainage ditch that crossed the pasture and emptied into Broad Run.

A winter storm began with heavy rain that turned to ice and snow that night. Seeking shelter, the other cows brought their calves to the barn. Geraldine tried to do this too, but with no success.

As was his habit, Black Molasses had lain down in the drainage ditch earlier in the day before the rain began, propping his feet on the incline of the bank and settling down for his accustomed nap. This time, he propped his feet a little too high, not careful to remember that the anatomy of cattle is such that they must get their feet under them to rise to a standing position, and that unlike horses, they are not able to roll over to gain a more advantageous footing.

When the rain began, Black Molasses was trapped. Geraldine tried desperately to nudge and push him with her nose to get him up, but he could not get his feet under him to move.

Hopalong, still dragging her crippled leg toward the barn, with little Halloween in tow, long after the other cows were gone, came over to help with Geraldine's distress and joined in the effort to push Black Molasses back to his feet. While they did, Halloween hung her head over the drainage ditch and looked on with increasing fear and horror at what was about to happen. As the storm gathered strength and poured torrential rain on the pasture, water gushed down the drainage ditch, and Black Molasses lay there and drowned.

Geraldine was beside herself with grief. She mooed and cried, and carried on, pacing back and forth in the pasture with unrelieved agony. Hopalong, with the frightened Halloween pressed close to her side, stood by to lend Geraldine, in her anguish, support and sympathy as long as she was able. As the storm worsened, and the rain turned to sleet and snow, Hopalong was obliged to look after her own. With reluctance and regret, Hopalong left Geraldine and took little Halloween back to the safety of the barn, looking back over her shoulder all the way as she slowly and painfully climbed the hill, now slick with ice.

Not until the next morning, when we woke to a world iced white as a wedding cake, did we realize what had happened in the pasture the night before. And we did so then only because as we looked from the warmth of the kitchen window onto the swirls of snow that had covered the fields and frosted the trees, we saw the buzzard flying, his silhouette black against a white sky.

We found Geraldine, oblivious to the cold and snow on her back, head, and eyelashes, still standing over Black Molasses, pushing and shoving his lifeless body, trying to get him to stand up again. As the buzzard circled overhead, Geraldine rushed toward him in rage and pain to ward off what she knew to be inevitable. Confused and crushed by her misfortune, Geraldine turned her anguish on Sassafrass, who had accompanied us to the fields. Charging Sassafrass like an enraged bull, Geraldine ran her out of the pasture and under the fence and just dared her to set foot there again. Othello, struggling with his own troubles of trying to negotiate his way through the hip-high snow, fared no better. When she turned on him, he was not able to move out of her way quickly enough and she stomped him on his fine plumage and denuded his tail, leaving him with a humiliating exposure.

Crazed with grief, Geraldine guarded her dead baby's body night and day, letting no one near it. When we tried to take it from her to bury it, she pawed the ground and charged forward with 850 pounds of rage. The other cows walked past where she held her wake, looking over their shoulders toward her with long-lashed sympathetic eyes . . . sorry for her, but glad for themselves that such a grief was not their own.

The buzzard, who had been circling for days, finally sat on the fencepost to wait. He knew that it was just a matter of time before Geraldine fell from fatigue and he could get on with his work. When Geraldine saw him sitting there, she rushed the fence, battering the post with all her might. The situation became impossible. Geraldine had simply gone berserk and something had to be done.

I went down to the country store and found Clarence and Claude pulled up to the potbellied stove warming themselves. Matthew, wearing his hat, red muffler, and mittens, was leaned up against the snuff shelf behind the cash register shivering and rubbing his elbows to keep his circulation going.

"Looks like you got trouble in your pasture," Clarence said when I came in. "I been seeing that buzzard fly for days."

When I told him what had happened, he crimped the corner of his mouth and leaned over to brood over the problem. "I seen that happen once before. Cow lost her calf and went slam crazy. Had to shoot her."

I looked at Claude, who was pulling a plug of tobacco out of the layers of sweaters and coats he was swaddled in. He bobbed his head up and down to verify what Clarence had said.

"Well, I'd sure hell hate to shoot Geraldine," I told them. "She's got trouble enough already. There ought to be something else I can do. Maybe if I got her another calf. . . ."

Clarence cocked his head, his eyes fixed with exasperation. "If I done told you once, I done told you twice, ain't no Angus goin' to accept another cow's calf."

Claude leaned over and spit a stream of brown tobacco juice in the syrup can by the stove. "Ain't it the truth!"

"Like I told you, ain't nuthin' to do but shoot her."

Matthew, still propped against the wall, motionless and mute throughout the conversation, nodded his head in agreement. I simply could not accept that what they said was so. I went home and got Luther Stokes on the telephone.

"Sho' we can," Luther said when I suggested substituting a calf for the one Geraldine had lost. "Me and my daddy done it plenty of times."

"And it worked?"

"Ever' time."

"The other farmers say it won't work. That an Angus will accept only her own."

"They went about it wrong," Luther explained, telling how he and his daddy had successfully substituted an Angus calf on an Angus cow by skinning the dead calf and tying the hide on the substitute. "Cows identify their own calves by scent. Once Geraldine smells the odor of her own calf on the substitute," Luther predicted, "she'll accept it, let it nurse, and raise it for her own."

Claude and Clarence slapped their knees and doubled up laughing when they learned this. "You ain't got a snowball's chance. I've seen a forgery like that work on sheep, but I ain't never seen it work on no Angus cow . . . never will either. What's gonna happen," Clarence said, with Claude joining in the grinning, "is that *you* gonna be the one bottle-feeding that substitute. I bet you my next bottle of Pepsi-Cola that cow ain't gonna have nuthin' to do with a substitute calf."

"I lay my next plug of tobacco right along side it," Claude snickered.

Claude and Clarence had seen it all and done it all. They had lived on the land and worked it all their lives, like their parents before them and their parents before that, but so had Luther. For Claude and Clarence, some things were inevitable and long ago they had had the sense to accept those things, but to Luther, there was always one more chance to try. Others' efforts against the inevitable amused Claude and Clarence because they already knew how it was going to come out. They were still chuckling when I left the country store.

But Luther had said we could, even if they said we couldn't. All I could do was hope. I could not, for my life, see shooting Geraldine. When I called Luther, he offered to do the graft on the counterfeit calf and pawn it off on Geraldine. At the sales barn, he found a black Angus calf whose mother had died, purchased it, brought it to our barn, and put it in a stall.

It was early morning when we began. Larry had already driven off to work and the yellow school bus had taken Wayne and Billy-Wade off to school. There was only me, Luther, and Sassafrass to deal with the distraught Geraldine, who still stood guard over her dead baby's body.

Since it was necessary to get Geraldine out of the way to get the job done, Sassafrass was pressed into service and used as a decoy. While Geraldine was busy running Sassafrass back to the barn,

Luther quickly and expertly skinned the dead calf with his scalpel-sharp knife.

Geraldine, with her mind on demolishing Sassafrass, ran her straight into the paddock and I slammed shut the gate, locking her in the barnyard. Back in the pasture, Luther, with a handful of rawhide, looked up. "You gonna have to help me. Hold this so I can finish cutting it loose."

The odor was awful and the ooze of the rotting rawhide between my fingers was so revolting that I could feel nausea rise in my throat. I tried not to close my eyes, but only look away and try not to think about what was happening. I could still remember china teacups and polished nails and afternoons at the bridge table and as I stood there in the raw November wind in rubber boots and a field jacket, helping to skin a dead calf, I thought about how far I had come from that, and whether there was any way back, and if there was, would I really want to go.

When the hide was cut loose, we raced back to the barn and Luther laced it with hay string and tied it on the new calf's back like a saddle. This done, we opened the stall door and let Geraldine in.

Immediately, she smelled the scent of her dead baby. Her big, bullfrog eyes bulged out like marbles. Utter astonishment registered on Geraldine's face, followed by delight. She hurried over and began to sniff the back of her resurrected calf. Satisfied, she licked its head. Watching this from the shadows of the barn, Luther began to smile. Success was certain.

Encouraged by this reception, the little calf, half-starved from improvised feedings since the death of its mother, wanted to nurse right away, but Geraldine, just to make certain, decided to investi gate further. Sniffing underneath where the hide did not cover the calf's stomach, she smelled a scent that was not her own, and indignantly kicked the calf in the belly.

The little calf's stiltlike legs collapsed and he sank in a heap on the stall floor looking hurt and confused and protesting with weak little moos. Geraldine was so angered by this impostor that the topknot tuft of hair on top of her head trembled with rage. She stalked over to give him another kick when she smelled her own baby's scent again. Torn by indecision, Geraldine's eyes darted suspiciously back and forth, from me, to Luther, to the baby calf on the barn floor, and back again. She couldn't think what to do.

While she was trying to make up her mind, we gave her a heaping bucket of grain for distraction. Unaccustomed to such bounty and half starved to death from days of denying herself food and water while she guarded her dead calf, Geraldine gave herself up to gorging grain. Seizing the opportunity, the little calf crept up behind her and began to nurse. Geraldine looked back, gave him a warning glance, but decided to deal with him later. Concluding that she might not ever have the offer of so much grain again, she continued to eat. The little calf did, too.

Satisfying her hunger for food and another calf seemed to settle Geraldine down. Every once in a while she would remember that there was something not quite right with her resurrected calf, but whatever the problem, it was not nearly so bad as before. Just for good measure, however, every once in a while, she would give him a half-hearted kick.

"You don't have to worry about that," Luther said in response to my distress over Geraldine's occasional kick. "Geraldine ain't mean with her feet. You can see she ain't gonna hurt him and pretty soon she's going to settle down and accept him for her own."

Every word Luther said was true. By afternoon, they were both full and had settled down in the hay for a nap. This calf did not prop his feet up but curled them under him in proper cow fashion. Nodding her head while she chewed her cud, Geraldine seemed genuinely pleased.

The next day when the cows came up to the barn, Geraldine began the protective mooing indicative of acceptance. Unlike Black Molasses, *this* calf obeyed immediately. Pleased with the response, Geraldine nuzzled him with her head and gave him a gentle lick of approval with her tongue.

She called the other cows over for inspection. Watching them give the newcomer a look and a sniff, Geraldine stood proud once more. She, too, had a calf again, even if it was a counterfeit calf.

At the country store, Claude and Clarence offered me the Pepsi and plug of tobacco that they had bet, but I refused.

"I don't drink and I don't chew."

Clarence shook his head, still finding Luther's success hard to believe. "That beats all I ever heard."

"If it was me," Claude concluded, "I'd put it in the paper."

We did, and Geraldine became the most celebrated cow in the herd. She was known throughout the county as "the cow with the counterfeit calf."

We would have liked to bask a while in Geraldine's reflected glory, but by then, Ismene had become the barnyard I.R.S.

CHAPTER 20

Ismene Was the I.R.S.

ISMENE was a scraggly white chicken with long yellow feet and a bad disposition. She was one of the bunch we originally bought from Effie back in the summer.

Is-me-ne in no way resembled Sophocles' noble character in the Greek play, *Antigone*, for whom she had been named. Ismene was chosen because it seemed euphonically appropriate.

Incredibly, and without cause, Ismene, suddenly became the I.R.S. of the barnyard. She kept a sharp eye on every transaction that took place and knew every available store of grain and feed, and extracted from whomever whatever she chose.

Even though she was only a chicken weighing barely two pounds with negligible strength, she tolerated no truck from any of the animals out in the barnyard. Her fury, once stirred, was so great that she would fly into a fit, hold the horses—uncertain of who or what she was—at bay, and make the dogs back off their own feed dish while she walked around in their bowl with her feet plucking off whatever morsel she wanted before allowing them to feed.

At night, when the other chickens found warm roosts in the barn, Ismene took the tower position in a treetop in the turnaround circle near the barn, an island that afforded full view of what was going on in the house, barn, and pasture. Every night at sunset, Ismene flew up into the tree and clutched the top branch with her big, bony feet. No matter how the rain fell, the snow swirled, or the storm winds blew, nothing could persuade Ismene out of her perch in the treetop.

When morning came, and she fluttered down out of the tree, her feet were still knotted into the clutch she had on the tree branch, and for most of the day, she walked around with a disagreeable look on her face and her feet drawn up into two fists. Her self-imposed discomfort added to her aggravated attitude, and everyone gave Ismene wide berth.

There was never a fight if another chicken had worked hard at scratching up a worm and Ismene ran over and snatched it away. Ismene was the I.R.S. of the barnyard. She took what she wanted and no protests were tolerated. The chicken that had been pillaged slumped with despair and turned back to scratching the ungiving ground in hopes of finding another worm to assuage hunger.

The more the animals in the barnyard gave way to Ismene's wants, the more she demanded. When the horses' corn was put out, Ismene flew up on their feed boxes and flapped her wings with such fury that they allowed themselves to be frightened away. Startled and stunned, they, who weighed one thousand pounds, stood back and watched while Ismene, who weighed two pounds, ate their corn.

Ismene became an outrage who was regarded with resentment by the others, but it never occurred to any of them to do anything about it. Watching Ismene stalk around the farm, assured and arrogant, they thought they couldn't. She did just one hateful thing after another, and the resentment grew, but still, they did nothing.

"That ain't no natural chicken. She ain't got no bidness sleeping in that tree and going around taking things off them others."

This observation came from Mrs. McWillie, a little farm woman of extraordinary strength and character whom I had found to help me with the overwhelming household chores. Having raised ten children and presided over all their growing-up disagreements, Mrs. McWillie had a singular sense of justice and didn't hesitate to make a pronouncement when somebody or something had overstepped its bounds.

Watching Ismene's activities in the barnyard, the lines around Mrs. McWillie's thin lips tightened. "That chicken's done crossed the line."

In her early sixties, Mrs. McWillie had long since earned her rest but refused to take it, because she was determined not "to give over" to age, illness, or circumstance.

"You have to fight it out," she told me two days after a hemorrhoid operation when she wanted to come back to work.

"I won't have it, Mrs. McWillie. I won't let you come do housework for me when you should be in bed recuperating. The doctors will tell you that a hemorrhoidectomy is one of the most painful operations a person can have."

Mrs. McWillie belittled what I knew was so. "It just stings a little."

"Nevertheless . . ."

It was the only disagreement we had in all the time she worked for me. By my not letting her come scrub the walls, windows, and floors, she felt I was contributing to her early disability and demise. She tried to forgive me for that since I was her junior and had no understanding or experience with debilitating illness and age.

I had found that with work in the house and work in the fields and animals and children and chickens to take care of, there just weren't enough hours in the day to make rounds and take care of them all. It was then that I found Mrs. McWillie. She came to help with the housework, but became instead my dear and trusted friend. She dyed her hair black and powdered her face white and her one small vanity was refusing to tell her age. When asked, she fluttered her grey eyes shyly and replied, "There's some things ladies don't tell."

Mrs. McWillie had grown up with and always known problems

aplenty, but she addressed herself to life with a force and a determination not to be overcome. She had a special quality of earth wisdom that made her wiser than many people I knew who held Ph.D.'s. There was never a situation or problem that she, her children, or her relatives had not experienced, and there was always the value of knowing how someone else had trod the path that I was presently on.

On the farm, in the days that Mrs. McWillie grew up, there was little opportunity for formal schooling, but this only disadvantaged Mrs. McWillie when she tried to understand her insurance contract, which was written in obscure language and was incomprehensible anyway. She had a strong sense of propriety in how things should look and how they should be done, and she took pride in her work because she knew it was important and necessary. She had five houses that she took care of every week, and I was her "Friday lady." None of us had names, only assigned days of the week.

She arrived for work in the morning with her pocketbook in her hand and a silk scarf tied around her head. She always wore slacks and spotless white sneakers and did a prodigious amount of work. By the time she finished her eight-hour day, she had washed and ironed the clothes, vacuumed the rugs, dusted the furniture, washed the windows, scrubbed the kitchen, cleaned the stove and refrigerator, polished the floors, and cooked the dinner for that night. An efficiency expert could have learned a lot from Mrs. McWillie, and I myself took notes.

When I drove her home in the late afternoon, she sat in the car with her work-roughened hands folded over her pocketbook, tired but satisfied with what she had done, and turned the conversation to her favorite topic: politics and government intervention.

Mrs. McWillie never discussed the people she worked for, but her absorbing interest was Washington and what went on there. "They's always medlin' in somebody's bidniss. Working folks got it hard enough without the gov'mint makin' it worse."

She was a dyed-in-the-wool Republican and had nothing but scorn for the Democrats and their programs to underwrite, aid, and assist those disinclined to work.

"Them Democratz ain't got no bidniss givin' money to them that won't work. If them unimplawed was hungry, they'd find somethin' to bring bread on the table."

Mrs. McWillie had had experience with this all her life and remembered the times when she and her children picked blackberries in the woods, walked five miles to town and five miles back, and sold them for fifty cents a gallon.

What riled her most were the exorbitant taxes taken from her hard-earned pay to finance these programs sponsored by the Democrats. "I done worked for my spending money," she would bristle indignantly, "Ain't no reason for me to work for theirs."

Her husband, a maintenance man retired from civil service now doing maintenance on his own, had voted the straight Democratic ticket all his life. He was born a Democrat, planned to die a Democrat, and defended whatever the Democrats did. Mrs. McWillie never referred to Mr. McWillie by name, but always as "the old man."

"I done tole the old man as long as I'm able that them Democratz don't do nothin' for you. They just put money in one hand and take it out of the other."

Even though they had raised ten children and lived together all those years, their political differences were such that they could no longer watch television together at night. Mr. McWillie watched from seven to nine, and Mrs. McWillie watched from nine to eleven. This was the only way, she said, to avoid points of contention and political disputes.

They lived in a little jewel of a house down a winding road they had themselves restored and repaired, polished and shined. When they wanted to buy it, they had trouble at the bank because they had no credit record. In all their years they had always paid cash for everything they bought, figuring that until they earned it and saved it, they should not go borrowing money to buy it.

"Don't that beat all?" Mrs. McWillie demanded, outraged by the bank's policy. "Folks that ain't never had nothin' and borrowed it all is the ones they want to lend money!"

Her discussions on how the country had gone from a cash economy to a credit economy were as astute as any I had ever heard, and for all her lack of formal education, she spoke with eloquence and passion about the pitfalls of a country whose consumer products were bought before the money was earned, and worn out before they were paid for. She got her loan to buy her house because her character alone was enough for collateral. No one who knew her would have refused to cosign her note.

Every Friday when she came, Mrs. McWillie looked up in the tree and saw Ismene still sitting there keeping an eye on the world. She always clamped her lips together and shook her head. For Mrs. McWillie, Ismene was something in nature that had gone wrong.

"Ain't right her sitting up there in that tree showing her underneath clothes. Worse'n that, is the way she goes around treating them other animals. What's the matter with them other animals? Don't they see she ain't nuthin' but a chicken?"

Mrs. McWillie's face was stiff with exasperation.

"Ismene," I explained, "has so awed them with her fury that all they see when they look at her is trouble, and to avoid that, they just give over to anything she demands."

"You wait and see," Mrs. McWillie predicted with a satisfied snap of her head, "before first and last, somebody's gonna have gumption enough to put a stop to it. She's gonna overstep one time too many."

Ismene was a special distress to Puttie because Ismene had brought dissension where there had been peace before, but, like the others, Puttie couldn't quite figure out what to do to stop Ismene's outrages. She could in no way stop what was going on in the barnyard, but when Ismene came to foul the kitchen steps, Puttie drew the line, bowing up her back and spitting in Ismene's face. Ismene pecked Puttie right on her pink little nose, and Puttie took her paw and slapped Ismene's face. When the skirmish attracted Mrs. McWillie's notice in the house, she snatched open the door and ran Ismene away.

Giving her cleaning cloth an exasperated snap, she went back to the window she was washing. "Somebody needs to put that chicken in a pot and cook her."

I shook my head. "Nobody wants to eat a tough old bird like that."

"Mark my words, somebody will," Mrs. McWillie said, watching Ismene stalk off to look for more trouble. "I seen a lot of tyrannizing in my lifetime, and I ain't never seen it last. That chicken's just like them Germans and Eye-talians in the World Wah Two, and look at what happened to them. Them that tyrannized finally got it."

Ismene did too, but from the most unexpected quarter. Surprisingly, Sassafrass, who had had to leave home before for eating chickens, never laid a tooth on another chicken again once she returned. No matter what Ismene did, Sassafrass, guilt-ridden by her earlier activity, would slink away, head down, shoulders slumped, eyes on the ground. Puttie did what she could, but then she later got busy nursemaiding the four black Border Collie puppies that Sassafrass had one cold November morning out in the barn, and Ismene was left to her own devices.

The four black fluffs with white collars and white-tipped tails were Puttie's absorbing joy. Sassafrass had chosen for her babies a nest of hay behind the stairs leading to the barn loft. It was here that Puttie took up her station on the stairs, crouched on all fours, with her head peering through the rung of the steps, to watch below all that happened. When Sassafrass had to leave for food or water, Puttie did the baby-sitting. Attended constantly, the puppies grew into four fat butterballs, rolling and tumbling and chasing each other around the barnyard. Puttie looked on with undiminished pleasure, as though she shared the triumph. We had named them Puddin, Petunia, Pancake, and Dunkirk, the latter being a disaster, no matter what she tried to do.

One day, in a moment of play, Ismene stalked by and gave Dunkirk a painful peck on the head, and for that, the other three, without a moment's pause or a consideration for caution, jumped to Dunkirk's defense, and chased Ismene down and ate her.

The puppies were too young to know who or what Ismene was or that they should be afraid. They had not yet learned fear and were not intimidated by Ismene, for they saw her for what she was and not what she was supposed to be. There seemed to be something profound about that, a lesson about fear and becoming accustomed to being afraid, a lesson about being persuaded and investing too heavily in what others think of themselves, a lesson that the old and experienced sometime need to relearn from untried and un-damaged youth.

There was another lesson, brought vividly to life, that took its roots back in the purchase of Effie's chickens. When Jake, her husband who had done the killing, came to trial, Effie came back and asked would I take her to court. I said I would and went to pick her up the morning of the trial at the farm where she was staying.

She got in the front seat of the station wagon beside me. "Would it be all right if my uncle comes too?"

I agreed and she leaned out the window and yelled, "Hey, Mohill, come on."

The farmhouse door opened and a huge, 300-pound man rolled out the door, tugging his belt up and arranging his coat. As he sank in the backseat, I heard the springs screech and felt the tailgate give way.

Effie fixed me with a solicitous look. "Can my two nephews come too?"

With Mohill's weight sagging one side of the car down, a counterweight seemed a good idea. When I nodded, she leaned out the window and yelled again, "Y'all come on."

Instead of two, there were three black men and only room for two. "Them's my nephews," Effie explained, flinging her hand toward the first two, "and this here's Moten, my tenant from back at Dr. Grawson's place."

Remarkably, Effie, who had been a tenant herself, had had a tenant of her own, and he needed a ride to work in town. The car was already filled up with Effie and all her relatives.

"I'm sorry," I told him, "there's just not any more room."

"How 'bout if I hang on the back?"

I could just imagine what the sheriff would have to say if I arrived at the courthouse with the car full of people, the tailgate dragging, and one hanging on the back.

"I'm sorry," I repeated. "I just can't do that."

I was done with doing good deeds, but his face was creased with concern, and he tugged at his overall straps.

"If I don't gets to work, I'm gonna lose my job. How 'bout if I just scrunch up in the tailgate?"

His was the real need, and I didn't have the heart to say no. All of Effie's relatives got out, he crawled across the backseat into the tailgate, they got back in, and I drove them all to the courthouse in town. I never expected to see Effie, her relatives, or her tenant again.

It was coming Christmas, and one cold, winter afternoon, I was standing in the kitchen paying Ewell Early for repairs he had made on the barn. As I did so, I saw something flash past the window outside.

"Oh, my God! There's Sabre . . . there's Brandy . . . there's Winchester . . . there's Pride!"

All four horses were loose and running down the drive toward the road and not a one of them had on a halter so that they could be caught. Ewell's ancient red pickup truck was parked outside and we ran to the barn, got halters and ropes, jumped in his truck, and started off to catch the horses now running down the road and over the hill toward the railroad. I couldn't even imagine how the two of us were going to catch the four of them, but it somehow had to be done before they got hurt or hurt someone else running across their path on the highway.

Ewell and I were in his truck headed down the driveway when a car pulled in. "Damnation! Who is that blocking the way?"

The car door opened and Moten, whom I had not seen since the day he wanted to hang on the back of the station wagon, got out.

"Ain't them yo' hosses running down the road?"

"Yes," I replied, anxious to be gone before the horses reached the railroad.

"Me and my frins," he gestured toward the two black men in ragged overalls in the car with him, "will help you catch'em." Seeing my anxiety, he grinned a reassurance. "Don't you worry none. It won't take us no time. We'se used to this."

I was never so glad to see anybody in my whole life. I had already been calculating in my mind how much the damage suits might be if some unsuspecting driver were suddenly overrun by four rampaging horses. I couldn't even think about the amount of tears that would be shed if any one or all of the horses were killed on the railroad by a train going by. I was just seized with dread and anxiety, and then along came Moten and his friends.

Moten hurried back to his car, the paint gone and the upholstery coming loose. "Come on, boys, let's go catch them hosses."

In no time, they and Ewell Early had the horses caught and penned up in the paddock. Ewell shook hands with them and thanked them, and I did too.

"Moten, I really appreciate what you and your friends did," I told him as we shook hands. "You were a Good Samaritan today."

Moten grinned. "Ain't no more'n you done for me. You know what the Good Book say about bread cast on the water. Well, you put some bread out on the water that day you give me a ride to work when I didn't have no way of gettin' there. I'm just proud I could bring a piece of it back today."

There was a brotherhood in our handclasp, for we had both known trouble. I had helped him and he had helped me, and it had meant something to both of us.

Half teasing, but meaning it too, I smiled and told him, "Moten, you did the Lord's work today."

Moten knew what I meant, and he stood tall and grinned back with a flash of white teeth. "You gotta pass it along," he said, satisfied with what he had done.

We were warmed and moved by the experience and it added to the glow of the holidays that were on the way. This special time was extra special to us in the country. The preparation and participation were unlike anything we had ever experienced in the suburbs. There were no red-suited Santa Clauses standing on street corners, no piped Christmas carols, and no streets strung with tinsel. This was going to be a real, down-home, honest-to-God, Country Christmas.

Matthew had already decorated his store. The two little red-tinsel wreaths surrounding yellow candles with orange flames that hung in each of the store windows must have already seen forty Christmases, but Matthew had them up again, along with a strand of tarnished silver tinsel across the door. On top of the cash register was a bunch of holly brought in from the woods, and a picture of Santa Claus was taped to the glass candy case.

Matthew, proud of his effort, was grinning from ear to ear. "See how I prettied it up?"

I could hardly hear what he said because when I walked in, Clarence and Claude were rolling around on their nail kegs howling with laughter. Clarence's face had the purpled look of one in the last stages of strangulation, and he had his arm wrapped around his stomach, trying to hold himself together. Claude had banded his thin arms around his bony knees and was rocking back and forth, gasping for air.

I figured somebody new must have moved into the neighborhood. I hadn't seen them laugh like this since I arrived. "What's the matter with them?" I asked Matthew.

"A bald horse!" Clarence cried, slapping his knee and doubling over again.

I looked back at Matthew. "What's he talking about?"

Merriment lit Matthew's eyes. "We had a dentist in here a while ago looking for timothy."

Timothy was the very best horse hay and sold for a premium price. In our area, the farmers raised only enough to feed their own horses. Their fields, like mine, were a mixture of orchard grass, clover, and timothy for cattle.

"What's so funny about looking for timothy?"

"This here dentist fellow moved out from the city," Matthew explained, "bought three horses for the family to ride, and when it come time to worm them, decided to do it himself. Went out and bought some worming powder and put it in the horses' feed boxes with the grain."

Just hearing it again sent Clarence and Claude into spasms. Clarence took out a greyed white handkerchief from his back pocket and wiped his eyes, and Claude wiped his nose on the cuff of his jacket.

Matthew caught his breath and continued. "Seems like this one horse he's got named Stranger is the hog of the bunch. He ate all his grain and then the other horses', too. All that much worming medicine made his hair fall out and now he's bald as an eagle . . . hadn't got a hair on his hide nowhere."

Clarence raised himself up long enough to add one more line. "Had to go out and buy a blanket for him."

"So he wouldn't catch cold," Claude hee-hawed.

I could only feel the deepest amount of sympathy for the dentist. It would have been just my luck to have the same thing happen to me. I just hadn't thought to try to worm my own horses. "I think it's just awful about that poor horse," I told them. I didn't think it was funny a bit, and it began to put a chill on the warm Christmas spirit that had so recently begun to grow.

"Well, you see," Clarence said, interrupting his orgy long enough to explain, "he's one of them city fellows that moves out here and figgers he can do any man's job. All he had to do was call Doc Caldwell and he wouldn've ended up with a naked horse."

"Ended up having to go to Doc anyway." Claude grinned. "That's how come he was here looking for timothy. Doc said he had to build that horse up so he'd grow hair again."

"Did you sell him the timothy?" I asked.

Clarence threw his big St. Bernard head back. "Naw. What do I want to fool with a fool for?"

It was the country conspiracy and I knew what it felt like. "Well, you can tell him I'll sell him some."

Clarence and Claude looked at me as if I had broken ranks. If I was going to be one of them, it wouldn't do to consort with outsiders. Clarence had opened his mouth to say as much when the door opened and Mrs. Turner and her brood of thirteen children came in and filled up the store. She flashed her jack-o-lantern smile, handed Matthew a dime, and dug in her purse for the other three pennies.

"Give every one of them a piece of candy," she told Matthew. "They got their report cards back today and they done fine."

Tommy tugged at her elbow. "Mama, I don't want any candy. I want to save mine."

A sort of pain came in Mrs. Turner's plain, kind face. "It's only a penny, Tommy. Go on and have some candy with the others."

He shook his head. "I want to save it."

Matthew, fishing candy out of the glass case for the others, smiled and asked, "What you doing, Tommy, saving up for Christmas?"

Tommy shook his head and slid the penny in the pocket of his faded jeans. "No, for something special."

Mrs. Turner handed over the other two pennies. "I can't get that boy to take a thing for himself."

Seeing me, Tommy came over and asked, "Have you got some work you need done at the barn?"

"Not now, Tommy. We don't have much going on." I told him, and then I remembered the dentist and said, "I may have some hay to load. If I do, I'll give you a call."

When the dentist phoned, we made arrangements for him to come out to pick up the hay and Tommy came up after school to help load. While we waited for the dentist to arrive, Tommy took a ragged handkerchief out of his back pocket, tied on all four corners, and began to unwind it.

"Do you think I've got enough money to buy Mama two teeth?" he asked, holding the handkerchief up for me to see. There was the roll of bills I had given him in the summertime for helping make hay, and a bunch of nickels, dimes, and quarters, and a whole lot of pennies. Altogether it wasn't nearly enough to buy one tooth, much less too.

"Is that what you're still saving for, Tommy?"

Tommy grinned shyly. "Yep, and I'm gonna get 'em too." His young face glowed with purpose and enthusiasm. "Mama's always happy and smilin' but it makes her ashamed to smile 'cause her front teeth are gone. I'm gonna get Mama some teeth so she won't have to be ashamed anymore."

I didn't have the heart to tell him that he had nowhere near enough money to buy what he had his heart set on having, but I didn't have to because the dentist, Dr. Zaggle, had arrived.

Dr. Zaggle was a big man with a flat head and a thick neck that seemed to be driven down into his shoulders, and hair cut so short it only left a shadow on his head. All his weight seemed to be in his upper torso, as though he had his breath all drawn up in his chest and was tiptoeing around on his feet.

He got out of his brand-new, just-bought green pickup truck and walked up the ramp to the barn. The most striking thing about Dr. Zaggle was the chastened look he wore on his face. He was clearly a man in pain. He told me how really bad he felt about what had happened to his horse, and that Stranger was his favorite, even though now he was ruined.

As he talked, he kept his hand on his hip and his eyes on the ground and when I asked him how much timothy he needed, he said, "A ton."

I really wasn't prepared to let that much timothy go. We had one small field that we had cut in the summertime and set off separate from the other hay. There was only enough for our own horses, and my effort today was to help him over an emergency.

"I've just *got* to have a ton of timothy," he told me. Then, thinking that money might be my object, he said, "I'll pay whatever you say."

Dr. Zaggle looked like a reasonable man, and I figured we could work out a trade. "Would you swap two front teeth for a ton of timothy?"

"Sure," Dr. Zaggle agreed, holding out his hand to clinch the deal. "Who needs the teeth?"

The Christmas spirit began to come back. It was truly going to be a real, down-home, honest-to-God, Country Christmas.

CHAPTER 21

A Country Christmas

BEFORE THANKSGIVING, Father Feagin asked that all the ladies save their Clorox bottles for the midnight Christmas Eve services. These were not to be crafted into jolly little doorstops, or such as that, but would be used in lieu of the fire truck that was stationed more than twenty miles away. As rector of our Episcopal Church, his plan was to collect enough plastic bottles, fill them with water, and set them under the pews so that if the church caught on fire during the candle-light service on Christmas Eve, everyone could pick up a jug of water and put out the fire.

Even though there were two churches in Minniesville, we had chosen this little rural church in the wildwood because we were Episcopalians accustomed to "the comfortable words" in our prayer-book, and like travelers too long from home, we longed to return. We searched out and were lucky to find this historic little church in the

Virginia woods that had been burned during the Civil War and re-
built afterwards by the conscience-stricken Yankee captain who had
ordered its firing.

The church was old, but so was Father Feagin. There was a bit of
Old England about him and he was frail and slightly stooped from
the snows of so many winters, with a cap of close-cropped silver
white hair, and eyes that twinkled behind gold-rimmed spectacles.
He had a deep sense of community and caring, and figured that
everyone had some sort of talent, and that more than money, the
church needed the talents of its parishioners. He pressed them all
into service and had people cooking church dinners, polishing silver,
pressing altar cloths, chopping wood, cutting grass, and planting
trees.

His only error in judgment was in getting three of the parishioners to take down an enormous dead oak tree that towered over the
church and that he feared might fall and crunch the roof. The three
chosen, for whatever other qualifications, were a doctor, a cattleman,
and an insurance agent. The guide ropes were attached, the tree was
cut, and when it fell, it crunched the roof, the windows, and the
stained glass just as he had feared it might. The only comment from
his ash-white lips was, "Blessed behold! I expected it to fall the other
way."

Fortunately, this happened in the summertime so that when we
sat in church on Sunday mornings and looked at the sky, weather
was no discomfort. By pressing every available hand into service,
when fall came, the church was once more as it had been, and we
had an early Thanksgiving service in addition to the traditional one
in November.

Maintenance was not his only roster. The children, as soon as they
were able, served as acolytes, assisting with the bread and wine of
Communion while their parents took turns with tea on the tailgate.
This was served on linen cloths off the backs of station wagons in
the churchyard under the shade of the giant oaks when the congregation spilled outside after service on Sunday. It accomplished a
sense of community, and since we all lived on the land or out in the
country, the conversation usually ranged over horses, cattle, and crops.

Whenever there was a signal event—a horse winning a race, a child winning a ribbon, a lost cow being found, or a difficulty being overcome—Father Feagin wrote about it in the church bulletin that was mailed out mid-week to all parishioners. Geraldine and her Counterfeit Calf made the pages of the church bulletin, as did our goat Dooma Lee in the Christmas issue.

Father Feagin wrote voluminous notes, advice, and news in the bulletin, not only of coming events and accomplishments but also of illnesses and accidents. It was here we learned why Ed Ames was not in church one Sunday morning. Having risen early to climb atop his silo to throw ensilage down to his Black Angus cattle below, he had not taken note of the early morning frost underfoot. Losing his balance, he fell down the chute of the silo and became wedged there until hours later someone was sent to find out why he wasn't in church.

Father Feagin clucked over us all like a mother hen, reminding us to remember when he himself usually forgot. There were Sunday mornings when he rushed out the rectory door and forgot his vestments, and sometimes he forgot the church key. One Sunday morning as Larry, Wayne and Billy-Wade and I drove up to park under the trees in the churchyard, we saw the congregation all standing out on the church steps.

Larry, who had been pressed into service as a vestryman, sighed. "I'll bet he forgot the church key again."

But this time it wasn't so. The church windows had been opened earlier to air out the interior and a skunk had climbed inside, spewing his scent up and down the aisle. The congregation remained on the steps outside until enough spray cans of deodorizer could be rounded up to overcome what the skunk had done.

Before Thanksgiving we were reminded that services would be held at eleven o'clock and that "the Dear Lord will not look with disfavor on those who interrupt their cooking and come in their aprons or those who wear their boots and spurs to church . . . as long as they come."

This was the Virginia hunt country, and the opening hunt officially beginning the fox hunting season, with the Blessing of the

Hounds and the stirrup cup served to mounted riders in silver cups, was traditionally held on Thanksgiving Day. After prayers at the church, Father Feagin joined the riders in the field. He stood among them in his long black cassock with his prayerbook in hand, blessing the hounds and riders who would take the field that day, ending with the petition that "when the evening comes, let them be like the harvest, safely gathered in."

A blast on the brass horn by the Master of the Hunt, wearing a scarlet coat, mounted astride a silver horse, and the hounds, with a bellow, took the field and ran up and over the fence and out of sight. A thunder of hooves, and the riders, correctly called "the field," followed at a gallop, disappearing over the fence one by one.

Since we weren't riding, we joined the others who were "hilltopping," driving from vantage point to vantage point to watch the progress of the hunt on the hills beyond. As much as we would like to have hunted with the others, it just wasn't possible because Sabre was such a fool about loading. He had clipped his ankle on being unloaded from the horse van when he was brought to the farm and ever after that he violently resisted any efforts to get him in a horse van again. When it was absolutely necessary to transport him any place, it took four strong, courageous men, each one lifting a leg and placing it one step forward to get Sabre in the van. Sometimes this took repeated efforts and all day and by the time it was done, there wasn't strength enough left to ride, let alone hunt.

As preparations for Christmas began, all of us decided what we most wanted to do. Larry wanted a giant two-foot-diameter yule log to burn for the Christmas fire. Wayne and Billy-Wade wanted three-foot red flannel stockings to hang outside like "The Night Before Christmas" across the upstairs veranda. I wanted to have a Christmas party—not the accustomed kind to pay back social obligations and dinner invitations, as had been the requirement during all the years before, but a party just for our farmer friends whom we had gotten to know during our almost-year on the farm, and who had shared our experiences. We all agreed to what each of the others of us wanted and set out to get it done.

I went about mine in completely the wrong way. I had been

brought up by a Southern mother who believed that the very best in effort and hospitality should always be offered to one's guests. This meant full dress: the Brussels linen, the family silver, and the finest china. "That's the tribute," she always said, "that one makes to one's guests. If you don't go to a lot of trouble, they might figure that you figure they aren't important enough to make the effort." So, it was going to be the whole nine yards. Invitations were sent out on folded white informal notes, and the only alteration from what was usually done was to change the time of the party from four to six to three to five so that the farmers could all be home in time to feed their stock.

I was terribly disappointed when I began getting refusals one by one, all for the most obscure reasons. Down at the country store, Claude and Clarence said they wouldn't be able to come.

"Why?" I wanted to know.

"Well, you see, we got this sick cow." They looked at the floor and I knew they were lying. They didn't have a sick cow, they just didn't want to come to my party.

"Well, surely, you can leave her for a little while, long enough to come to the party."

Clarence gravely shook his big St. Bernard head. "Naw, she's awful sick. Me and Claude gotta tend to her."

I turned to Matthew, backed up against the snuff shelf behind the cash register. "You're coming, aren't you, Matthew?"

Lying came hard for Matthew. It gave him an attack of conscience, and made him feel guilty. He shuffled his feet around, and pushed his glasses up on the bridge of his nose to hide the truth behind the smudged lenses. "I gotta help Claude and Clarence," he said, trying to make it sound truthful.

Henrietta Early called up and said she wouldn't be able to come to the party either.

"What's the matter?" I asked.

"I broke my toe and can't get on my shoes."

"We're not going to stand on ceremony, Henrietta," I told her. "Wear your bedroom slippers."

Henrietta gasped as if I had suggested something obscene. "Oh, I couldn't do *that!*"

Hers was the most transparent fabrication yet, but then Luther came by and said he thought his mother was coming for a visit the day of the party and he wouldn't be able to attend.

"Bring her to the party, too." I suggested.

"Can't," Luther said, trying to make it sound convincing. "She's too old."

Something was wrong and I knew it, but I didn't know what. In our little village, whenever the need arose to gather or transmit information, the place to go was the post office. Matthew's store might be the public forum and Central Information, but the post office was Central Intelligence. Here, the postmistress, Mrs. Roundfield, knew everything that was going on and didn't mind telling it.

She was a well-padded, pigeon-breasted woman who always wore black so that people would know that she took her job seriously. She knew all the federal rules and regulations by heart and all the penalties that could send you away to Alcatraz if there was the smallest infraction of the federal statutes, such as putting only one stamp on a letter when you knew very well it would require two.

There was only one parking space in front of her one-room post office beside the railroad because she had had a flagstaff with a round cement base built that was so big that it took up the other two slots. It wasn't important to Mrs. Roundfield that the post office patrons had no place to park; what was important was the flag on its fifty-foot pole and letting the surrounding countryside know that *here* was the post office.

She made a real to-do about the raising and lowering of the flag every day. At the beginning of business and at the end of business, she had her one male mail carrier standing at attention and performing the ceremony of putting up and taking down the flag while she stood outside and watched with her chest thrown out. She didn't salute, but you could always tell she wanted to.

Inside the post office, she sat in a cage with the steel bars drawn down over the window in case some gunman were to come in and try to take her cash receipts. She wore bifocals and whenever she spoke, she lowered her chin to her chest, thereby terracing all her double chins. She already knew all the names on the guest list for my party because she had taken note of everyone who was mailed an invitation.

"I'm really distressed," I told her when I went to the post office to find out what was happening. "I'm getting all these refusals. I don't think anyone wants to come to my party."

She dipped her chin down, looked up at me over the frame of her glasses with squirrel-bright eyes, and shook her head. "It's not that," she told me quite seriously. "It's who they might see there."

It didn't make sense. "What do you mean?"

Mrs. Roundfield took a quick look over her shoulder to see if the mail carrier in the back was listening. Then, lowering her voice to a confidential tone, she said, "They think you got a whole bunch of fancy folks coming out from the city and that makes them uncomfortable and ill at ease."

"That's not true!" I protested. "This party is only for my farmer friends who live out here in the country."

That afternoon, the phone began to ring. Claude and Clarence's sick cow had suddenly gotten better. Henrietta Early had discovered that she could get her broken toe into a pair of boots, and Luther's mother had decided not to visit.

The party was a smashing success. They all arrived in their Sunday best, stiff as store mannikins, in three-piece suits, white shirts, and string bow ties. Maude Hardy, whom I had never seen outside her red and black lumberjack jacket, wore a red silk dress with big yellow flowers and a flounce ruffle on the bottom. My next-door neighbor, Marvella Mason, came in with her hair done up in ringlets and the fox stole that she wore to the races on Tuesday. Her husband, Heywood, took one look at me in high heels and silk stockings and said, "If I'da met you on the street, I wouldn't even have known who you were. I ain't never seen you wear nothing but blue jeans and boots."

"Same here, Heywood." He was grand in his Robert Hall suit, so new that he held himself rigidly straight as though the seams might break. "I may even have to get name tags so we'll all know who we are."

"Ain't it the truth!" Claude added, standing at my elbow and admiring the arriving company.

The yard was filling up with cars, pickup trucks and cattle trucks. Having gotten over the anxiety of arrival in their Sunday-best clothes and the comments this elicited, they now crowded around the dining room table laden with fruitcake, Christmas cookies, tea sandwiches, candy, and nuts. To make certain that everyone's taste and preference was accommodated, I had punch bowls of eggnog laced with brandy and eggnog laced with vanilla, spiked fruit punch and plain fruit punch, coffee and tea.

Henrietta was standing there in her dark Sunday silk over her rubber barn boots seemingly unable to find what she wanted.

"What can I get for you, Henrietta?" I asked.

"Oh, I'll just have a cup of warm water."

Henrietta could never step out of the frame she was in. She always had to be a stand-out in any crowd. "Warm water?" I couldn't believe it.

"Yes," Henrietta said, as though she had the answer to civilization. "It's very satisfying."

I looked at Claude, Clarence, and Matthew across the table looking at me. They had that look of: "Henrietta's just thata way." I wanted to reply, "Ain't it the truth!" Instead, I went to the kitchen and got Henrietta a cup of warm water. Without blinking an eye, she drank it down and then went over to the dining room table and began inspecting the silver and checking the markings on the bottom of china plates.

Joe Frost, no bigger than a bantam, in a coat too big with leather patches neatly sewn on the elbows, was standing there sliding a few sugar cookies inside his vest pocket. He looked up at me with his long nose that pulled his eyes almost shut, and grinned. "You don't mind if I take a few of these home for supper, do you?"

Ewell was smiling a "That's Joe, for you," smile, and out of range of Henrietta, sipped eggnog laced with brandy from a silver punch cup, each time taking his napkin and polishing away the lip print on the cup. Luther, seeing him do this, decided this was probably protocol and what was expected, so he took his napkin and polished his lip prints away, too.

More comfortable out in the field than here in the house holding a silver punch cup, Luther, nonetheless, was enjoying the experience in spite of himself. He nodded to me and grinned. "One thing you can say," he paused to give it emphasis, as though it were a phrase borrowed from the ancient sages, "a good time was had by all."

Probably the best time of all was had by Mrs. Turner, who arrived with her husband and their thirteen children. She flashed a dazzling white smile with her two new front teeth and had all the others gathered around admiring them.

"Where," they asked her, "did you get two such beautiful teeth?"

Mrs. Turner looked down at Tommy with love in her eyes. "Tommy done it," she said proudly, "for my Christmas present."

Embarrassed by all this attention, Tommy stuffed his hands in his back pockets and blushed down at the floor. "Aw, Mama, you didn't have to say that," but we all knew that no present would ever be laid under the Christmas tree that would mean this much to him again.

Wayne and Billy-Wade whisked all the Turner children upstairs where they had their own party going on, and Larry kept the punch cups filled while trading jovialities with the company. Even the sheriff came by. "I saw all those cars and trucks parked outside and figured I might need to pull a raid," he said with a twinkle as he took off his Smokey Bear hat and had a cup of fruit punch.

It was the kind of good fellowship and camaraderie that you want to keep forever, but it was almost five o'clock. Time to feed the stock and time for the party to be over.

Carlyle Hayes, the dairyman from Minniesville who had been a friend from the beginning, apologized for being the first to leave.

"I have to take my animals to church," he told us.

"Take your animals to church!"

Carlyle, a tall, middle-aged man with merry blue eyes who loved to tease, raised his right hand in testament. Ruth, his soft-spoken, ivory-faced wife, nodded a silent affirmation.

I could just imagine Carlyle in the congregation with his cows crowded all around. "All of them?"

"No," Carlyle grinned, "only the babies. They are to be part of the manger scene tonight."

Instead of the usual cardboard figures, Carlyle explained, every Christmas, the Minniesville Methodist Church had a live manger scene with members of the congregation taking the parts of Mary, Joseph, the Wise Men, and the Shepherds. Farmers provided baby animals for the manger, and Carlyle was to bring calves, lambs, and baby burros for the performance that evening.

It sounded so splendid, I wanted to participate, too.

"Have you got a goat for tonight's performance?" I asked Carlyle.

"No."

"Oh, I wish Dooma Lee could go!"

Carlyle, always courteous and accommodating, said, "Why we'd be glad to have Dooma Lee in the Christmas pageant."

I should have known that I would live to regret it, but at the moment, I was trying to figure how I could get Dooma Lee to church in the station wagon. Carlyle, ever generous, offered to come back in his pickup truck and take her over with the other animals.

Wayne and Billy-Wade were delighted that our goat would be part of the live manger scene. Dooma Lee was not. When Carlyle arrived with the pickup truck, we all went to the barn to put her aboard for her trip to church. At first, Dooma Lee was annoyed that her dinner hour had been interrupted. She flattened her ears out in opposite directions like airplane wings and wore a cross look. This changed to alarm when she realized that she was going to be seized, and immediately, she jumped into the hayrack on the barn wall. A bucket of grain and comforting words coaxed her out of her corner and into the tailgate of the truck. Once there, something happened in Dooma Lee's head, some dim recollection from memories past. Dooma Lee didn't want to go. She panicked and backed off the truck with such force that she ended up sitting on the ground and refused to be moved. Four strong men gently lifted Dooma Lee back onto the truck. Her resistance defeated, she stood on the truck looking down at me, her golden eyes a mixture of accusation and sadness. Then I realized: Dooma Lee thought she was going to be sold. This was the dim memory that had surfaced in Dooma Lee's brain. This was the way it always happened. They came to get them on the truck.

"Oh, Dooma Lee!" we all cried, "you're only going to church."

Neither reassuring pats nor gentle tones could assuage the hurt on Dooma Lee's face. She turned away and wouldn't look at me anymore.

In Minniesville, the cast for the Christmas pageant had arrived. The church bells in the belfry were ringing, calling the faithful. On the lawn in front of the little white frame church, Mary and Joseph, in brown homespun, took their places near the manger. The shepherd boys, in short, belted sheets, leaned on their crooks. The Three Wise Men, resplendent in flowing cloaks of purple and gold, knelt, offering their gifts to the Christ Child.

Dooma Lee, the baby burros, calves, and lambs were penned in the enclosure around the manger. In this unstructured situation, Dooma Lee became very nervous. As always, it affected her bladder. As usual, she made no effort at restraint. The other little animals were placidly eating their hay and blinking their big, daisy eyes; Dooma Lee was busy messing up the churchyard. I went over to try to reassure her, but she was no longer speaking to me. She turned her face aside, closed her eyes, and hiked her nose in the air to indicate clearly that what I had done was irreparable.

Inside the church, the organist began the first strains of "O, Little Town of Bethlehem." The spotlights were turned on the manger scene, and the members of the congregation, visitors, and spectators circled round the manger and sang the Christmas story.

To hear the long-loved hymns sung in a country churchyard under the stars on a cold winter's night in Christmas week was a warm and moving experience. Even Dooma Lee forgot her stage fright and began to enjoy being in the spotlight. During the singing, she joined in a few choruses with loud "Bahs." She found her audience so receptive that she smiled and posed and hammed it up, disgracefully dominating center stage. The memory of her performance at the County Fair was coming back and she began to enjoy it.

After the Christmas program was finished, those gathered round in the audience came over to see Dooma Lee. All this attention and the friendly pats on the back went to Dooma Lee's head like a shot of raw whiskey. She waved her beard and tossed her head and became vain, haughty, and proud. The crowd laughed and Dooma Lee, deciding that this was a request for an encore, did it all again.

When it was time to go home, Dooma Lee sashayed onto the truck and held herself aloof from the other little animals who had not elevated themselves out of their humble status. They looked at her with soft, timid eyes, but Dooma Lee only drew herself up more haughtily and stood apart. *She* was a star.

The Christmas pageant was not a one-night stand, but a performance that was given nightly through Christmas week. By the time Dooma Lee had taken her last bow and arrived home, she was such a celebrity that she had become insufferable. She scorned the dog, kicked the cat, and created such havoc in the barnyard that the ducks flew away to the pond. Even the chickens, who usually gathered round for any bits of grain she dropped while eating, would have nothing more to do with her. She was pretentious and preposterous. Her former friends in the barnyard, having endured Ismene's tyranny, were not now going to abide her inflated ego. They regarded her antics with hard eyes and sullen looks waiting for the day of deliverance.

Dooma Lee's arrogance ended the day she boldly struck a pose blocking the horses' entrance into their stall. Sabre lowered his head and with one swift blow with his nose, flipped her over backwards. Dazed and deflated, Dooma Lee picked herself up off the barn floor. There was a smile on every face in the barnyard.

After that, Dooma Lee was cured of her theatrics, but not of her desire to return to the stage. Thereafter, anytime a truck arrived, Dooma Lee, with ears alert and anxious eyes, tried to climb the fence and get aboard.

By Christmas Eve, all was in readiness. Larry had found and rolled his two-foot-diameter Yule log in for the Christmas fire, and little black Suzie was already lying on the hearth waiting for the blaze to begin. Wayne and Billy-Wade had helped Larry finish decorating the tree inside and putting the Christmas lights on the giant cedar outside. From the upstairs veranda, decorated like a mammoth mantelpiece with green garlands and gold ornaments, hung four three-foot red flannel stockings initialed for each of us. In the kitchen, the turkey was ready for the oven and the house was filled with the spicy odor of mincemeat and pumpkin pies.

Puttie's little heart was full to overflowing with love and the Christmas season, and she ran from one to the other of us pressing her head up against us and wrapping her little paws around our legs in an embrace as we all got ready to drive to church for the midnight Christmas Eve service.

"Is it going to snow?" Billy-Wade asked for the fortieth time.

The weatherman had promised snow, and all day long Wayne and Billy-Wade had looked at the sky hoping for a white Christmas, but as we drove the twenty miles to our little Episcopal Church in Fauquier County, the stars in the midnight sky shone with a brilliance that only seems possible on Christmas Eve.

The double arched doors of the church, ancient with age and scarred by the storms of so many winters, were hung with holly wreaths and red velvet ribbon. Inside was the smell of spruce and candlewax burning in the banked window wells under the blood colors of the stained glass windows.

Down the center aisle of the church, the old brass kerosene lamps, hung from the ceiling in an age before electricity, dimly lit the red carpet down to the altar, its path worn thin now by the tread of so many feet. Beneath the pews, side by side with the green prayer cushions, were the Clorox bottles filled with water, ready for use should a fire occur.

Father Feagin had chosen Wayne and Billy-Wade as acolytes for the Christmas Eve service, and as the processional began with the old seventeenth-century English carol, "Greensleeves," the congregation raised its hearts and voices: *"What Child is this . . ."*

Wayne and Billy-Wade, scrubbed shining clean, dressed in the church's white cottas over long red cassocks, leading the men of the church down the aisle, looked, for once in their lives, like God's own angels, and I began to cry. Larry reached over and squeezed my hand, but he wasn't much better off because there were tears in his eyes too.

This only lasted for a moment because as I watched Billy-Wade, carrying the heavy oak cross, almost too much for his strength, down the aisle, it began to weave from side to side like a pendulum, and all I could think was: *Oh, God, on Christmas Eve night, don't let Billy-Wade drop the Cross on somebody's head.*

Mercifully, he made it and the service began. From all over the countryside, the faithful had come to hear again the story of the Christ Child and Bethlehem. Standing in the golden glow of the altar candles, Father Feagin began: *"And it came to pass in those days that there went out a decree from Caesar Augustus. . . ."*

The words were new to no one. They had long since been engraved on our hearts by Christmases past, but they were savored all the same and listened to with love.

Wayne, his face serious and intent with the work of the church, held the vessels of bread and wine as Father Feagin administered Christmas Communion to those who came to kneel at the altar rail. Laying a gentle hand on the heads of children who knelt beside their parents, Father Feagin blessed them with: "Go out in the world and find God's peace."

When it was over, lights from the altar were brought to the congregation who had been given candles with cardboard cuffs to take home to light their own Christmas candles. With flickering flames and dripping wax, we poured out of the church to the strains of "Silent Night" and found, to our surprise and delight, that fluffy white snowflakes had begun to fall from the midnight blue sky.

"Let's go for a Christmas ride," Wayne insisted on the way home.

Billy-Wade, who planned to keep the legend of Santa Claus alive as long as possible, with an eye on his late fifties, objected.

"Now! Just when Santa Claus is supposed to come!"

The devil was in Wayne's eyes. "Maybe we'll meet him in the pasture."

A Christmas ride seemed like a triumphant idea and Billy-Wade was persuaded that Santa Claus would have plenty of time to deliver all the things he wanted before morning. We changed into riding clothes and boots and took the horses completely by surprise when we flipped on the barn lights.

Inside the barn, the startled chickens stood up uneasily on their roosts, jerking their heads from side to side to see what was going on. The cows, uncertain of what was happening at this hour of the night, watched silently with fifty pairs of eyes as we saddled the horses to ride to the field. Sassafrass, overjoyed with this unexpected opportunity, was wagging all over from head to foot, and the puppies were running around in circles like four little whirlwinds. Dooma Lee, never one to be left alone, insisted on joining the party, and we all galloped off to Broad Run to watch the dark water run through the banks of snow.

Suzie and Puttie, with their noses pressed to the frosted pane, watched out the window for our return. Around the pond and back again with the ducks quacking a greeting, and we turned for home, riding up and over the snow-covered hill until we saw the blue, red, green, and gold lights of Christmas falling through the window and lighting up the snow-covered lawn like jewels in the night. The bay window, lit with candlelight, framed the hearthside, blazing with the Yule log, and the Christmas tree beside it glistened and glowed, spilling warm light on the presents below.

At that moment, on this night before Christmas, we all knew that we had come home at last; that despite all the work, worry, and aggravation, that here, at last, was Camelot.

CHAPTER 22

A Buzzard Is My Best Friend

CHRISTMAS MORNING we woke to a silent world blanketed by snow, with rooftops iced over and swirls of blue smoke coming from red brick chimneys. Outside, the winter-green spruce trees bent under their burden of snow, and a red cardinal stood on a bare black branch of the oak tree over the well and waited for crumbs from the Christmas table.

Later in the afternoon, our farmer friends came to call, each with presents like we had never received before. Always on Christmas, they offered their very best . . . the finest gold jellies, the purest red jams . . . all made with loving care from crops gathered in their fields during the fall. Ewell Early gave us a piece of old and unusual barbwire found buried one day while he was building a fence. We, in turn, gave him one of our roosters with his legs tied together with red Christmas ribbon to replace the one he had lost. And Claude and Clarence brought us a package of paper napkins with the word "Welcome" printed across the corner in green.

That night, by the fire, with Christmas almost over, we heard a noise in the driveway. Going to the door, we found Ewell Early on his big, red tractor with his family on sleds attached by tow lines.

"The ice is right," he yelled over the roar of the motor. "Come join us in sledding to the top of the hill and then we'll go skating on my pond."

Wayne and Billy-Wade hurried to get their new skates and sleds and we all four wrapped up in stocking caps, scarves, and mittens against the ten-degree cold. We added our sleds to the scraper blade on the back of Ewell's tractor and rolled down the driveway like a centipede with a lot of unwieldy legs.

The fields were white under the light of a full moon and the trees stood like dark sentinels against the sky. The red taillight from Ewell's tractor shone on those sledding behind, giving them a rosy glow and lighting up laughing faces as we scudded across the frozen road at what seemed a breathless speed, trying to keep the tow lines untangled. Our dogs had joined their dogs in running alongside barking and yipping and adding to the squeals and laughter that rang out across the silent hills.

"On to Richmond!" we cried, but Ewell laughed and shook his head. Too often the ponds weren't frozen solid enough for safety.

"We've got to skate while the ice is right."

Down by the edge of his pond, Ewell had built a fire with long, dark logs of wood that burnt bright orange against the night sky. From his big red barn nearby we brought up bales of hay to the pond's edge for skaters to sit down, change their shoes, and warm their feet. The surrounding snow was a luminous blue in the moonlight and lanterns that had been set out to mark the pond's limits cast a warm yellow glow on the frozen white surface of the pond.

After hours on the ice, hot chocolate, and cookies, we crawled back home, utterly exhausted.

"Nothing," Wayne said, stripping off his red muffler and mittens, "beats Christmas in the country."

Glowing beside him, Billy-Wade added, "Do you know it's only 364 more days 'til Christmas comes again?"

"Go to bed!" we told them and Christmas was over.

Before the holidays ended, we had a call from our former suburban neighbors, Clara and Charlie, whose son, Nootie, had been Wayne and Billy-Wade's playmate. Nootie had gotten a .22 rifle for Christmas and with the city's ban on firing weapons, Nootie had no place to shoot it. They wanted to come out to the country for target practice.

Charlie, big and affable as always, with a growing paunch and a balding head, told Larry all about his latest golf scores and who passed out at the nineteenth hole. Clara, chic and slim in high heels and fashion's latest skirt, described in detail her everlasting delight when her bridge contract, doubled and redoubled, was won by the clever finesse of a king.

I sat listening for a long while, not able to believe that these things that vitalized them once marked the perimeter of our own world. It was hard to remember how far we had come, how much we had done, and how much more meaning life had for us now.

Nootie was nagging to go outside and shoot his rifle, and Larry set up a barricade of hay beside the barn with a target cloth over the top. We watched as the boys all took turns at marksmanship, but Nootie soon tired of this, and seeing the buzzard fly over making his turn of daily surveillance, Nootie pointed at the sky.

"Hey, Dad, let's shoot that buzzard up there."

"Don't you dare!" I shouted with such severity that it startled Clara and Charlie out of their complacency and left Nootie with his jaw hanging open.

Nootie recovered enough to nag and ask, "Why not?"

Why not! I was outraged by the question and so angry with Nootie that I wanted to take him by his scrawny little neck and shake some sense into him. I looked up at the buzzard who was looking back at me and Nootie was saying, "He ain't nothing but a buzzard."

Nothing but a buzzard . . . lowly, despised, ugly to look at, doing the work disdained by others, but so necessary and essential to me.

Come crisis or chaos, he was the one constant I could depend on to always be there, doing his job as I was trying to do mine.

During the year on the farm, we had become partners, and then one day, more than that. Out in the pasture, I had seen him trying to teach his young offspring to fly. When the baby buzzard faltered, he swooped down and lifted his wing with his own until the baby buzzard regained his balance.

Watching, I then felt a common bond with the buzzard, for I realized that the buzzard's efforts were no less than my own—which were to somehow give the young their wings and teach them the ways of the wind currents, and the downdrafts and the exhilaration of soaring skyward.

After that day in the pasture, I knew we were all in this thing together . . . me and the buzzard and the cows and the grass, and if somehow we could make it all mesh, we could make the whole thing work. It was so easy to say, so hard to do, but the buzzard was one of my strengths to be relied upon.

I looked at Nootie, with his face turned up waiting for an answer to why he should not shoot the buzzard.

Impatient, he demanded again, "Why not?"

I knew there was no way for me to explain so that he could understand the importance of the buzzard and what he meant to me. So I told him, quite firmly, leaving no margin for doubt, *"Because . . . that buzzard is my best friend!"*

Charlie looked puzzled, and Clara looked perplexed, and Nootie pouted and looked put out. Unable to understand the changes that had come over us, they soon left and drove back over the hill to the city. The buzzard dipped a salute and continued to circle, keeping his watch from high in the sky, and I waved back an acknowledgment.

Shortly thereafter, the decision on the one-year lease of the farm had to be made: whether to return to the city or remain in the country. We, of course, chose to remain in the country, not one year, but seven in all, until Wayne and Billy-Wade grew up and drove over the hills to college at the University of Virginia and William and Mary.

During the years in between, Luther helped us with the hay and the cattle, and the three Turner boys—Timmy, Tommy, and Tad—became our hay crew and grew up in our fields putting hay on the wagon and stacking it in the barn. Mr. Finley continued to come by and check on progress, and the final act of acceptance was the day that Clarence and Claude bought one of my purebred bull calves for their nephew to raise and show in the 4-H Club ring. The ribbon he won was his, but the pride was ours.

We had finally become farmers, and while we did we watched the suns set and the moons rise—but not often enough, for we did not remember that one day . . . like everything else . . . it would end. But in memory, it's always four o'clock on any golden afternoon and we're back again galloping across the green. The barn is silhouetted black against a red setting sun and the ponds are pink. In the distance on the hill is Camelot.